"The second edition of *Exploring Psychology and C*
Moes and Tellinghuisen invite the reader to reflect as Christians on an array of topics in the field of psychology. This is an excellent resource for introducing students to the relationship between their faith and the study of psychology."

—**Mark Yarhouse**, Wheaton College

"Speaking as an undergraduate professor of twenty-five years, I can say that writing a book aimed at beginning college students is not for the fainthearted! It requires the ability to communicate complex concepts with clarity and to do so in a way that engages students and, ideally, invites self-reflection. Moes and Tellinghuisen have checked all the boxes. My undergraduate students have been enthusiastic about the first edition, and the second edition shows promise of being even more inspiring."

—**Elizabeth Lewis Hall**, Biola University

"Psychologists Paul Moes and Donald Tellinghuisen are uniquely equipped to engage and critique psychological science from a distinctly Christian perspective. Their five-theme approach offers a systematic strategy for Christians to think seriously and productively about the implications of their faith for understanding contemporary psychology, one of God's great gifts for those curious about human nature. This is a cogent, thorough book that will prove insightful and illuminating for Christians seeking a deeper and more comprehensive understanding of themselves and others. Strongly recommended."

—**Bryan J. Dik**, Colorado State University; author of *Redeeming Work: A Guide to Discovering God's Calling for Your Career*

"In this fresh edition, Moes and Tellinghuisen provide a faithful and fruitful framework for rigorous engagement with the psychological science of human behavior and mental processes. They emphasize five themes of human nature. These themes are used as a framework that aids readers in considering psychology research and theories spanning neuroscience and cognitive, developmental, social, personality, experimental, and clinical psychology. An excellent resource with lasting value!"

—**Charlotte V. O. Witvliet**, Hope College

"Moes and Tellinghuisen do an excellent job of exploring the sometimes difficult issues raised by faith and psychological science. The text is accessible and interesting while being thoughtful and sophisticated. There are no easy answers here, just careful thinking about the issues with an even-handed presentation of multiple perspectives. They make a good argument that Christians should be thoughtful and engaged people of faith and science, of Scripture and psychological research. This book is useful for both introductory courses in psychology and upper-level courses in the integration of science and faith."

—**Laird R. O. Edman**, Northwestern College, Iowa

"*Exploring Psychology and Christian Faith* fills a need for an introductory resource to help students think holistically about faith and learning in a way that values and respects Christian faith and the modern discipline of psychology and its diverse subfields. In this second edition, Moes and Tellinghuisen improve on an excellent text by making it more succinct, accessible, and effective. It is a superb companion text for any introductory psychology course."

—**David N. Entwistle**, Malone University (emeritus)
and North Greenville University

Exploring Psychology and Christian Faith

AN INTRODUCTORY GUIDE

Second Edition

Paul Moes and
Donald J. Tellinghuisen

Baker Academic
a division of Baker Publishing Group
Grand Rapids, Michigan

Published by Baker Academic
a division of Baker Publishing Group
Grand Rapids, Michigan
www.bakeracademic.com

Printed in the United States of America

Library of Congress Cataloging-in-Publication Data
Names: Moes, Paul, 1955– author. | Tellinghuisen, Donald J., author.
Title: Exploring psychology and Christian faith : an introductory guide / Paul Moes and Donald J. Tellinghuisen.
Description: Second edition. | Grand Rapids : Baker Academic, a division of Baker Publishing Group, 2023. | Includes bibliographical references and index.
Identifiers: LCCN 2022049306 | ISBN 9781540964687 (paperback) | ISBN 9781540966537 (casebound)| ISBN 9781493441648 (ebook) | ISBN 9781493441655 (pdf)
Subjects: LCSH: Psychology and religion. | Christianity.
Classification: LCC BL53 .M5595 2022 | DDC 150—dc23/eng20230117
LC record available at https://lccn.loc.gov/2022049306

23   24   25   26   27   28   29   7   6   5   4   3   2   1

This book is dedicated to our families
and to all students exploring the relationship
between faith and psychology

Contents

Five Themes of a Biblical View of Human Nature

The following five themes describe how the Bible depicts human nature. They serve as the backbone of this book and will be referred to throughout as we explore the relationship between Christian faith and psychology's perspectives on persons. These themes are described more fully in chapter 1. The Bible shows humans to be:

1. *Relational persons*. We are made in the image of God, and we are meant for relationship with him, others, and creation.
2. *Broken, in need of redemption*. We are sinners in need of salvation through Christ, living in and as part of a creation that suffers the consequences of all humanity's sin.
3. *Embodied*. We bear God's image in real bodies in a real world.
4. *Responsible limited agents*. We make choices (within constraints) that result in actions for which we are both individually and corporately responsible.
5. *Meaning seekers*. We seek to make sense of our surroundings, experiences, and purpose through our perception of patterns, through creative meaning making, and through a desire for a deity.

Preface

When we told friends that Baker Academic had requested a second edition of this book, a common response was "That means people are reading it!" In the years since the first edition, many students of psychology have explored how scientific psychology and Christian faith can relate. And we've heard that our book's approach to integrate psychology and faith has helped students take both pursuits seriously, just as we had hoped when we started work on the first edition.

With this revised edition, we wanted to produce once again a useful companion to introductory psychology textbooks for students who are interested in the intersection between Christian faith and psychology. The general format of the book remains the same. In chapter 1, we outline five themes about persons that we believe are evident throughout the pages of Scripture and that should resonate with a wide variety of Christians. While many of these themes appear to be compatible with a variety of approaches in psychology, conflicts also exist. Although there are no simple answers to the real or apparent conflicts between biblical assumptions and psychological theories, we attempt to help students critically analyze various theories from a biblical perspective. Through the remainder of this book, we relate these themes to the many subfields in psychology in a structure like that of college-level introductory psychology textbooks. We have designed this book so that, after reading the introduction and chapter 1, students can read the remaining chapters in any order, allowing flexibility in studying topics as they come up in an introductory psychology course.

Psychology is a broad discipline with many disparate findings. By relating these findings to the five themes of this book, we hope to help readers develop a more cohesive Christian approach to the field and gain a better understanding of both psychology and a biblical view of persons. We also hope that by distilling many themes and findings into a more cohesive approach, we will provide a fresh way of examining past, present, and future ideas within psychology.

Scientific psychology and religious faith differ in how they explain the nature of humans and their goals in doing so. However, they both carry assumptions about human nature. These assumptions, which are sometimes implicit and sometimes explicit, serve as the common threads that are woven throughout the chapters of this book. The questions raised about human nature in this book are not unique to Christians, since people from very diverse perspectives have sought to understand our basic nature. And while the principles provided to answer these questions are drawn from Christian theology, people from differing backgrounds will likely find agreement with at least some of these principles.

As for the perspective we take in the book, we hold scientific methods in high regard and believe that Christians have an obligation to identify truth regardless of the source. We also hold steadfastly to the truth of Scripture and the power of the Word to convict us of our need for and the way to salvation. We also believe that Christians should live out their faith commitment as they develop theories in psychology. As Nicholas Wolterstorff has said, "Only when the belief-content of the Christian scholar's authentic Christian commitment enters his or her devising and weighing of psychological theories in this way can it be said that he or she is fully serious both as scholar and as Christian."[1]

Our goal for this second edition was to make the book more concise, readable, and relevant. Introductory psychology textbooks are already loaded with information, so we believed that adding additional information from other books would be burdensome for students. We made five major changes in this edition:

1. We reduced the length. Every chapter is shorter relative to the first edition, and we combined what had previously been two chapters on brain and behavior into one.

2. We clarified the writing throughout. We made changes in prose on practically every page. Hopefully this made the writing clearer and more succinct.

3. We highlighted vocabulary terms. Important terms appear in bold, followed by definitions in italics. This should make it easier for readers to note new terms and ideas.

4. We updated many references. We included new studies and different examples in several places.

1. Wolterstorff, *Reason within the Bounds of Religion*, 77.

5. We evaluated evolutionary psychology and responses to it in a new appendix. This foundational theory of the discipline is typically addressed only briefly in introductory psychology textbooks, yet it raises significant issues for Christians. We explain evolutionary theory and discuss its implications regarding sex and gender. In addition, we outline various perspectives that Christians have in regard to this theory and the relationship between faith and psychology more broadly while also exploring these issues in the context of the five themes used in this book.

We pray that you will find this book beneficial in thinking about how psychology and Christian faith can be better understood.

Acknowledgments

This book would not have been possible without the incredibly helpful comments of current and former colleagues in the psychology department at Calvin University: John Brink, Laura DeHaan, Marjorie Gunnoe, Emily Helder, Blake Riek, Alan Shoemaker, Scott Stehouwer, Glenn Weaver, and Julie Yonker. These colleagues joined us in two intensive gatherings (sponsored by the Calvin Center for Christian Scholarship) where we discussed the ideas of this book, reviewed chapter drafts, and discussed the broader topic of how to teach psychology's relationship to Christian faith. William Struthers and Scott VanderStoep joined one of these two-day discussions and provided invaluable feedback on chapters. In addition, several other reviewers, including Laird Edman, Elizabeth Lewis Hall, Christopher Koch, and Angela Sabates, provided insight that helped shape earlier drafts of specific chapters. Thanks also to Cathy Parks for her work in editing footnotes and references.

We also thank the Board of Trustees of Calvin University for funding sabbatical leaves for both of us and for the funding from the Calvin Center for Christian Scholarship. We also wish to thank our wives, Phyllis Moes and Becca Tellinghuisen, for supporting us through this project and for Becca's proofreading of earlier drafts.

Introduction

Why Did I Do That?

▶ SUMMARY: We all have questions about our own actions. This chapter introduces the basic questions that psychologists, people of faith, and all of us ask about our everyday behavior. It also addresses the fundamental ideas that we have about human nature that influence how we answer questions about our own behavior.

> I have the desire to do what is good, but I cannot carry it out. For I do not do the good I want to do.
>
> Romans 7:18–19

> Psychology keeps trying to vindicate human nature. History keeps undermining the effort.
>
> Mason Cooley, *City Aphorisms*

Jasmine had no fear of flying, and she thought people who did were completely irrational. Then two events changed her attitude. The first involved flying through a terrible storm in a twenty-passenger jet. The storm was so violent that, even with her seat belt buckled, Jasmine hit her head on the ceiling several times. The second event was when Jasmine flew out of an airport where there had been a plane crash just a few weeks earlier. The national news had repeatedly shown horrific scenes of a DC-10 crashing in a ball of fire on this same runway. The wreckage of that aircraft was still visible to Jasmine as the plane ascended. She felt very anxious and uneasy the rest of that flight, and afterward she grew increasingly anxious about flying. At one point, she

1

considered taking a train on one of her trips to avoid flying. Even though she could identify the events that had changed her thoughts, she still wondered why she couldn't just overcome this irrational fear of flying. She was also a Christian and wondered why her faith had not sustained her more through these events. Wasn't her trust in God enough to overcome these feelings?

Likely you have had similar questions about something you have done or felt, asking yourself questions such as "Why did I do that?" or "Why do I keep doing that?" You may recognize that the questions we ask about behavior often have both psychological and religious overtones. That is because both psychology and religion have a lot to say about why we do what we do and about our basic human nature.

In this book, we, as Christian psychologists, approach questions about human behavior from a biblical point of view and then apply the answers to issues addressed by contemporary psychology. Some people believe that this mixing of psychology with Christian faith or any other religion is not valid or even possible. Their approach has religion and psychology operating in parallel, with religion answering questions about the next life and morality, and psychology addressing scientific questions about everyday behavior.[1] Others feel that religion is of far greater importance in answering basic questions about human beings and feel that psychological science is of little value.[2] Still others value psychological explanations and feel that religious faith has little to say about our behavior.[3] (See the appendix for an expanded discussion of these issues.)

While difficult issues can arise when we try to relate a faith perspective to psychological science, we believe that a Christian worldview or faith perspective can and should inform our understanding of psychology. This approach is not simply about overruling psychological science with religious ideas whenever research findings appear to contradict religious teachings. Rather, in this book, we examine basic Christian (and nonreligious) beliefs, assumptions, and presuppositions about human nature and explore how these beliefs may influence a deeper understanding of research and practice in psychology. The approach we are using is not common in psychology since most psychologists rarely raise deep questions about human nature or consider how these issues influence their approach. In fact, psychologist Noel Smith states that "psychology may be the sorriest of all disciplines from the point of view of hidden biases"[4] because psychologists rarely state or even acknowledge their presuppositions—despite being influenced by them. So religion and psychology address different aspects

1. Carter and Narramore, *Integration of Psychology and Theology*, 91–101.
2. See Farber, *Unholy Madness*.
3. See Pinker, *Blank Slate*.
4. N. Smith, *Current Systems in Psychology*, xiv.

of life and operate at different levels of analysis, but both have explicit or implicit insights about the basic human condition that sometimes contradict and other times show considerable agreement. For example, religion addresses directly, and psychology indirectly, ideas about whether we are basically good or evil; whether we can make free choices and act responsibly; and how we relate to God (or some "cosmic" idea), to one another, and to the natural world.[5]

To see how these basic assumptions might influence our explanations for human behavior, consider this story. Ethan was a bright kid in elementary school, but he often ran out of time or lost interest in his work. By fourth grade, his grades had started to slip. Ethan brought his work home, but he would often get answers wrong because he didn't follow directions. His ability to tell funny but inappropriate jokes helped his popularity with other students but also made him a regular in the principal's office. His pediatrician diagnosed him as having ADHD (attention-deficit/hyperactivity disorder) and prescribed medication to help with his attention. The school psychologist set up a plan in which the teacher gave him specific rewards for positive actions like finishing assignments on time and remaining in his seat at school, and mild punishments (e.g., a time-out) for misbehaviors. Ethan also received tutoring in reading, math, and homework completion. The medication, the behavior-improvement plan, and the tutoring all helped, but he still struggled with social behavior and academic issues. After more testing by the school psychologist, Ethan was diagnosed as having a learning disability in addition to ADHD. The school social worker interviewed his parents and discovered that Ethan's dad probably had some of the same academic and emotional problems as a child.

Although these interventions helped Ethan improve in school, by the time he was in high school he began to have more social difficulties. His circle of friends started to shrink, and he spent most of his free time playing video games. He seemed to lose interest in a variety of common activities. For example, he rarely went with his parents to their church, even though he said that he still believed basically the same things. His parents began having marital problems, and Ethan struggled emotionally following their divorce. A private counselor helped Ethan cope with his personal and social issues, but after high school he continued to struggle with mild depression and eventually started abusing alcohol. Now in his late twenties, Ethan has become a relatively responsible person whose alcohol abuse problem is under control and who works at a full-time job. However, many aspects of his life continue to be a struggle for him. Looking forward, he wonders if the rest of his life will be such a struggle and if there might be something more for him than just holding down a job.

5. See Jeeves, *Human Nature at the Millennium*, 156–57.

Many of you may find Ethan's circumstances familiar, either because you know someone like Ethan or because you yourself have experienced some of these difficulties. You probably have your own ideas about why Ethan has problems, but let's consider some common explanations that friends, family, and professionals may suggest (key thoughts are emphasized). You may find yourself agreeing with at least some of these explanations.

1. Shawna, a friend of Ethan's family, feels that Ethan did not need medication or therapy. She believes that Ethan was a spoiled only child and that his parents should have disciplined him more. He is just *making bad choices*, and it is time for him to grow up and *take on adult responsibility*. Shawna also feels that this is a good example of *the apple not falling far from the tree*, since Ethan's dad had similar issues. Finally, and most importantly, Shawna feels that the main issue in anyone's life is the *condition of their heart and soul*. If Ethan's family had more faithfully given their problems over to Jesus through prayer, working on their spiritual lives instead of spending a lot of time and money on counselors and doctors, they would have all been a lot better off.

2. Ethan's counselor feels that Ethan's problems are the result of him having *low self-esteem*. He never learned to *accept himself* because other people set expectations that were impossible to meet. Deep down *he is a good person* just waiting to come out—all he needs is more love and acceptance. Ethan has also struggled to find some greater meaning for his life, so he lacks direction and drifts from one problem to another. While the main cause lies with how other people treated him, only he can *freely choose* to be the person he would like to be in the future.

3. The school psychologist believes that Ethan is *neither good nor bad* (deep down); *his brain just works differently* from other people's. This problem was likely *passed on genetically* from his dad. His *environment* is also part of the problem because he has received a lot of rewards from others for misbehaving (e.g., attention for his inappropriate jokes), which leads to more misbehavior in the future. He needs to take his *medication*; receive better *feedback* (e.g., rewards and punishments) from family, friends, and professionals; and practice better (e.g., more logical) *thinking patterns*.

4. The social worker concludes that Ethan's problems result from *a bad social environment and damaged relationships*. Ethan *can't be blamed entirely for his problems*; his problems are the result of the way the whole *social system* works (or doesn't work). It's obvious from his parents' divorce and his lack of friends that *his relationships became toxic*. In other words, each person

involved was fine individually, but the relationships themselves became distorted.

5. Ethan's friend Ryan (who recently took two psychology classes) believes that Ethan is *driven to satisfy his unconscious and primitive motives*. This is not an immoral tendency but simply an *instinctive drive to put his own needs first*. However, because social and moral rules conflict with these motives, he has become anxious and conflicted. This conflict comes to the surface without his awareness and results in troubled behavior. He needs to dig deep inside himself to find all the inner demons and release them by just letting repressed anxieties out and cleansing himself from all these unconscious influences *that determine his actions*.

Take a minute to ask yourself how you would explain Ethan's problems. Do you think that one of these five responses, some combination of them, or something completely different accounts for Ethan's difficulties?

If you are familiar with the field of psychology, you may recognize that some of these ideas match various psychological theories. Your choice for the best explanation of behavior may depend on research evidence, but it is also likely influenced by the way you view human nature. Most of us, including most psychologists, are not consciously aware of how we view human nature. In other cases, we rarely give such beliefs much thought, and we are not sure why we believe such things. Sometimes we may actually hold two beliefs that are opposites, but we don't notice that we use both beliefs. For example, Shawna believes that Ethan is very much responsible for his actions, yet she also attributes his problems to his dad (i.e., the apple doesn't fall far from the tree).

Let's examine the explanations given for Ethan's behavior to get a better idea of the impact these views have on human nature. If you focus on the italicized phrases in the explanations given above, you may notice some themes or dilemmas that arise. While we now present these dilemmas as opposing views, keep in mind that they represent a continuum of beliefs for most people, where their beliefs fall on neither one extreme nor the other. We believe the dilemmas can be summarized this way:

Dilemma 1: Are we complete as individuals, or do we depend on one another? The individualistic view stresses that each person is a unique personality and that each person is individually accountable and responsible for their actions. On the other side of the coin, being dependent on others suggests that we are not simply individuals acting in the world but that we are defined relationally, as part of a social system, and are embedded in community or cultures.

Dilemma 2: Are we good or bad? We all have implicit ideas about whether people are basically good (i.e., deep down they desire to do the right thing—whatever that is), basically bad (i.e., they are mostly interested in themselves and do not really care too much about others), or essentially neutral (i.e., they are neither self-centered nor caring; they are just trying to get by).

Dilemma 3: Are we simply part of the natural world, or are we something more? The vast majority of people in the world believe that the mind—and perhaps a related thing, the soul—is what makes us human. Most often this mind or soul is thought of as a separate "thing" from the physical body—and it is this thing that ultimately controls our behavior. Others believe that human beings are nothing but highly "intelligent animals," shaped by their physical and social experiences.[6]

Dilemma 4: Do we have free will (and responsibility), or are we determined? Determinism suggests that many different forces act on us to create who we are and what we do.[7] Some combination of genetics, brain function, evolution, the physical or social environment, and/or our unconscious minds destines us to think or behave in certain ways. The free will idea suggests that we can freely choose our own destiny and set our own path despite internal or external forces acting on us.

Dilemma 5: Are we motivated by survival, or do we seek something higher? Most people will certainly acknowledge that we are motivated to survive, but is that the only motivation we have? Some psychologists believe that we are simply responding to the conditions that we experience and nothing more.[8] Others believe that we are also motivated to find meaning at a basic level (i.e., to explain why things happen) and at a deeper level (i.e., to find a bigger purpose or deeper meaning).[9]

Most of us tend to be somewhere in between these competing positions, or we alternate at times between various views. However, going back to the various responses to Ethan's problems, if you emphasize our individuality over our relationality and believe that people are more evil than good, you are likely to agree more with Shawna, who stresses Ethan's individual responsibility and his tendency to be self-centered. If you emphasize group membership, believe that people are basically good, stress free will, and feel that we are motivated to find

6. Crick, *Astonishing Hypothesis*, 4.
7. Farnsworth, *Whole-Hearted Integration*, 86–88.
8. Crick, *Astonishing Hypothesis*, 3–12.
9. N. Smith, *Current Systems in Psychology*, 113–14.

meaning, then you might agree more with the counselor and social worker. If you feel that people are basically neutral (i.e., neither good nor bad), stress our physical existence, and believe that humans are motivated only to survive, then you might agree more with the school psychologist, who believes that Ethan is just responding to his genetic inheritance and his environment.

Of course, it's possible to agree with the school psychologist or any other response without accepting all the underlying ideas about human nature. You may feel that one approach is good simply because it offers a practical solution, or you may only partially agree with some of the basic perspectives. However, the main point is still that our views of human nature push us to favor certain approaches more than others.

So hopefully you can see that everyone has views about human nature, determinism, the mind, individuality, and so on. All introductory psychology textbooks proclaim that psychology is an "empirical" (i.e., observational) science—and indeed it is. But because the subject matter is human behavior, we can also see many philosophies, worldviews, and personal interpretations influencing the larger theory. Sometimes these worldviews are implicit and well below the surface; other times they are very explicit and promoted strongly. Either way, it's hard to be completely neutral in psychology given that psychologists make statements about human behavior that cut to the core of who we are.

Most major religions and philosophies also address these fundamental questions.[10] This is why we believe that the best starting point to explore psychology in the light of Christian faith is to focus on these fundamental questions. Some Christians in psychology focus instead on interesting applications of faith to practice. For example, over the years, Christian therapists have raised questions related to the Holy Spirit in therapy, therapy as evangelism, the use of prayer in therapy, and so on.[11] These are certainly worthwhile and important questions, but we feel that we should first answer questions like "To what extent does a faith perspective promote a more individualistic or relational view?" or "If we use a scientific approach to studying human beings, does that mean that we necessarily accept the notion of determinism?" Answering these questions of human nature first allows us to build a foundation for addressing practical issues as we move to applications and practice.

In chapter 1, we articulate basic biblical principles of human nature that relate to the dilemmas posed in this chapter. These principles do not settle all questions in psychology, but they can guide us in grappling with complex theories and research in psychology and life. The remaining chapters in this book expand

10. See discussion in Miller and Delaney, *Judeo-Christian Perspectives*.
11. For examples, see McLemore and Brokaw, "Psychotherapy as a Spiritual Enterprise."

on these principles and are an attempt to apply them to many of the specialty areas in the study of human behavior.

DISCUSSION QUESTIONS

1. If you are familiar with various movements or schools of thought in psychology (e.g., psychoanalytic, behavioristic, humanistic, cognitive), can you match these ideas with the explanations given by number 2 (counselor), number 3 (school psychologist), and number 5 (friend Ryan)?

2. Do you think that psychology can be or should be a science?

3. Do you agree that religious faith should be used to answer questions in psychological science? What are some of the dangers or benefits to psychology of trying to relate these areas? What are some of the dangers or benefits to religion?

1

Who Am I?

Themes of Human Nature

SUMMARY: This chapter describes major themes that address the basic questions and dilemmas raised in the introduction. We have based these themes on scriptural principles about human nature that are relevant for addressing pressing issues in psychology. In the remaining chapters in this book, we seek to apply each of these themes to various areas of study within the field of psychology. Our approach with this chapter is to assume that doing psychology from a Christian perspective requires that we start with a biblical foundation to answer the question "Who am I?"

> What is mankind that you are mindful of them,
> human beings that you care for them?
> You have made them a little lower than the angels
> and crowned them with glory and honor.
> You made them rulers over the works of your hands;
> you put everything under their feet.
>
> Psalm 8:4–6

If you're a student, you are used to being asked, "Where do you go to school?" or "What's your major?" These questions are attempts to get a sense of your identity—who you are and who you want to be.[1] While these are common questions, it's interesting that the Bible focuses on who *God* thinks you are

---

1. Kroger, *Identity Development*, 34.

rather than who *you* or *other people* think you are. Starting with the first words of Scripture, "In the beginning God created" (Gen. 1:1), we can see that the Bible describes humans as *creatures*. Genesis 1:27 also says that humans are made "in [God's] own image." Through the early chapters of Genesis, humans are called to bear God's image by being his agents, acting on his behalf, in the world he made.

The introduction to this book presents many of the dilemmas we face when trying to explain behavior. Various psychological theories, religions, and world-views provide different answers to these questions, so we believe that people of faith need to start by exploring basic themes about human nature found in Scripture. While Christians debate how these themes should be applied, there is wide agreement among biblical scholars and laypeople alike about our basic nature and our condition.

Throughout the rest of this book, we will come back to these themes to explore the relationship between Christian faith and psychology's perspectives on persons, including addressing the basic dilemmas outlined in the introduction. These themes suggest that humans are (1) relational persons; (2) broken, in need of redemption; (3) embodied; (4) responsible limited agents; and (5) meaning seekers. We freely admit that not every aspect of human nature is captured by these five themes, but they cover many of the key aspects of human nature that are relevant to psychology. We assume that each of these characteristics is distinct, but they are also interrelated, as we will discuss throughout the book. This chapter describes these five characteristics and offers a brief discussion of how each is addressed in psychology. The rest of the book explores in greater depth how these characteristics relate to major areas of psychology.

Theme 1: Humans Are Relational Persons

While Scripture speaks of our individual nature, uniqueness, and responsibilities, it also makes clear that we cannot be understood apart from our relationships. In the book of Genesis, God says, "Let us make mankind in our image, in our likeness. . . . It is not good for the man to be alone. I will make a helper suitable for him" (1:26; 2:18). The phrase "Let us make mankind in *our* image" reveals the relationality within the very nature of God. God's essence is relational, shown in the interrelatedness of the Father, Son, and Holy Spirit. God extends this relatedness to humans, as seen in the Genesis story. God created Eve for Adam because "it is not good for the man to be alone" (1:26). In addition, just as God creates things, humans are called to the task of being fruitful and caring for God's handiwork (1:28). Humanity has creative work to do within and as a part of creation. As one theologian puts it, humanity is tasked by God to be his "authorized representatives on earth,"[2] bearing God's image as a collection of people, not just individually.

Being made in God's image has traditionally implied that we are made for at least three kinds of relationships.[3] These relationships are described by Christian psychologists David Myers and Malcolm Jeeves, who write, "The biblical account is a God-centered view and is preoccupied with relationships—first and foremost the relationship of God to humanity, but also of person to person, and of humankind to the created order, of which it is both a part and a steward."[4] Let's explore the implications of each of these three relationships: with God, humanity, and creation.

First, we are made to be in relationship with God, not as equals but dependent on God as his treasured creation. God made us for himself, out of his love and for his glory, to be in fellowship with him (Isa. 43:7). As theologian Philip Hefner states, "God does not deal with us only impersonally through deterministic processes, or treat us as things, but rather carries on a history with us."[5]

Second, rather than focusing on individual differences between persons, the Bible strongly emphasizes that humans are part of something much larger—the human family (Gen. 5:1) and, for Christians, the body of Christ, which is the church.[6] This church is much bigger than an individual congregation, as it includes all Christians, both now and throughout all history—the holy catholic (universal) church.[7]

The apostle Paul uses the analogy of a body to describe how Christians are to live and work within creation: "Just as a body, though one, has many parts, but all its many parts form one body, so it is with Christ" (1 Cor. 12:12). He goes on to say that one part of the body cannot live without the other parts. Being just a head or just a foot is useless. Paul implies that our fundamental relationality leaves us unable to go it alone. The parts need to work together,

---

2. Middleton, *Liberating Image*, 289.

3. Hoekema, *Created in God's Image*, 81; R. Roberts, "Parameters of a Christian Psychology," 77.

4. Myers and Jeeves, *Psychology through the Eyes of Faith*, 33.

5. Hefner, "Imago Dei," 86.

6. By "the church" here, we are not referring to just the nearest one down the street or even particular denominations or branches such as Protestant, Catholic, or Eastern Orthodox.

7. Note that "catholic" is not capitalized, as it refers to being universal. This notion goes back to ancient statements of faith, such as the Apostles' Creed, written in the first centuries of Christianity (which can be found here: http://www.ccel.org/creeds/apostles.creed.html). There is a very similar line in the Nicene Creed, which is used by Catholics, Protestants, Anglicans, and Eastern Orthodox churches (and can be found here: http://www.ccel.org/creeds/nicene.creed .html). Given the conflicts that happen among Christians, it may seem impossible that this is a "group," but through God's Holy Spirit, the church is a fellowship that extends through time and across the diversity of races and countries.

and when they do, the body of Christ (the church) can function as intended. Being in relationship with one another and with God allows us to be fully human, what theologians call personhood.[8] **Personhood** *is the full humanity that God intended for each person, which comes only in the context of the body of Christ, where we collectively bear God's image and fully love each other in each other's personal uniqueness.*[9]

God's relationship with humans is both personal and communal. This is clear in the interactions between God and his people recorded in the Bible. There are times when God blesses individuals as well as families, tribes, or nations. For example, God establishes a promise or covenant with Abraham *and* all his descendants to make them a "great nation" (Gen. 12:2) so that "all peoples on earth will be blessed through you" (12:3). There are also times when people are condemned as groups or nations. In the case of Israel, the prophet Ezekiel proclaims, "Now this was the sin of your sister Sodom: She and her daughters were arrogant, overfed and unconcerned; they did not help the poor and needy" (Ezek. 16:49). Although the city of Sodom may be most associated with its sexual sins,[10] it's the community's indifference to the poor and needy that is the real focus of condemnation. Likewise in the New Testament, members of the early church are treated as a unified body. Even though the apostle Paul names specific persons when writing to the churches,[11] his letters are addressed to groups of Christians: he praises the Philippians as a group (e.g., "I thank my God every time I remember you" [Phil. 1:3]) and condemns the Corinthian church as a group (e.g., "Brothers and sisters, I could not address you as people who live by the Spirit" [1 Cor. 3:1]). God calls out particular persons to fill specific roles, but God's interactions with humans emphasize the fundamental interrelatedness of humanity.

The third core relationship implies that just as God created and sustains the creation, so people are also to be creative and care for creation (Gen. 1:28). God set up a perfect creation from the outset and called humans to continue the creation project—to "take care of it" (2:15). Humans are endowed with capacities to learn and develop, and the human role of caretaker includes our development of science and social institutions that allow us to better care for each other and the world.

To sum up, being made in God's image "represents God as commanding us to love him with all our heart, our neighbor as ourselves, and to be faithful stewards of the creation."[12]

---

8. Hefner, "Imago Dei," 87.
9. Yannaras, *Freedom of Morality*, 23.
10. *Sodom* is the basis of the word *sodomy*.
11. Paul pleads with Euodia and Syntyche to agree with each other in the Lord in Phil. 4:2.
12. R. Roberts, "Parameters of a Christian Psychology," 77.

Human Relationality and Psychology

Relationality is also a central topic of psychology. Ethan from the introduction to this book is in a series of relationships with others, including friends and family, and these relationships doubtless influence him as he has influenced them. Many areas of psychology explore how we interact with, influence, and are influenced by our environment (people as well as things). How we learn from others, the ways our brains recognize another person's face, why we laugh, and why individuals suffering from anxiety may fear others all reveal an interest in relationships. The biblical emphasis on relationships is very compatible with many ideas and research findings in psychology.

There are, however, at least two emphases of relationality that differ between psychology and the Bible. First, by allowing only natural explanations of behavior (only physical explanations count; supernatural explanations aren't allowed in science), psychology doesn't directly study how God relates to people. Psychologists sometimes study religious behaviors and thoughts of people but not the behaviors and thoughts of God toward us. Second, psychology places a great deal of emphasis on a type of relationality barely mentioned in the Bible: relationship to oneself. The fact that the Bible says little about how we relate to ourselves may surprise you—it surprised us when we were doing our research for this book. Terms like *self-concept* and *self-esteem* are common in psychology, and therapy emphasizes self-awareness and self-fulfillment. The Bible seems far less concerned about these notions, and although some think the phrase "know thyself" is found in the Bible, it's not.[13]

Despite an increased emphasis on relationality in recent years, some psychological perspectives as well as some religious perspectives have stressed the individual apart from our relational nature. Christians in the Western world have all too often stressed our individual accountability but have ignored the larger collective nature of brokenness. Should the Bible's emphasis on interrelatedness have any impact on how we approach psychology? Knowing that we hold a unique place within creation as collective image bearers of God might influence how we study group behavior, worker motivation, and gender differences, and how we conduct therapy—to name just a few.

Theme 2: Humans Are Broken, in Need of Redemption

God designed us to thrive in the three core relationships we just described. What would it look like if humans lived out God's image in God-intended

13. One place it appears is in Shakespeare's *Hamlet*.

relationships? Every day would involve a guilt-free, harmonious relationship with God and people, tending God's flawless creation, at peace with each other, creation, and God. Everyone could live to their full potential. Summing up the situation at the end of the creation narrative, Genesis 1:31 says, "God saw all that he had made, and it was very good."

Of course, that's not our situation now. Our world has war, selfishness, and disease. Why? Christian theology and the Bible teach that rather than trusting God's plan, humans chose instead to trust their own. The essence of **sin** *is putting our will and our plans before God's*. God created us, but we rebelled against our creaturehood and our Creator, declaring ourselves the "creators" of our own lives, choosing self-determination instead of living in creaturely obedience as God's representatives on earth. This rebellion is known as **the fall**: *humanity moving from its original state of goodness and obedience to one of disobedience*. In the fall, the full relational interconnections of "God, humans, and all creation in justice, fulfillment, and delight,"[14] mentioned by theologian Cornelius Plantinga Jr., were rejected. Instead, humans took up an individuality that creates a gulf between God and each person. As one Greek Orthodox Christian writer puts it, "From the moment when the human person rejects this call and this communion in which he himself is grounded, . . . he becomes alienated from himself."[15] Theologian Miroslav Volf writes that humans "affirm themselves in contrast to others (other human beings, other creatures, and God), necessarily creating distance between themselves and all others."[16] As a result of this fallenness, "The natural needs of the individual being, such as nourishment, self-perpetuation and self-preservation, become an end in themselves."[17] We try to go it alone, but we're not up to the task. Because of sin, "we live anxiously, restlessly, always trying to secure and extend ourselves with finite goods that can't take the weight we put on them."[18] Pastor Timothy Keller writes, "The reason even the best possible worldly goods will not satisfy is because we were created for a degree of delight and fulfillment that they cannot produce."[19] We are estranged.

This separation through sin is universal—everyone gives priority to someone or something other than God. "If we claim to be without sin, we deceive ourselves," says 1 John 1:8. Sinfulness shows up in what we do but also in what we think; while you may not steal, who doesn't envy? The Bible states

14. C. Plantinga, *Not the Way*, 10.
15. Yannaras, *Freedom of Morality*, 30.
16. Volf, *After Our Likeness*, 81.
17. Yannaras, *Freedom of Morality*, 31.
18. Yannaras, *Freedom of Morality*, 61.
19. Keller, *Making Sense of God*, 90.

that the only sinless person—the only one not totally self-centered—was Jesus Christ.

But this condition is more than a set of personal sins or a tendency to sin. Unfortunately, all of creation is in "bondage to decay" and "groaning" (Rom. 8:21–22) because of the curse that was placed on the world through sin. The pain, suffering, and difficulty of life we experience result from damage to a created order that is now "not the way it's supposed to be," as Plantinga writes in his book of the same title.[20] It's not just that each of us sins; the *world* is broken.[21] **Brokenness**, *the impact of sin on all of creation*, affects not only each person's life now but also the lives of people in the future.[22] Plantinga writes that sin is "a polluted river that keeps branching and rebranching into tributaries," a parasite that keeps tapping its host (humans and all of creation) for survival. This continual stream "breaks down great institutions and whole societies."[23] Roman Catholic theology similarly concludes that the fruit of sins in social structures and relationships can affect people,[24] as "every sin has repercussions on . . . the whole human family."[25] A good creation is spoiled.

The result? We can expect (and do find) that patterns of human living and even the functioning of nature itself show brokenness. Sin damages how relationships operate, but it also damages how bodies function. Disease, genetic abnormalities, brain damage—the list goes on—were not part of the original creation but are the result of brokenness, as nature is distorted. A child of a convicted felon suffers from the parent's crime by being without that parent, and a child born with the genetic disorder Tay-Sachs disease will suffer progressive destruction of the nervous system and be unlikely to survive childhood. Natural disasters claim lives and livelihoods. Well-intentioned desires by a group to protect itself may result in discrimination against others, leading to violence that leaves scarred environments and systematic racism that causes animosities between groups well after physical fighting has ended. In a sin-free world, nature functions as God intended, and desires to follow God, to love others, and to care for creation are pure; in a broken world, things get pretty messed up. Each of us has suffered the consequences of being in a world with sin.

20. C. Plantinga, *Not the Way*.

21. This is different from having "a broken and contrite heart" in Ps. 51:17. That sense of brokenness means having a sincere remorse for sin and giving oneself up to God, realizing that sin is an offense against God's holy goodness.

22. Sins can affect future generations. In Exod. 20:5 (part of the Ten Commandments), worshiping other gods in place of God is unfaithfulness toward God, and this results in breaking the covenant with God. If a father rejects God's promises and takes his family into sin, the children will suffer the consequences.

23. C. Plantinga, *Not the Way*, 55.

24. *Catechism of the Catholic Church*, 103.

25. John Paul II, *Reconciliation and Penance*, 52.

This is getting depressing! But there is hope. Although damaged by sin and existing in a broken, fallen world, the relational core of God's image remains in us. The good news of the gospel is that the story does not end with our sin. God provided a way out of this mess through the death and resurrection of God's Son, Jesus Christ. Although we sin in this broken world, we are not in a state of despair. Romans 3:23–24 clearly indicates that "all have sinned and fall short of the glory of God, and all are justified freely by his grace through the redemption that came by Christ Jesus." As C. Stephen Evans writes, it is God who "created us in his image, who sorrowfully allowed us to reject him and break fellowship, and who sacrificially became one of us and suffered the effects of our rebellion so as to bring about a triumphant reconciliation."[26] **Salvation,** *making right the relationship between humanity and God,* is possible for people who accept Christ's death on their behalf.

Despite this gracious reconciliation, sin's consequences remain in a creation that is still "not the way it's supposed to be." Creation itself is damaged and needs renewal. On a community level, **structural sins**—*sins that are built into the very fabric of a society through laws and customs,* as is the case with racism—infect human institutions and groups. Structural sins need a structural solution. An entire organization may need to make broad changes or perhaps even disband and start again. On a personal level, old habits die hard, and better ones aren't always easily acquired. God desires better of us and for us than continuing to sin; he wants us to lead more Christlike lives. What theologians call **sanctification,** *becoming Christlike,* is a lifelong process (described more in chap. 9). As Paul writes, a "good work" was begun in believers by God, and it will be carried on "to completion until the day of Christ Jesus" (Phil. 1:6)—that is, when Christ returns. Writing to Christians, the author of Hebrews encourages fellow believers to "run with perseverance the race marked out for us" (Heb. 12:1) and to battle against sinful desires, making "every effort to live in peace with everyone and to be holy" (12:14).

What are God's people called to do in this life? Going back to the task given in Genesis, they are to transform God's creation by being his representatives (Gen. 1:28). This involves taking on Christian virtues and behaviors (Col. 3:12–13) as part of the body of believers (the church). Christians aren't alone in this: the Holy Spirit empowers and guides believers (Rom. 8). A Christian's life is a long-term transformation by God, not an instant change. And God makes this change possible. This change is personal and requires individual action, but it doesn't end there. It includes collective efforts to restore justice and love mercy in order to transform a broken society.

26. C. Evans, "Concept of the Self," 4.

Human Brokenness and Psychology

What does all this talk of sin and salvation have to do with psychology? Biblical truths about sin profoundly influence how Christians think about a host of issues, such as how predictable we are; how we perceive, learn, and think; how our personalities are formed; how we relate to others around us; and even how we conduct therapy. Human brokenness brings in some tricky questions about human behavior. For example, when children misbehave at age three and then gradually learn to be more obedient, is this a case of sin followed by sanctification, or is it just normal learning? Does Ethan—as described in the introduction—simply need to pray more and be more devout, as family friend Shawna suggests, or are his problems the result of flaws in genetics and environment? Pressing the issue even deeper, is sin an "extra ingredient" added to the source of his problems, or is brokenness woven throughout his relationships, his mental processes, or even his physical being?

To be perfectly honest, as Christian psychologists we have struggled to understand how our sinful tendencies are to be understood in the context of psychological theories. We don't have simple answers for these complex questions. However, we are fairly certain that psychological approaches that strongly emphasize ultimate human goodness or complete neutrality of human nature (tendency toward neither good nor bad) are going to fall short when trying to comprehensively explain human behavior. We will provide specific examples of these shortcomings in many of the chapters that follow.

Theme 3: Humans Are Embodied

We've all done it: we are trying to find something, only to discover it was right before our eyes all the time. An obvious but often overlooked characteristic about ourselves is that we are **embodied**: *we are physical beings living in a physical world, not just souls or spirits unaffected by our surroundings, circumstances, or health.* The Bible clearly confirms that our physicality is central to our humanity. In fact, it may be much more important than contemporary Christians have generally assumed. Genesis 2:7 says that God breathed life into dust, and Adam became a living being. Our relationships all have a physical dimension. Like Jesus, we touch, change our gaze to look someone in the eye, or even throw things when we're angry.[27] People physically interact with God—kneeling to

---

27. Just a few examples: Jesus touched to heal people (e.g., Matt. 8), he looked at his disciples to address them (e.g., Mark 10), and he threw over the tables of money changers in the temple (e.g., Matt. 21).

pray or audibly speaking praise, just as Christ did.[28] Physical existence impacts our way of interacting, making our relationality shaped by our being embodied. A comforting touch is pleasing, while a harsh look hurts. Made in God's image, we have a unique relationship with him, occupying a special place in his creation. This status comes to us, however, as creatures made from the "dust of the ground" (2:7), and we have much in common with the rest of creation (e.g., hunger, pain, emotions, etc.).

Physical activities are really important; some activities may bring people closer to God (e.g., prayer, giving food to the hungry), while other actions may widen the gulf between people and God (e.g., withholding care for others, failing to offer God what is his).[29] In the Lord's Supper (or Eucharist or communion, depending on church tradition), believers physically eat and drink as Christ commanded his disciples (John 6), and Christ said that by doing so, one "remains in me, and I in them" (6:56). There appear to be important spiritual consequences of physical behavior, in addition to the more obvious physical outcomes. Many of Jesus's interactions were with people who were born with physical disabilities like blindness (e.g., 9:1) or who had contracted diseases like leprosy (e.g., Mark 1:40). And of course people in the Bible became old, physically suffered, and died—just as we do.

Human Embodiment and Psychology

Psychology takes bodies seriously, focusing on phenomena such as how our physiology changes in response to the environment and what our brains do when we experience thought. Researchers increasingly examine our most intimate thoughts within the working brain and explore how hormones and bodily functions influence our everyday behaviors. Obviously, embodiment raises some interesting questions about how humans function.

For example, can we overcome our physical existence or mental problems by using some nonphysical part of us? Is it even possible or necessary to talk about body, mind, and soul given that research shows that our thoughts are tied to brain function? Can God work through physical mechanisms by altering brain activity when we relate to him?

These deep questions will be addressed in chapter 3, but at this point, we want to emphasize that Christians need to affirm that our earthly and creaturely

---

28. Jesus fell to the ground in prayer, e.g., in Mark 14; he spoke thanks to God, e.g., in John 6.

29. James 2:15–17 shows the interrelationship between physical behavior and faith: "Suppose a brother or a sister is without clothes and daily food. If one of you says to them, 'Go in peace; keep warm and well fed,' but does nothing about their physical needs, what good is it? In the same way, faith by itself, if it is not accompanied by action, is dead."

nature appears to be both scriptural and very consistent with contemporary understanding of human beings. Christians can also be a prophetic voice in the field of psychology by stressing that, despite our physical nature, we are more than the sum of our physical parts.

Theme 4: Humans Are Responsible Limited Agents

Scripture is clear that we can make choices and act responsibly. Adam and Eve chose to rebel against God, and they were held accountable for that choice. We have **limited agency**, *meaning we can make free choices and act in the world, but this ability has boundaries* and is perhaps far more restrictive than we would like to admit. The Bible clearly teaches that humans have choice, but we're constrained by our physical nature, our social environment, and even God's sovereign plans.

Responsibility implies that a person has some degree of choice in their behavior, so responsibility and agency are intertwined. The ability to choose, however, doesn't always imply responsibility. Being **responsible** *means being accountable relative to someone else.* If you betray a friend's trust, you feel responsible for that situation. However, you wouldn't feel as responsible for the broken trust experienced by someone you have no relationship with. Responsibility outside the context of a relationship makes no sense.

We need to look at both limited agency and responsibility a little more deeply because there is more to each than meets the eye. First, having agency implies not only that we make choices but also that we can change ourselves in some way. The Bible contains countless stories of people changing. Change can be a gradual, lifelong process, as in the life of the disciple Peter in the New Testament. Sometimes change occurs due to God's sudden and direct intervention (like the apostle Paul's experience in Acts 9). Other times change happens through deliberate choices people make ("Choose for yourselves this day whom you will serve. . . . As for me and my household, we will serve the Lord" [Josh. 24:15]).

People exist in a particular time and place, limiting how much they can change (there's that idea of limited agency again). In the case of the Israelites, as much as they might have wished to be free of Roman rule at the time of Christ, there wasn't much they could do about it. When the apostle Paul and his gospel coworker Silas were in prison for preaching (Acts 16), their choices were few. Embodiment limits choices.

But our limitations are deeper than just external factors like physical space and time. Past choices set us in directions that dictate present and future consequences, thereby restricting our future options. Each time we make a choice, we are set on a path. Think of heading down a trail and coming to a point where the trail forks to either the east or the west. If you take the west branch, that necessarily means you don't take the east one. Taking one path eliminates other alternatives—you don't, at least at that exact time, get to go down the other path, as life is lived only once. This concept gets ramped up considerably in Romans 6, where Paul emphasizes that we live life as slaves—not a slavery involving physical chains but a slavery of the mind and behavior. Paul emphasizes that we can be slaves of sin or slaves of righteousness. Slavery seems a little extreme, doesn't it, when we're just talking about choosing a trail? The idea here is that if someone were, for example, a slave of righteousness, some choices (trails) may not even come to mind or might be so offensive to that person that they never pursue them. It's like the choices have mental "trail closed" signs. God is at work in people who put their faith in him, bringing people to become more and more like Christ (Rom. 8:29). On the flip side, slavery to sin means that righteousness is not our default behavior. One's moral character, often developed through habits, further limits thoughts and behavior. So either righteousness or sinfulness can limit our freedom because we are fundamentally limited by our earlier choices.

There's a paradox with these limitations, however. Going back to the branching trail, while taking one path means others aren't taken, the path pursued opens all the possibilities of that path—possibilities unavailable if the other path had been taken. Keller has written that "the modern definition of freedom is the ability to do whatever we want."[30] He counters this notion with the story of a cardiac patient who loves his grandchildren but also loves to eat whatever he wants. His doctor tells him that if he doesn't restrict his diet, his heart problems will worsen and lead to a heart attack. Desires are in direct and grave conflict for this man. The question this man faces is not how to live completely free. "The proper question is: Which freedom is the more important, the more liberating?"[31] There is a freedom that comes from knowing limitations and then thriving within them.[32] To thrive in his life as a grandparent—to make all of it that he can—this man must necessarily turn away from something else.

One more comment is needed here: *being limited isn't sinful*. We are not God— the creature is not the Creator. We are not all-knowing or all-powerful, and God made us that way. Not paying attention to everything, forgetting where we left something, and needing to sleep are all part of being an embodied human, with no sinfulness necessarily attached.

30. Keller, *Making Sense of God*, 101.
31. Keller, *Making Sense of God*, 102.
32. Christ is recorded as saying, "Take my yoke upon you and learn from me, for I am gentle and humble in heart, and you will find rest for your souls. For my yoke is easy and my burden is light" (Matt. 11:29–30).

Now to the second issue: responsibility. The biblical view of responsibility is that it occurs both at the individual level and at the group level. A clear example of personal responsibility can be seen in Acts 5, in the story of a couple named Ananias and Sapphira who lied about money they were giving to the church. The result? Each of them died after telling their lie—definitely a stiff and very personal penalty! Focusing solely on individual responsibility, however, misses the Bible's bigger-picture view of what it means to be human. As described earlier, groups in the Old and New Testaments were praised or condemned for their collective responsibilities. This means that the response to sin is both personal and corporate, just like the consequences of sin. Myers puts it very clearly: "Because evil is collective as well as personal, responding to it takes a communal religious life."[33] Humans, together, have choices to make, and humans, together, are responsible for those choices. To the extent there is agency, persons are responsible for their behavior.

People may experience success or failure on their own, but the fate of the individual is always bound up within a group because humans are interconnected. This characteristic of human nature therefore implies that how we live out our lives is shaped by being persons *and* by the groups with which we align ourselves—our families, religious groups, and countries of origin, to name a few—and for Christians, this also includes the body of Christ, which is the church. People have responsibility to others, whether it is just one person or a nation. God's desire is for humans to have personal and corporate relationality that is harmonious and mutually uplifting.

Human Responsible Limited Agency and Psychology

Questions of responsibility and agency come up all the time in psychology. Obviously, if a psychologist concludes that someone has no ability to choose, then the notion of responsibility is irrelevant; it is impossible to be responsible without real choice.

Psychologists disagree about our ability to choose;[34] it naturally follows that they would also disagree about how responsible people are for their behavior. Some psychologists (e.g., B. F. Skinner) assume that we have no ability to choose, which impacts the kind of research questions they ask. Rather than looking at situations in which people make choices, these psychologists study how changes in the environment change behavior. Other psychologists (e.g., Carl Rogers) assume almost unlimited agency for humans, so these theorists

33. Myers, "Levels-of-Explanation View," 61.
34. Just one of a number of books that debate this question is Baer, Kaufman, and Baumeister, *Are We Free?*

might design studies to help determine what choices people make or to understand the impact of choices.

Psychological research shows that several factors may influence the degree to which people exercise the limited agency they have and whether they take responsibility for their behavior. A variety of experiments, for example, indicate that some conditions and situations make it easier to follow moral codes, while other conditions and situations make doing so more difficult, as discussed in chapter 12. In addition, differences in brain development and the consequences of brain injury show that people differ in their ability to consider choices and even to understand the consequences of their own behavior (discussed in chap. 3). Psychological science, when it acknowledges the agency of persons and their potential for responsible behavior, gives insights into how to be responsible and how responsible we can be. Responsibility, like agency, can be limited. Understanding that we have limitations should lead to a sense of empowerment. The more we know about influences (internal and external), the more effectively we can assert and reassert agency because we know the boundaries within which we work. Those believing that behaviors are uninfluenced by forces outside their control are the ones most limited by these forces because they fail to recognize them. In the case of our limited agency, knowledge is power.

In later chapters, we will see that debates over the extent of personal agency are pervasive in psychology. Recall Ethan from the introduction: To what degree are his behaviors the products of his choices, and to what degree are they determined by factors in his environment, like his home life and school situation?

Theme 5: Humans Are Meaning Seekers

The previous four themes provide a basis for describing who and what we are, but as psychologists, we also want to explore *why* we act. We may be relational, broken, embodied, and responsible limited agents, but if we have the capacity to make choices, why do we choose certain paths over others? Are we driven forward mindlessly by our past and present relationships, sin, bodies, and limited minds, or can we direct our thoughts and actions with something more? We propose a fifth characteristic of human nature, that humans are **meaning seekers**: *we consistently try to make sense of our surroundings, experiences, and purpose.*

At least three aspects of meaning seeking are fundamental to human nature. First, at a most basic level, we *perceive patterns*. We sense and take in our world in ways that are virtually automatic and fundamental to understanding what events in the environment mean and how to respond to them. But we don't just see or hear things; we interpret them. Sights and sounds are perceived as patterns, so we can recognize a friend by their shape and voice, for example. In addition, to care for creation we need to be able to navigate our environment, understand how it works, and plan next actions.

Second, we seek meaning through *creatively understanding experiences*. Creativity is seen in how we often work at making sense of our experiences to understand how things work (including ourselves!) and plan what to do next. What did an event mean? Why did I do that? What should I do now? In the Bible, people are described as understanding (and often misunderstanding) Jesus's words. For example, when miraculous events occur, the disciples try to interpret their meaning (e.g., Mark 9:10), but their creative interpretations could be wrong.[35] They, like us, want to figure things out. We, like the disciples, gain fuller understanding through God revealing his truth to us, particularly when trying to understand God (e.g., Matt. 16:12; 17:13). Nevertheless, as Evans has stated, part of our nature is to be thinkers.[36] This leads us to seek meaning.

The third dimension to meaning seeking is the human *desire for a deity*. Christians believe that because we are made by God and meant to be in relationship with him, ultimate meaning comes from God, who created and redeems his people. The Bible also makes clear that we are built to worship something, and although God clearly deserves that worship, we turn to other things. Here's what Romans 1 says about this:

> For since the creation of the world God's invisible qualities—his eternal power and divine nature—have been clearly seen, being understood from what has been made, so that people are without excuse. For although they knew God, they neither glorified him as God nor gave thanks to him, but their thinking became futile and their foolish hearts were darkened. Although they claimed to be wise, they became fools and exchanged the glory of the immortal God for images made to look like a mortal human being and birds and animals and reptiles. (Rom. 1:20–23)

People have a sense of there being some higher power, pushing them toward worship, but that sense gets misguided. Under theme 2, we talked about the effects of sin separating us from God and of us trying to make ourselves individual gods. Attempts at individual self-fulfillment dominate people, but those individual desires can never fill the gulf that sin has created between God and each person. We look for ultimate or even just intermediate levels of meaning

---

35. E.g., in Mark 8:14–21, when Jesus's disciples misinterpret his cautions about Herod, thinking they need to bring more bread.
36. C. Evans, "Concept of the Self," 5.

in our individuality rather than in God. Note the turnabout that occurs in the last sentences of the passage from Romans 1. Rather than worshiping God, people turn to worship other things—perhaps things more easily understood, tangible, and possibly manipulated by people. The point is that, for humans, it's easy for something to take the place of God.

In the end, meaning seeking is more than just how we think about things; it is what we do, and it ties directly to our propensity to worship. James K. A. Smith emphasizes that our worship takes up our reasoning and emotion and that a Christian view of persons must emphasize our desires, those fundamental intentions that can occur in mostly unconscious and strongly emotional ways.[37] As Smith has stressed, humans cannot be reduced to just their rational characteristics. We have desires, and we direct them toward what is and becomes most important to us. These desires show what we worship—what is our god.

Human Meaning Seeking and Psychology

Psychologists debate the degree to which humans are meaning seekers, just as they debate whether people have agency. Those with a more limited view of agency are also likely to argue against extensive meaning seeking in humans. Behaviorists like B. F. Skinner acknowledge that we reflexively respond to patterns but would reject the idea that humans actively seek meaning. However, Carl Rogers would emphasize not only that humans *do* pursue meaning in all situations but also that they *should*. One group that would fall somewhere between these two is cognitive psychologists, some of whom emphasize our unchanging responses to simple events in the environment, like responding to a bright light, while others focus on how expectations shape our interpretations, such as when we misidentify a stranger as the friend we expected to meet (see chap. 5 for more examples).

We believe that people make meaning all the time and that psychological theories without that perspective will underestimate humans. In our desire to "make sense of our world," as David Myers and C. Nathan DeWall write, "people are prone to pattern-seeking."[38] This brings together both our simple pattern perception and our creative meaning making. Humans don't let events go unexplained—we demand explanations for everything from the cause of car accidents (traffic investigations) to why a team won the Super Bowl (the postgame interview and analysis).

While perceiving patterns is apparent, even in animals, the propensity to look for gods is utterly human. Developmental research in the cognitive science

37. J. Smith, *Desiring the Kingdom*, 51.
38. Myers and DeWall, *Psychology*, 22, 23.

of religion echoes the Bible's notion that people are born to believe. Researchers, having studied children's beliefs and citing developmental evidence that "religion is natural,"[39] have proposed that children may be "intuitive theists"[40] or "born believers,"[41] as we discuss in chapter 9. In many ways, however, psychologists have neglected to consider this basic aspect of personhood, maintaining a mechanistic ("person as machine") view of humans. That perspective suggests that we are driven by simple, practical goals like survival, avoiding pain, seeking pleasure, and learning. Other psychologists, however, believe that humans are the only species strongly motivated to understand why they exist and are driven to find deeper purposes. Humanistic psychologists such as Carl Rogers and Abraham Maslow proposed that people are moved to attain self-actualization, which includes meaning and purpose.[42] Positive psychologists such as Martin Seligman likewise propose that the happiest people are those with a deep sense of meaning in their lives.[43] There may be helpful elements in all these perspectives. Most people do generally try to avoid pain. But we believe that Scripture points to a strong internal tendency not only to seek meaning but also to act based on what we feel is meaningful. How the issues of meaning and purpose (and even worship) play out in psychology will be addressed further in several chapters.

A Look Forward

What does psychology tell us about these relationships with God, others, and creation? Psychological science is all about the exploration of our interactions with and understanding of the world—its things and inhabitants, including ourselves—and tries to characterize them scientifically. Christianity asserts that we're made not only for such physical interactions but also for a spiritual relationship with God. There are some things that psychology can tell us about our relationship with God. Psychology can empirically (e.g., using scientific observation) study our attempts to relate to God. It's possible to objectively observe activities like church attendance, gather self-reports of how much one prays, or measure on a scale of 1 to 10 how important one believes God is in life, yet this gives us only part of the story. We *cannot* study God's interactions with us in an empirical way. Claiming that God's actions are responsible for

39. P. Bloom, "Religion Is Natural."
40. Keleman, "Are Children 'Intuitive Theists'?"
41. Barrett, "Cognitive Science."
42. Rogers, *Way of Being*, 120; Maslow, *Motivation and Personality*.
43. Seligman, *Authentic Happiness*, 14.

what someone does simply isn't a scientific explanation—it doesn't count by science's rules, as we will discuss in the next chapter. So psychology's understanding of our relationship with God and, even more, God's relationship with us has a significant limitation. However, psychology's abilities to look at how we relate with humans (who are physical) and the world (also physical) are much more promising. When dealing with objectively measurable causes and consequences, science works. These relationships and the characteristics of humans that are pertinent to them will be our focus as we proceed with this book.

In this chapter, we began with the significance of being made in God's image. "If humans are created in God's image, we should expect to see certain characteristics appear in psychological studies of humans."[44] The biblical truths about human nature will not always allow us to accept or reject the multitude of specific theories, research, or practices in psychology, but they can direct us to accept or reject certain presuppositions or views that inform our theories and practices. Each of the major areas within psychology has a particular focus when describing humans. The remainder of this book will look at how major areas of psychology—biological, clinical, cognitive, developmental, social, and others—approach humans and how these approaches fit with the biblical depiction of humans.

DISCUSSION QUESTIONS

1. Can psychology add further insight to a biblical view of human nature? If so, how do we take up the findings of psychology yet remain true to the Bible's view of human nature?

2. Do people differ in their level of agency, depending on their psychological status? Do people with limited intellectual capacity have less agency, and if so, do they also have less responsibility?

3. Is it possible to measure God's action in this world through physical evidence?

4. How does our drive for meaning influence how we interpret actions in the world? Does our drive to make meaning influence whether we perceive physical events as supernaturally caused?

5. Did our fundamental drive for meaning lead to science? Why or why not?

44. Seligman, *Authentic Happiness*, 183.

6. Identify behaviors that show the difference between having limited agency and being broken, in need of redemption.

7. What constraints are on your life? What has held you back if you ever wanted to change yourself—your study habits, your weight, your exercise patterns, perhaps something as seemingly simple as how often you say "um" in a sentence?

2

People Predicting People

Research Methodology

▶ SUMMARY: Psychological science assumes that through observation and testing, predictions can be made about human behavior. In this chapter, we discuss how these methods and assumptions relate to a Christian view of human nature. We then explore how psychology's attempts to predict human behavior correspond to responsible limited agency. In addition, we discuss how psychological science draws conclusions, particularly as related to our being meaning seekers. Finally, we look at ways that Christians might have a unique impact on psychological research through their choice of research topics.

Test them all; hold on to what is good.

1 Thessalonians 5:21

Psychologists love a good test. We're not talking about course exams; they're no more fun for professors to grade than they are for students to take. No, psychologists love a good test of a hypothesis. Typically, this means getting data (numbers indicating behavioral characteristics), such as scores on a scale of personality, speed to detect traffic changes, or happiness ratings when spending money on yourself versus someone else. Testing is so loved because it gives concrete results that address specific questions psychologists investigate. This lets psychologists explore how we recognize a friend's voice in a noisy crowd, or whether caffeine makes people more productive (or just makes them believe they are).

Psychological *Science*?

Examining the kinds of questions mentioned above might not fit the popular image of what psychologists do. In our experience as psychologists, a typical reaction when telling someone you're a psychologist is "Well, I guess I'd better watch what I say!" People sometimes ask if we are trying to "analyze" them. Such responses are indicative of what psychologist Keith Stanovich has labeled "the Freud problem."[1] Stanovich writes that if you ask one hundred people on the street to name a psychologist, "Sigmund Freud" would be the top answer. They're partly right—Freud was interested in psychology, but his training was in medicine. Among the problems with this answer, however, is that modern psychology looks almost nothing like Freud's practice. Today, only a tiny minority of psychologists are concerned with Freudian psychoanalysis. Freud actually steered clear of the sort of experimental basis that is the foundation of today's psychology.

Current psychology is well characterized by the sort of definition given in today's introductory psychology textbooks, which boils down to this: **psychology is the science of behavior and mental processes**. Let's look at the components of this definition. First, *science* means that psychology uses systematic observation (also known as the empirical method) and repeatable, verifiable findings.[2] Psychology explores questions that can be tested using methods currently available to give natural (versus supernatural) explanations for those questions. In fact, this method is the common factor that holds together the diverse topics that psychologists study. How does playing violent video games influence one's sense of smell? It probably doesn't, yet both video games and smell are studied by psychology! What puts them under the umbrella of psychology is that they are mental and behavioral phenomena studied using scientific methods. The word *behavior* means the externally observable actions of a person—what people do alone or with others. *Mental processes* are internal functions, particularly ones in the brain, that can be inferred from behavior, self-report, or brain-scanning techniques.

1. Stanovich, *How to Think Straight about Psychology*, 2.
2. Stanovich, *How to Think Straight about Psychology*, 6.

Science's Assumptions

Predicting Natural Phenomena

For their science to be possible, psychologists must make assumptions. First, science specifies the focus of its study: **natural phenomena**, *which are events that can be detected by the senses and are assumed to be predictable or regular*. Psychological science assumes that humans have a large degree of uniformity or regularity. Further, psychology must assume that nature is real (what we see, hear, etc., actually exists) and that these regularities and reality can be discovered.[3] These assumptions are the same ones chemists use when studying the molecular structure of any substance. Chemists assume that atoms function in regular, predictable ways so that when two parts hydrogen are combined with one part oxygen, water results. If behavior was not regular in any way, as we tell students in psychology research methods courses, we may as well pull down the Psychology Department sign and go home—there would be no point in trying to figure out how humans generally act. We can't talk about what is likely to happen if *anything* is likely.

People tend to be of two minds about this notion of the regularity of human behavior. On the one hand, we act as though we believe people will behave as expected. We predict other people's behaviors all the time. For example, if you drive a car, you expect that everyone else will act "normal"—they will obey traffic lights, drive on the proper side of the road, and generally not cause mayhem. When people fail to follow these rules (as we have all experienced at times), we are surprised, frustrated, or even scared. We also anticipate consistency in ourselves—that studying for an exam or practicing a skill will improve our performance. We assume that usual circumstances and behaviors will lead to expected outcomes.

On the other hand, while you may be okay with predicting the behavior of yourself and others, you may not like it when the situation is reversed and someone else is predicting *your* behavior. Psychologist John Gottman and colleagues developed a series of tasks that, when completed by married couples, allowed them to predict with an amazing 93 percent accuracy which marriages would end in divorce over the next fourteen years.[4] They did this by seeing whether a couple was behaving like couples from one of their earlier studies who had divorced versus those who had not.[5] They determined which group a couple belonged to, and based on this, they predicted likelihoods of divorce

3. Christensen, Johnson, and Turner, *Research Methods, Design, and Analysis*, 7.
4. Gottman and Levenson, "Timing of Divorce."
5. Buehlman, Gottman, and Katz, "How a Couple Views Their Past."

with great accuracy. Although we may not like the idea that someone can tell us what we will do before we do it, this research suggests that in the case of divorce, Gottman and his colleagues can.

Naturalism versus Methodological Naturalism

Christians may have an objection to this notion of regularity in behavior, as it appears to conflict with the Bible's view of humans and God. Within the assumption of uniformity can be an additional notion known as **determinism**: *the belief that mental processes and behaviors are caused only by preexisting factors (there is no free will or choice involved in a behavior)*. One understanding of how everything works that can follow determinism is **naturalism**: *a worldview that assumes only natural causes to events, with no room for spiritual or supernatural explanations or characteristics*. While a Christian view holds "that each and every thing that exists, other than God, exists because of God and God's creative activity," as philosopher C. Stephen Evans has stated, a naturalist believes that "all of these things exist 'on their own,' so to speak. . . . There is no reason or purpose behind the existence of the universe as a whole or the individual entities that compose it."[6] According to this perspective, your beliefs about God are entirely explained by your environment (e.g., childhood experiences and ideas you were exposed to) and your brain's response to it. God played no role either in creating you or in how your environment responds.

Many psychologists, and certainly most Christian psychologists, would have a problem with pure naturalism and choose a different approach: *methodological* naturalism. **Methodological naturalism** *uses the methods of science, as naturalism does, but does not necessarily assume that the reasons for how the universe functions and why events occur are solely natural*. The methods of naturalism are used, but the philosophy of naturalism isn't fully embraced. This position is not anti-scientific because one doesn't need to accept all of naturalism to accept the effectiveness of the scientific method. Science's tools aid in studying the regularities of the world and human behavior, but like all tools, they have their limits. While a hammer effectively drives a nail through wood, a piece of cloth would be lousy at that job because it isn't designed to be effective on nails. Science studies the natural world, but it's not set up to study whether reality consists of more than just what science can investigate—it's not designed for that—so supernatural explanations are outside the boundaries of what science can study.

Boundaries affect what people study, but they also extend into how they interpret what they study. Both theists (believers in God) and atheists (nonbelievers)

6. C. Evans, *Why Christian Faith Still Makes Sense*, 22.

can agree that scientific findings, even scientific laws, apply to the natural world and to people. However, as Evans has written, the interpretation by these folks will differ: "The theist believes those laws hold because of God's creative activity; the atheist can give no such explanation." Importantly, Evans adds that "there are no scientific experiments that can decide the question of whether the natural world is all there is. Such questions are philosophical in nature."[7] Science, by its very method and restrictions, can neither prove nor disprove God's existence. The supernatural is outside its territory. People from a variety of faith (or non-faith) backgrounds, cultures, and worldviews who accept the methodological naturalism perspective can affirm the use of the scientific method while still embracing realities beyond just what we see. This perspective allows for a difference in interpretation of why people exist and do what they do, such as being created by God or living in a broken world. It's the difference between seeing humans as a result of random circumstance (naturalist's perspective) and seeing them as being part of God's divine creation and purpose (theist's perspective).

What about Supernatural Phenomena?

Christians claim that God and supernatural phenomena are real (avoiding naturalism) and that humans have some degree of free choice (avoiding determinism), so why are they doing science at all? For people of faith, aren't God and spiritual life all that really matter? Science can help Christians in living out a life of faith in at least two ways. First, along with our relationship with God, core human relationships include those with other humans and with creation.[8] God made people physical beings in a physical world. Learning more about how that creation works and how we work should make us better caretakers of each other and creation, fitting our nature as relational persons bearing God's image (theme 1). Second, understanding influences on our behavior can increase agency. Not knowing what changes our behavior leaves us more vulnerable to that influence and less in control of our behavior.

Studying creation also tells us about God. This is a theological notion called **general revelation**: *God shows something of himself in what he has created.*[9] Creations you made as a child, whether scribbles on paper or more elaborate glue/paper/glitter self-portraits, reflect who you were in terms of abilities, interests, and more. Creation reflects who God is; he made it entirely[10] and out

---

7. C. Evans, *Why Christian Faith Still Makes Sense*, 23.

8. Jesus called his followers to pray for each other and also to take care of their physical and emotional needs (Matt. 25:43–45).

9. Worthington, *Coming to Peace with Psychology*, 76.

10. See, particularly, the first portion of Ps. 19.

of nothing (Heb. 11:3).[11] We are part of creation, so the image of God carried by us reflects God. Studying ourselves tells us more about God (Rom. 1:20).[12] Malcolm Jeeves describes creation as *theocentric*—it is meant to reveal God so that people can know God better. God is deeply interested in his creation, and humans in particular. Jeeves writes that the Bible has a theocentric emphasis that primarily deals "with humankind in relation to God their Creator, Sustainer, and Redeemer."[13]

Doing science does not conflict with Christian faith; in fact, it can reinforce faith as God's infinite abilities and care are seen in creation.[14] A note of caution is necessary here, however. Theme 5 suggests that we have a tendency toward worship—we are meaning seekers looking for a god. Enjoyment of creation may turn to a worship of creation or even a worship of ourselves in making discoveries (being infatuated with ourselves for ingenuity in discovery) if we overlook God's creating all of creation, including us. The theologian John Calvin advised, "To be so occupied in the investigation of the secrets of nature, as never to turn the eyes to its Author, is a most perverted study; and to enjoy everything in nature without acknowledging the Author of the benefit, is the basest ingratitude."[15]

Predictably Human?

The order and regularity seen in creation reflect the orderliness of its Creator, and these properties are sustained by God's action. This regularity and thus potential predictability have clear benefits in fields such as chemistry and biology. Obviously, it helps that salt consistently dissolves in water. Cooking, for instance, would be a lot harder to pull off if we never knew what salt might do in water. But is human behavior *that* predictable? Does science see humans as machines that respond to laws of nature like salt dissolving in water? Can all of psychology achieve the level of success that Gottman has had in predicting divorce?

Failures in Prediction Due to Insufficient Knowledge

We believe the short and correct answer to each of these questions is no. Here is the beginning of one reason why: salt doesn't always dissolve in water.

11. Clear statements of God's creating everything are found in several other Old Testament and New Testament verses, including Neh. 9:6; Ps. 146:6; Acts 14:17; Rev. 4:11.
12. Yet this knowledge of God through creation does not bring salvation—Christians believe that Jesus Christ brings salvation.
13. Jeeves, *Human Nature at the Millennium*, 100.
14. See Myers, "Levels-of-Explanation View," 50–51, for further discussion of how Christians have been leaders in science and how they search for truth.
15. Calvin, *Commentaries on the First Book of Moses*, 60.

If the temperature is below fifteen degrees Fahrenheit, salt just sits on top of water (which would then be ice). Living in a snowy part of the United States, we are well aware of the fact that salt doesn't melt ice on sidewalks when it is too cold, so one must tread carefully. Known chemical reactions, like salt dissolving in water, are altered depending on circumstances. When important dimensions of the future are not known, results are **nondeterministic**: *the idea that more than one possible outcome could occur.* In the example of salt meeting water, our inability to predict what happens to the salt is due to our lack of knowledge about the situation in which the salt exists (in the cases outlined above, the key variable is temperature). This kind of nondeterminism is due to insufficient knowledge.[16] If all conditions were known beforehand, this kind of nondeterminism could be eliminated. In the case of Gottman's research, the reason that predicting marriage outcomes isn't 100 percent correct may be that he and his researchers did not identify all the factors that influence marital success. If they did, perhaps their prediction would be perfect.

Failures in Prediction Due to Humans' Limited Agency

A second kind of nondeterminism occurs due to **real chance**:[17] *when what is being studied has at least some degree of unpredictability or apparent randomness built into it.* Unpredictability or randomness is part of how humans work. People may work to defy prediction, such as when a couple, after having their marriage quality reviewed by a Gottman-type study, says, "Forget them saying that we're getting divorced; we're staying together!" and works to do so, perhaps picking up John Gottman and Nan Silver's book, *The Seven Principles for Making Marriage Work.*[18] This couple would be exercising free will—humans have agency, limited though it is (theme 4).

How much agency humans have is definitely debated by psychologists. The main issue is whether we make real choices on our own or whether what appear to be choices are caused by factors over which we have no control, leaving us with no real choice. Freud thought that if we understood the animalistic drives that motivate humans, things such as sex and hunger, it would be clear that humans have no freedom.[19] B. F. Skinner assumed that we are simply products of our environment, and once the environment is fully understood, we can discard any idea of free will.[20] They had different starting points, but both Freud and

---

16. This is otherwise known as epistemic chance.

17. What we have called *real chance* here is known among philosophers as *ontological chance.* See chap. 5, "Chance," in Howell and Bradley, *Mathematics through the Eyes of Faith.*

18. Gottman and Silver, *Seven Principles.*

19. Freud, *Complete Introductory Lectures,* 49, 106.

20. Skinner, *Beyond Freedom and Dignity,* 98.

Skinner thought that free will is at most very limited—more likely nonexistent. Humanistic psychologist Carl Rogers,[21] on the other extreme, saw free will as virtually limitless. The Bible's perspective, as stated in theme 4, is that people have some real choices and real responsibility. Joshua, speaking to the tribes of Israel, gives a clear example: "Choose for yourselves this day whom you will serve, whether the gods your ancestors served beyond the Euphrates, or the gods of the Amorites, in whose land you are living. But as for me and my household, we will serve the LORD" (Josh. 24:15). In this case, choice allows for chance, what is known as **nondeterminacy**: *more than one outcome is possible*. Chance doesn't mean absolute randomness. Joshua knows that people will worship *something* (the human nature of meaning seekers being what it is). Humans show limited agency but also very regular patterns in how they behave. Choice happens, but always within constraints.

God has given people some degree of agency. One way of thinking about this, argued by Russell Howell and James Bradley,[22] is in terms of God as the primary cause of all things in the universe. In addition, God created secondary agents, including people and natural processes in the universe (as well as the laws that govern these processes), to maintain his creation.[23]

God did more than just set up the rules and let the universe run; God is actively involved in the world, with people also playing an active role. The Bible records God's acts as speaking with people through various means,[24] directing natural phenomena,[25] and sending Jesus Christ to save believers from sin (1 Tim. 1:15). More broadly, God also shows **providence**—*God's continued preserving and upholding of creation*—using natural phenomena and the circumstances provided by them.[26] God doesn't micromanage every single step, however. God set up the way creation works and can guide its unfolding, but humans are God's image bearers who steward creation and can act in creation in ways that are not fully preset. Chance exists in the world, but it is not purposeless or without any direction.

21. Rogers, *On Becoming a Person*, 203.

22. Howell and Bradley, *Mathematics through the Eyes of Faith*. Their argument here follows the logic of Thomas Aquinas.

23. This big-picture view of God's activity fits with the idea of methodological determinism, described above.

24. E.g., God spoke directly to Moses (e.g., Exod. 19:19) and Abraham (e.g., Gen. 17), as well as through the prophets and Jesus (Heb. 1:1–2).

25. E.g., God's assurance in Gen. 8:22: "As long as the earth endures, seedtime and harvest, cold and heat, summer and winter, day and night will never cease."

26. God upholds all of creation. Acts 17:24 states that God "made the world and everything in it" and that God continues to be "Lord of heaven and earth." God maintains this world regardless of human worthiness, as shown in Matt. 5:45, which says that God "causes his sun to rise on the evil and the good, and sends rain on the righteous and the unrighteous."

Limited Nondeterminacy

Chance is real, but we don't want to overstate the nondeterminacy or un-predictability of human behavior. People act in systematic, regular ways, and psychology does a marvelous job of helping us understand those regularities—many of which are outlined in introductory psychology textbooks. Human agency is limited, as we simply can't contemplate all choices at once (we get overloaded by choice possibilities, as we discuss in chap. 8 on thinking), and we can follow through on only one choice at a time (i.e., we live each moment only one time—no do-overs). It's interesting, then, that we often give up the opportunity to exercise choice by just doing what we usually do (without con-sidering alternatives). A simple example of this comes from classrooms. Neither of us uses assigned seating in our courses, yet by the second week of classes, most students have self-assigned themselves to a seat. People sit, habitually, in the same place day after day, despite no request to do so and there being several other empty seats. By going to the same seat every day, no decision needs to be made. But in doing so, each student, usually unknowingly, gives up an opportunity to exercise free will. This happens term after term; it's a very predictable pattern of not choosing.

One semester, one of us brought this pattern to a class's attention to highlight how we limit our free will through habit. The next time the class met, some students switched to a new seat, although only for that day. Then it was back to usual. Two students, however, sat in different seats every day for the rest of the term! The rest never changed, saying that they could have moved but, after thinking about it, were happier where they already were. Bottom line: choice opportunities may or may not result in a change of behavior, even when agency is involved. People have a choice about using or not using choice.

This variation in individual behavior gives some insight into the fact that psychological science isn't generally designed to predict the behavior of any particular person. Instead, psychologists compare groups with other groups (or occasionally they compare a single individual with a group, in the situation of a case study), knowing that individuals within groups differ from each other. For example, not all couples with marital difficulty are alike. While most couples that show unhealthy communication patterns in a marriage eventually divorce, not every single couple that showed that behavior did divorce.[27] Psychologists may be very good at predicting the behavior of a group but less accurate when it comes to predicting the behavior of any single individual.[28]

27. Gottman and Levenson, "Timing of Divorce."
28. Group versus individual prediction is apparent in insurance rates, which are based on group membership. E.g., single people pay more than married folks. Of course, marriage ceremonies don't include lessons on better driving, but married people tend to have fewer accidents than

To summarize, two factors, (1) insufficient knowledge and (2) human's limited agency, are fundamental in why predictions in psychology are **probabilistic**: *a prediction in terms of what is likely but not guaranteed to occur*. Psychological scientists use their findings to predict what *most* people are *likely* to do in particular circumstances. That, however, is quite different from being able to predict what *all* people will *definitely* do.

Seeking Meaning through Science

Science generates facts about the natural world and natural phenomena. It is generally neutral regarding moral and ethical questions.[29] Psychological science, due to its method and reliance on only natural explanations, can't answer moral questions. Values and beliefs, not science, are the basis for morality. Science-generated facts can provide information relevant to moral questions, such as indicating what could occur if someone were to do one thing versus something else. Knowing likely consequences of an action is helpful, but it doesn't help us decide whether an action is right or wrong. Imagine a parent trying to decide whether punishing a misbehaving child by giving a time-out (separating from the child with no interaction for a few minutes) is better than yelling at the child. Psychological findings can provide statistics on the outcomes of these two parenting techniques—for example, how each affects the parent-child relationship or whether children tend to act more responsibly following one or the other. How the parent prioritizes relationships and being responsible, however, is ultimately a question of values. Scientific information can offer insights to help the parent make the judgment, but it can't actually judge what makes an outcome ultimately good or bad.

Psychology's findings regarding human behavior and moral questions are better seen as *descriptive*—telling or describing how things are—rather than *prescriptive*—telling us how things should be. As David Myers, author of a best-selling introductory psychology textbook, writes, the "ultimate" questions of life—How should I live? What is the purpose of life?—are not answered by psychology. "Instead, expect that psychology will help you understand why people think, feel, and act as they do. Then you should find the study of psychology fascinating and useful."[30] Questions about life's ultimate purpose are,

---

single people. If you are insured, your insurer doesn't know whether you, specifically, will have fewer accidents if you're married; they know that married people in general have fewer accidents than those not married, so such people cost less to insure.

29. See chap. 3, "Should There Be a Christian Psychology?," in Myers and Jeeves, *Psychology through the Eyes of Faith*, for further explanation of this.

30. Myers, *Psychology*, 10.

for Christians, addressed in the Bible and in the contexts of relationships with God and God's people.

Meaning Seekers Conducting Research

Values, therefore, are critical in determining whether to use scientific information. Philosophers of science have noted that the beginning of the scientific process is also full of values, and even the process of doing science is not as unbiased as may be presumed.[31] A **worldview**, *the fundamental values and commitments that are a person's guideposts for living and morality*, impacts questions of what should be studied, how people will interpret findings, and even how they might implement findings.[32]

Paging through an introductory psychology textbook shows this variability in what is judged worthy of time and effort. Just as students use individual criteria (like personal interest in a class, difficulty of previous tests, and current course grade) to determine how much they will study for a test, so psychologists use their own set of criteria to choose what they will research. Interests and research agendas flow from psychologists' worldview values, stemming from sources like one's nationality, current psychological state, and religious beliefs. Training and experience, along with practical matters like availability of funding to do studies, also influence which questions are asked. Looking at how different psychologists approach studying ADHD in people like Ethan (described in the introduction) provides a good example of how such influences play out. A developmental psychologist would likely focus on how ADHD changes over the course of Ethan's life, while a cognitive psychologist might study how his memory abilities differ from those of people without ADHD. A social psychologist may look at how people interact differently with people like Ethan if they think he does or does not have ADHD, while a physiological psychologist would likely focus on how Ethan's brain differs from that of someone without ADHD.

The reason for these differences in interests, we believe, goes back to theme 5: we are meaning seekers trying to understand the world. Past experiences and worldviews influence our priorities. For Christians, faith commitments should impact what is deemed worthy of study in psychology and what to do with

31. Kuhn, *Structure of Scientific Revolutions*, 77–79.

32. A more complete definition of **worldview**: "A commitment, a fundamental orientation of the heart, that can be expressed as a story or in a set of presuppositions (assumptions which may be true, partially true or entirely false) that can hold (consciously or subconsciously, consistently or inconsistently) about the basic constitution of reality, and that provides the foundation on which we live and move and have our being." Sire, *Universe Next Door*, 20.

those findings. A pivotal question for a Christian to ask when contemplating a potential psychological study should be "Will this honor God?" That can include asking whether core relationships will be built up in God-honoring ways by the work done. Myers and Jeeves give the following example: "Just as physics can be used to trigger nuclear explosions or to relieve suffering through radiotherapy, so psychology can be used to manipulate individuals or groups or to relieve anxiety and depression."[33] We believe that Christian psychologists must continually use their faith as a beginning point for psychological research.[34]

The research path of one of our colleagues, Blake Riek, shows the influence that a Christian worldview might have on research. He has specialized in studying interpersonal relationships and recognized that past research on forgiveness focused primarily on the effects of granting forgiveness, such as how health and happiness improve for the person who forgives.[35] Riek's Christian worldview influenced his research direction, as he understood that the Christian view of forgiveness is about the restoration of relationships, not just personal improvement. For a relationship to be restored following an offense, people may need to seek out and receive forgiveness.[36] The Bible repeatedly emphasizes seeking forgiveness from others and God to heal broken relationships.[37] Riek used that understanding to design studies that explored the components of a biblical picture of forgiveness.[38] His faith perspective led him to see additional components of forgiveness. It enriched his research and helped illuminate the conditions under which forgiveness is more likely to occur.

Meaning Seekers Interpreting Research

Differences in priorities, extending even to how we see the world, can be labeled biases: *simple prejudgments in favor of one alternative or another*[39]—that is, we like one thing or idea more than another from the outset, and that influences

33. Myers and Jeeves, *Psychology through the Eyes of Faith*, 12. Myers, "Levels-of-Explanation View," also gives helpful examples of how Christian faith can relate to psychological research.

34. In *Reason within the Bounds of Religion*, Wolterstorff strongly advocates that Christians take just this approach (105–6).

35. Riek and Mania, "Antecedents and Consequences."

36. "Forgive, and you will be forgiven" (Luke 6:37).

37. Many passages emphasize repentance—being sorrowful and contrite about past behavior. Repentance is tied to forgiveness. A great example of this is Ps. 51, where King David begs God for forgiveness following his adultery with Bathsheba.

38. E.g., Riek, Root Luna, and Schnabelrauch, "Transgressor's Guilt and Shame."

39. We have a lot more to say in chap. 8 about how psychology has studied human biases as they influence thinking and decision making.

the work we do. Biases also influence how people draw conclusions based on research findings.[40] Our general tendency toward seeking meaning deeply influences our interpretation of research.

Our biases can be apparent when we like or don't like what research "says." Because psychology is about you (and us), there may be ideas we personally hold that are confronted by psychological research, and the two do not line up. For example, classic research by Stanley Milgram shows that average people will obey an authority figure even to the point of acting immorally.[41] A person may look at such research and say, "People aren't like that; no one can make me do something I don't want to do," and reject it out of hand (regardless of the amount of evidence supporting it).

Similarly, what is a Christian to do if a research finding goes against their Christian beliefs? Here's an example: some research on prayer has shown it to be ineffective in helping physically heal people who were being prayed for,[42] concluding that prayer is ineffective. The Bible clearly stresses the importance and effectiveness of prayer.[43] In the research, both on obedience and on prayer, an important personal belief appears to be contradicted by research. Again, what should be the response?

Christian research psychologist Scott VanderStoep writes that the first gut response—"I don't believe it!"—is a nonstarter for taking any psychological research seriously.[44] The beginning point of critiquing research is to evaluate its scientific merit. If the research was poorly designed or conducted, rejecting it is appropriate. If, however, personal preferences alone dictate the validity of research and people pick and choose studies based on those preferences, then science has little hope of progress. Jeeves writes that when Christians encounter research findings that either contradict or confirm beliefs, they must above all tell the truth about what was found, honestly exploring what God shows in creation, even if they may not like everything they see.[45] When Christians are evaluating research, science's rules need to be respected. Christians must

40. Bastardi, Uhlmann, and Ross, "Wishful Thinking," 731–32, provides a good example of where people's evaluations of scientific evidence were strongly influenced by what they hoped to be true.

41. Milgram, "Behavioral Study of Obedience."

42. No positive effect of prayer was found by Benson et al., "Study of the Therapeutic Effects." Another study reviewed ten studies that had tested over seventy-five hundred participants; this study showed that in some studies, prayer was associated with positive outcomes, although the majority did not show prayer to have effects; see L. Roberts et al., "Intercessory Prayer."

43. First Thess. 5:17 encourages people to "pray continually"; James 5:16 encourages believers to pray for those who are sick, as "the prayer of a righteous person is powerful and effective."

44. VanderStoep, "Psychological Research Methods," 100–104.

45. Jeeves, *Human Nature at the Millennium*, 235.

examine whether a study's methodology allows for the conclusions that were made by the experimenters. That's playing by science's rules rather than according to personal preferences. Learning how to do that is a skill, and in our psychology department (as in most psychology departments), students are required to take a course on research methodology. How to do this assessment well, however, is beyond the scope of this book.

If the research was done well and the conclusions follow from the method used, then the consumer of the research can decide whether action should follow, keeping in mind that findings are descriptive, not prescriptive.[46] In the case of prayer research, even if prayer was not effective in that study's context, a person may well not give up prayer. One may decide that prayer is important regardless of whether a prayer is answered in the way the person praying had hoped. People may pray for additional reasons. Sometimes prayer may be less about making God do something (after all, God is not our servant) and more about recognizing one's own inadequacy and drawing closer to God.[47] Here's a case in which a researcher's expectations and worldview may influence the research question being asked *and* how to answer it. Evaluating the physical effects of prayer may not fit with a biblical understanding of prayer, particularly if trying to measure how it brings about healing, so from a Christian perspective, researching such effects might be asking the "wrong" question.[48]

In addition to critiquing scientific methods used, when approaching research that appears to conflict with deeply held beliefs, it's also reasonable to reexamine those beliefs.[49] In the example of research on prayer, what does the Bible say about prayer, and does that differ from what a particular person believes about prayer? As Everett Worthington writes in his book *Coming to Peace with Psychology*, all people—scientists, Christians, and Christians who are scientists—are living in a broken world. This means that humans may make errors in doing and interpreting science and also in their interpretation of Scripture.[50] Human understanding of Scripture involves potential errors in how God's Word is translated into modern language and in terms of how theologians and laypeople are influenced by their context, including politics, history, society, and culture.[51] People may also adopt interpretations that they personally like but that aren't actually biblical.

46. VanderStoep, "Psychological Research Methods," 102.

47. Jeeves and Ludwig, *Psychological Science and Christian Faith*, 211–17, has an insightful discussion of the research on prayer's effectiveness.

48. Jeeves and Ludwig, *Psychological Science and Christian Faith*, 211–17.

49. VanderStoep, "Psychological Research Methods," 102–3.

50. Worthington, *Coming to Peace with Psychology*, 116.

51. Worthington, *Coming to Peace with Psychology*, 117.

Seeking Clarity in Community

Taking a broad view of psychological findings, if values influence how research is done and the conclusions that are drawn, then is there any hope for seeing reality as it is, untainted by bias? Christian philosopher Arthur Holmes wrote a book titled *All Truth Is God's Truth*, in which he says that God is the author of all truth, so any truth that is discovered is from God.[52] While Holmes's book title has a great sentiment to it, is it possible for broken, sinful people to clearly discover that truth?

Sin has brought separation from God, others, and creation (theme 2)—the very relationships that would offer us clarity in understanding and reduce our bias. Bert Hodges offers helpful insights into the problems Christians face when dealing with bias.[53] He emphasizes that knowledge is always within a context that is meaningful at a certain time, to a certain group of people, biases included. Sin, however, has brought some degree of separation between us and everything that we are studying or trying to relate to. As we tend toward being individuals rather than persons (discussed earlier), we try to go it alone in our attempt to understand things, but God didn't design us to work in this way.

More lasting knowledge, moving toward the truth of reality and God, comes from embracing and living out lives as relational persons (theme 1). God revealed himself and the relationship between him and creation through multiple perspectives: creation, varieties of voices in Scripture, and the life of Jesus Christ. These multiple perspectives, coming together in community, allow humans to discover God's character and being. In terms of science, multiple, diverse viewpoints coming together bring understanding, says Hodges.[54] This would work out in Christians with various perspectives using their various gifts to pursue truth honestly and openly. The Holy Spirit's guidance leads people together in that pursuit (1 Cor. 2:6–16).

Implications and Applications

Psychological research can boost our knowledge. But can it help Christians who want to faithfully follow Christ? The apostle Paul says, "All Scripture is God-breathed and is useful for teaching, rebuking, correcting and training in righteousness" (2 Tim. 3:16). The Bible, Christians believe, leads people to God through Christ and informs them how to live life. As Christian philosopher

52. Holmes, *All Truth Is God's Truth*.
53. Hodges, "Perception, Relativity."
54. Hodges, "Perception, Relativity," 74–75.

Nicholas Wolterstorff has written, the Scriptures are "authoritative guides for the thought and lives of those who would be Christ-followers."[55] What could psychological research add to that?

We believe that psychology does have things to offer Christ followers. We want to mention three benefits. First, psychological science helps us better understand part of God's creation—us! Psychology can illuminate some of our abilities and the intricacy of the brain. We can potentially learn more about our Creator as we look at what God created.

Second, while the Bible's audience is all people for all times, as C. S. Lewis writes in *Mere Christianity*, Scripture does not set out a specific method of living that would be effective through all circumstances and all of history. Psychological science may be able to help with those details. Lewis writes, "When it tells you to feed the hungry, it does not give lessons in cookery. When it tells you to read scriptures, it does not give you lessons in Hebrew and Greek, or even ordinary English grammar. It was never intended to replace or supersede the ordinary human arts and sciences: it is rather a director which will set them all to the right jobs, and a source of energy which will give them all new life, if only they would put themselves at its disposal."[56]

Living Christianly is different in different times and situations. For example, the Bible consistently calls people to work for justice (e.g., Isa. 1:17; Mic. 6:8; Matt. 23:23), but how that is done in a democracy is going to look quite different than in a dictatorship. Psychological science, which studies the influence of an individual in a group and the impact of groups on an individual, can help address these questions, as we will see in chapter 11 on social psychology. Such understanding can help Christians to be Christ followers by increasing their understanding of people.

Third, psychological science can deepen our understanding of ourselves, giving us greater insight into what it means to be creatures made in the image of God. Along this line of thinking, Malcolm Jeeves and Thomas Ludwig gave their book, *Psychological Science and Christian Faith*, the subtitle *Insights and Enrichments from Constructive Dialogue*. They make the case that psychological science and Christian faith need not be seen as having conflicts but instead may add to each other. Science, of course, doesn't "prove" God or the rightness of the gospel. As we have written before, that's beyond what science can do for two reasons: science studies only natural phenomena (while God is supernatural), and science cannot answer moral questions (right versus wrong). However, we hope that throughout the rest of this book, you will see some of the benefits of

55. Wolterstorff, *Reason within the Bounds of Religion*, 71–72.
56. Lewis, *Mere Christianity*, 64.

informing psychological science with insights from Christianity as well as seeing how psychology may deepen our understanding of Christian faith.

DISCUSSION QUESTIONS

1. Why are people bothered by the idea that their behavior is predictable?
2. Why do we seldom experience the feeling of being predictable?
3. Will there be psychology (or perhaps any science at all) in heaven?
4. How is evidence for claims made in the Bible different from evidence in psychological science? How are they similar?
5. Should a Christian understanding of human behavior be different from a psychological understanding and/or require a different research methodology than psychology does because Christians take spiritual realities seriously?
6. Can scientists who are Christians learn from non-Christians, and vice versa? Why or why not?

3

Bodies Revealed

Brain and Behavior

SUMMARY: If we are embodied, what are the implications for understanding human behavior? Is this really a strong biblical perspective? Isn't the mind or soul what really counts? The answers will not only stress the biblical emphasis on embodiment but also explore how this needs to be understood in the context of relationality—our basic condition—and our other basic human characteristics.

> If the body be feeble, the mind will not be strong.
>
> Thomas Jefferson,
> to Thomas Mann Randolph, 1786

> After all, no one ever hated their own body, but they feed and care for their body.
>
> Ephesians 5:29

Darius was fascinated by the traveling exhibit *Bodies Revealed*.[1] If you are not familiar with this exhibit, it was a somewhat surreal display of plasticized human bodies designed to educate us about the human

---

1. *Bodies Revealed*, Premier Exhibitions, http://www.bodiesrevealed.com/.

body. As he observed these interesting but slightly disturbing displays, the bib-lical question "What are human beings that you are mindful of them, mortals that you care for them?" (Ps. 8:4 NRSV) came to his mind. He was taught as a child that God can see us on the inside, so as he looked at these displays, he imagined God being able to see our bones, blood, muscle, and internal organs all the time. How unattractive is that? This raised other questions in his mind, such as, "Why do we have these frail and somewhat disgusting bodies at all? Why didn't God make us more like angels or perhaps to be pure spirits?"

Think about all the advantages of not being a body. We wouldn't have to worry about being hot, cold, hungry, tired, and so on. Perhaps we could trans-port ourselves to distant places or walk through walls; the possibilities are endless! However, the Bible places a great deal of emphasis on bodies, so they must be important for something. For example, Christ's bodily resurrection and the bodily resurrection of believers are central themes mentioned in countless passages. Many other passages stress the value and importance of the body (see 1 Cor. 15:35–54; Eph. 5:28–30; Phil. 1:20; 3:21).

Rejecting the Body

Despite the emphasis placed on material bodies in Scripture, many Christians have downplayed the body. In the early days of the Christian church, **Gnostics** *believed that the creation was made not by a good God but by an evil being and was therefore distorted from the beginning.*[2] While the early Christian church rejected this first-century heresy (which was heavily influenced by Greek philosophy),[3] some writers believe that a number of Christians are still influenced in subtle ways by this thinking.[4] Christians with these leanings often cite passages that refer to the "fleshly desires," with the implication that the body itself is evil and that the physical world is to be avoided. As we saw in the first chapter, this view runs counter to the strong scriptural view that God's creation—including human beings—was created good.

This world-rejecting emphasis of Gnosticism has two important implications for psychology. First, it suggests that many activities of this world (e.g., science, psychology, technology, and cultural development) are of little value; we should focus instead on saving individual souls. Second, this perspective implies that bodies are of little consequence when considering human nature, and therefore we should focus on the spiritual. So while we may have difficulties as the result

2. Brakke, *Gnostics*, x.
3. Pearson, *Ancient Gnosticism*, 12–19.
4. See H. Bloom, *American Religion*.

of our weak and sinful bodies, we can rise above these realities by transcendence. **Transcendence** *refers to a person's ability to rise above physical existence and to experience ideas or feelings in an abstract world.* This transcendent view implies that science can tell us very little about human nature because the body is simply an imperfect vessel for the "real" me—the spiritual me. Furthermore, the "real transcendent me" is where I make moral decisions, make my faith commitments, and willfully decide the course of my life. By this view, since science cannot possibly address the nonmaterial aspects of my being, psychological science must be an extremely limited discipline, or perhaps it has no value at all.

However, we, the authors, assume that God did make a good creation, which includes human beings who are made of "dust" (see Ps. 90:3). Therefore, we believe that bodies should be taken very seriously and that our "earthly composition" should have a huge impact on our understanding of human nature, including what we call the "mind." We, the authors, do not believe that we are bodies who *possess* minds (or minds who possess bodies); rather, we believe that we are **embodied minds**: *we think, feel, and act with our bodies.* To quote David Myers and Malcolm Jeeves, "Without our bodies we are nobodies," and "We do not have bodies, we *are* bodies, bodies alive with minds."[5] Just as life is not a *thing* that combines with the body but a quality of a living body, likewise, a mind is not a *thing* that combines with the body but a quality that arises from our complex bodies and brains. But before we explore more about the implications of this perspective and what Scripture teaches about the body, let's examine some fascinating things that neuroscience and psychology have revealed about mindful bodies.

Embodied Experience

Consider the case of the woman known as "S" (her name is withheld to protect her identity). S was described by neurologist Antonio Damasio as a "tall, slender, and extremely pleasant young woman."[6] But two structures in her brain known as the amygdalae were completely calcified and ultimately destroyed because of a rare disease. The amygdalae are known to be involved in fear responses and other strong emotions. Surprisingly, S maintained good memory, and her general intelligence (e.g., language and problem solving) remained strong. The biggest change to her personality was with her emotions and social actions. For example, she became unusually cheerful and was eager to interact with almost anyone she met. She regularly hugged and touched people she had just

5. Myers and Jeeves, *Psychology through the Eyes of Faith*, 30.
6. Damasio, *Feeling of What Happens*, 62–67.

met and almost never showed anger, agitation, or fear—even when the situation called for it. Careful testing showed that she was not able to identify the expression of fear in pictures of faces, even though she could identify emotions such as surprise, happiness, and sadness. She also could not display a fearful facial expression on command—despite being able to display other emotions on command. When asked to rate the trustworthiness of several faces shown to her, she rated all of them as trustworthy, even though half the people in the pictures had been rated as untrustworthy by other people. S was good at drawing faces, and when asked to draw faces showing different expressions, she could do so easily, but she was unable to draw faces that displayed fear. Most surprising of all was that S seemed to lack any conscious understanding of the *concept* of fear. In other words, the problem went beyond the inability to express fear or to feel fear—she had no memory or awareness of fear. One real-life consequence of her disability was that she was often taken advantage of by untrustworthy people.

The case of S reveals some interesting features about our "mindful" brains. First, it illustrates that our conscious experience (the part of us that some consider to be the soul) is very much a part of what the body does. Emotions are known to be influenced by brain areas but are also very much felt in the body (e.g., increased pulse, blood rushing to the face). So, S lacks the normal brain regulation, the necessary body response, *and* the conscious experience needed to fully know fear. If conscious experience is related to only a transcendent, non-material "mind/soul," then S should be able to re-create the conscious experience in her mind even without the brain regulation or body response. However, S has no conscious mental experience of fear because of her *body's* inability to create this. S *was* able to intellectually describe situations that might cause a fearful response in others, but she simply couldn't create the mental experience for herself. She had lost the ability to transcend her bodily existence to create the abstract concept of fear.

The second issue illustrated by the case study is that S seems incapable of *willing* or forcing herself to experience fear, despite being able to show willfulness in other areas (e.g., she could will herself not to eat candy). This loss of willfulness can occur in other situations that are less drastic. For example, a very intelligent young woman whom one of the authors met several years ago was experiencing severe depression. After receiving medication and counseling, her symptoms of depression began to diminish. She communicated sometime later that, for the first time in her life, she knew what the experience of happiness was all about. She had observed this emotion in others and could intellectually describe what conditions would normally cause happiness in others, but she could not experience this emotion at what psychologists call a phenomenological (i.e., experiential, personal, internal, and conscious) level. Again, this young woman could not transcend her bodily experience to appreciate the abstract concept of happiness, nor could she experience happiness by sheer force of will or by greater self-determination. Asking this person to will herself into happiness, or the woman S to will herself into fear, would be like asking a woman born blind to will herself into imagining a visual scene.

What *Are* Bodies For?

Christian psychologist Elizabeth Lewis Hall, in her very thoughtful essay "What Are Bodies For?," indicates that we cannot understand any object or being until we know the purpose for which it was made. Her thesis is that bodies were designed for "interacting with the world around us, including other people."[7] She believes that both psychology and Scripture confirm that we were created *as* bodies because that is what allows us to have relationships. She provides several illustrations for how and why bodies work this way. For example, she describes how we form relationships with others in our infancy by first mirroring another person's actions mentally and then using that experience to understand the intentions of others. We learn about these intentions not through abstract mental reasoning but through observation and action. A large amount of research shows that when we watch other people perform an action, groups of cells in our brains, called mirror neurons, activate the circuits that normally produce the same movement we observe in others.[8] (If you want to experience this phenomenon yourself, demonstrate to someone how agile you are at pointing your tongue in different directions, and then watch their mouth and tongue as they unconsciously mimic you.) This mirroring of others is what allows us to understand what others are intending to do because our brains re-create their actions. Other research on child development points out how important it is that very young children mimic the emotional expressions of parents in close, face-to-face interaction. Children who are deprived of these forms of mimicking activities show poor development in brain circuits involved in empathy, and they show a lack of empathy in their behavior as they get older.[9] By mimicking the actions and emotions of others, we come to understand the meaning of actions and emotions. Clearly, this embodied response is a big part of the way we learn to experience and control emotions, and eventually to experience relationships.

7. Hall, "What Are Bodies For?," 165.
8. Rizzolatti and Craighero, "Mirror-Neuron System."
9. Schore, "Experience-Dependent Maturation."

Hall provides another intriguing example from studies on the hormone oxytocin. This hormone is released in response to a variety of specific types of bodily stimulation. For example, women release this hormone during sexual intercourse, childbirth, and breastfeeding. In all these cases, there are specific physiological benefits from the hormone (e.g., functions supporting labor and delivery, and the production and "release" of milk in the breast), but it also is known to activate emotion centers in the brain that promote bonding. In other words, it promotes a sense of emotional closeness and attachment to the baby or sexual partner. So women feel this emotion in their entire being (i.e., "embodied mind").

Another interesting functional explanation for bodies comes from studies on sexual attraction. During the course of a woman's menstrual cycle, various hormones fluctuate. The level of one hormone, estrogen, is high just before ovulation, when women are most fertile (i.e., most likely to conceive because the egg has been released from the ovary). In one study, women were shown pictures of men at times during their menstrual cycle when estrogen levels were highest or lowest.[10] The faces of the men were digitally altered to look more masculine (e.g., square jaw, more prominent eyebrows) or more feminine (e.g., softer jaw, less prominent eyebrows). During high estrogen periods, women thought the more masculine-looking males were more attractive, but during low estrogen periods, they rated the more feminine-looking male faces as more attractive. How and why would estrogen levels make a difference? First, we know from brain studies that estrogen can alter the function of neurons in areas of the brain devoted to emotions[11] and face perception.[12] Second, the functional explanation from evolutionary psychology[13] is that women prefer masculine faces during times of high fertility because masculinity most clearly represents the opposite sex, which represents the best possible mate. Masculine-looking males represent the best mate because they are generally the healthiest and most likely to produce a good amount of sperm. There may be additional explanations for this pattern, but it certainly suggests that some of our basic desires and tendencies (e.g., attraction to the opposite sex) are directed by deep-seated bodily processes.

10. Penton-Voak et al., "Menstrual Cycle Alters Face Preference."
11. Österlund, Keller, and Hurd, "Human Forebrain."
12. Hong et al., "Aberrant Neurocognitive Processing."
13. Evolutionary psychology goes beyond attempts to explain biological changes in species by also explaining why behavioral changes occur over time. While this theory is controversial, one facet of the theory that is less controversial is that it attempts to explain the function or purpose of any behavior. In other words, "What value does this have for our survival?" Such explanations can be useful regardless of whether the behavior evolved through natural means or through direct acts of a Creator God. See the appendix for additional discussion of this area.

So can we reduce all intentions, emotions, and desires to simple physical events? Damasio provides a thoughtful response: "Does this mean that there is no true love, no sincere friendship, no genuine compassion? That is definitely not the case. Love is true, friendship is sincere, and compassion is genuine, if I do not lie about how I feel, if I *really* feel loving, friendly, and compassionate."[14] Damasio is suggesting that while these amazing experiences are accomplished with bodies, we cannot fully reduce these experiences to the simple nuts and bolts of bodily function; in other words, they are greater than the sum of the neurobiological parts. This holistic approach means that these experiences are not somehow outside ourselves (i.e., in a separate mind/soul) but that the personal, subjective nature of mental experience is real and meaningful and that our whole being is capable of authentically choosing these feelings. As we described earlier, we are meaning seeking creatures (theme 5), and as such, our embodied minds are very capable of establishing the meaning and significance of our experiences.

What these examples of bodily functions *do* imply is that we understand our world and relate to one another with our whole being, not just with an abstract or disconnected mind. Can you imagine robotic beings or ghostlike spirits forming deep relationships the way we do? Without the intricate workings and interactions of brain and body in the context of personal experiences, how could they truly understand one another, relate to one another, and develop feelings about one another?

Body and Soul?

But many people around the world believe in something called the soul. What do we make of this "thing," and how does it fit into the picture? Does the soul govern our behavior and ultimately rule over the body? This is an important issue in psychology. In fact, the Greek word *psyche, used in the New Testament and sometimes (but not always) translated as "soul," is the root for the word* psychology. Some might wonder how psychology can claim to be a science when we cannot dissect the soul! The full discussion of this issue is beyond the scope of this chapter, but we can say that there are a variety of views on this issue among Christians in the field of psychology. Some consider themselves **dualists**, *which means they view the body and the soul (which includes at least some or all of our essential mental qualities) as separate entities or "substances" that can exist apart from each other (i.e., at death). In the most common version of this view,* called **interactionism**, *the body has self-regulating properties, such as habits and*

14. Damasio, *Descartes' Error*, 125.

instincts, but it can also interact with the soul/mind. However, other Christians in the field believe that this view is increasingly difficult to square with the ever-tightening link between brain and mind that research repeatedly shows. In addition, some biblical scholars have suggested that the words translated as "soul" in the Old Testament (e.g., *nephesh*) and the New Testament (e.g., *psyche*) are more properly translated as "living being" (i.e., "Praise the LORD, my *soul*" [Ps. 146:1 NIV] should be "Let my *whole being* praise the LORD!" [CEB]), as "mind," or simply as "person."[15] As a result, a growing number of Christian neuroscientists, psychologists, theologians, and philosophers lean toward **monism**: *the belief that there are not two things (body and soul) but just one—a living, breathing, thinking body.*

For example, the theologian N. T. Wright argues that many of the terms in Scripture, such as *mind, flesh, spirit,* and *soul,* are describing not *parts* of a person but simply different *qualities.* He refers to this as a **differentiated unity,** *meaning that these combined qualities make a human being.*[16] This is similar to the way we might describe a flower as red and having a certain shape, smell, and so on. These are qualities that make the flower what it is, not just a collection of separate parts. We can't have red existing apart from the existence of the flower! In the same way, we cannot have a *quality* called mind or soul that exists apart from the body—yet it's an essential feature of the body.

Likewise, Jeeves, a Christian neuropsychologist, suggests that mental activity arises or "emerges" from the complex activity of the brain. Therefore, the mind is not a separate thing that can exist apart from a body but an "emergent property" of matter.[17] While the mind may emerge from matter and be wholly dependent on matter, it is also greater than the sum of its parts. In this version of Christian monism, individuals are certainly constrained by their bodily function, but at the same time, they can still possess responsible limited agency even within an entirely material substance. Just as Damasio, mentioned earlier, believes that love is real, even though it is a part of our biological substance, so Jeeves feels that it is not necessary to invoke something called a soul in order for us to be fully human.

Clearly there are many complex theological, philosophical, and moral questions about body, mind, and soul that remain unanswered from this brief discussion. While we cannot answer all these questions here, we believe that it is essential for Christians studying psychology to continue exploring the nature of our embodiment and the importance of our embodiment in understanding behavior. We also believe that it is important to emphasize a more holistic view

15. Jeeves, *Human Nature at the Millennium,* 111–14.
16. N. Wright, "Mind, Spirit, Soul and Body." Also see J. Wright, "Mortal Soul," 447–71.
17. Summarized in Brown, "Cognitive Contributions to Soul," 102.

of the person—one that takes embodiment seriously—when trying to understand our nature.

The Embodied Church

A fresh reading of the Bible may awaken us to the "earthy" nature of our human existence and the purpose that God has for our bodies. Again, Hall provides beautiful language to capture this purpose: "We are told throughout Scripture that creation exists for God's glory (Isa. 43:4–7, Eph. 1:11–12, Rev. 4:11). In other words, creation, and humans as part of that creation, exist to show who God is in all His glory."[18] She puts some "flesh and bones" on this idea by showing that we reflect God's glory when we are in relationship with him. As 1 Corinthians 6:15 suggests, "Do you not know that your bodies are members of Christ himself?" Notice that the apostle Paul doesn't say, "Your *souls* are members of Christ," suggesting that it's not some transcendent part of you that belongs to Christ but *all* of you. As Christian psychologists Warren Brown and Brad Strawn state, "A more holistic and embodied view of persons would consider salvation as turning of the whole person toward Christ—a bodily and behavioral change and reorientation involving a change of the entire person in relation to the whole of God's physical and social creation. The whole embodied person is redeemed and transformed."[19]

In addition, the church is often described in Scripture as the "body of Christ" (Rom. 12:3–8; 1 Cor. 12:27). This is not simply an interesting metaphor, as Hall points out, but a deeply meaningful connection that illustrates ancient Hebrew thinking. The Hebrews viewed a cohesive group of people as a complete unity, not just a collection of individual bodies. So to be cut off from the body of Christ, like a finger cut off from the body, would be a truly horrible thing. Just as we cannot have a deep relationship with someone without being a physical body, so we cannot have a meaningful relationship with God outside of our bodily existence or outside of his collective body. As we discussed earlier, being made in the image of God is not simply an individual concept but a collective concept. In other words, it is not really the individual body that reflects God's nature but the unified body of believers in fellowship with their Maker. Applying this idea to the contemporary church, Brown and Strawn suggest that spiritual growth is about the "reshaping of whole persons," which is "unlikely to happen while one is merely sitting in a pew or on a mountain top." Instead, "this sort of growth happens in the

---

18. Hall, "What Are Bodies For?," 167.
19. Brown and Strawn, *Physical Nature of Christian Life*, 109.

embodied give-and-take of the ongoing life of a highly interactive community of Christians."[20]

Implications

What are the practical implications for revealing the purpose of bodies and our embodied relations? To start, let's go back to the story of Ethan in the introduction—who, you may recall, had many difficulties (e.g., ADHD, social isolation from others). His friend Shawna suggested that Ethan should just take on adult responsibility and that the real issue lies with his heart and soul. We have some sympathy for Shawna's view because, before the face of God, we ultimately bear responsibility for our actions (see chap. 1). However, we also believe that Shawna fails to appreciate that we cannot transcend our bodily selves. Our bodies and brains sometimes don't work the way they are supposed to. Just as S cannot *will* herself to experience fear, it's entirely possible that Ethan cannot *will* himself to act in a completely different way. This same idea applies to many individuals with brain disorders, drug addiction, or mental/emotional disorders of many types. Individuals who argue that people with such conditions should be able to transcend their conditions do not appreciate the ways that all of us are *limited* agents (theme 4). We are both enabled and constrained by our bodies in very significant ways. Even when bodies function optimally and we are more capable of freely choosing, many aspects of our bodily existence limit or shape our thinking and behavior (think about oxytocin and estrogen as two examples). This limitation does not imply some form of reductionism or determinism (i.e., all actions can be reduced to and are determined by brain cell functions) for all behavior, but it does imply that change will often require more than just sheer force of will.

In addition, if we understand that bodies allow us to be relational creatures, then we may come to appreciate that our relational experiences (e.g., the divorce of Ethan's parents) become part of us—in other words, part of our bodily function. Our thoughts, actions, memories, and learned patterns of behavior influence our hormones, bodily reactions, brain activity, and even how our brains are wired. These physical changes and internal responses in turn impact how we think about and relate to one another. Therefore, Ethan is embodied in community, and it is the community that should bear the struggles with him. So the "cures" for Ethan's problems come from many sources, not only from a pill—which may be helpful in restoring elements of his bodily function—but also from restored and renewed relationships and from new ways of thinking and behaving that come through these relationships.

20. Brown and Strawn, *Physical Nature of Christian Life*, 109–10.

In conclusion, the reason people—including Christians—should care about bodies is that we ultimately care about relationships, first our relationship with God, then our relationships with one another. God commands us to love him above all and our neighbors as ourselves. Applying this idea to our previous examples, the main reason we should care about S's problem is that her lack of fear results in her having difficulty being in healthy relationships with others. The young woman with depression is debilitated not only because she can't experience happiness but also because she has difficulty relating to others—including God—in her current state. While psychological science is unlikely to find ultimate answers to the deeper meaning of our existence, it can help us better understand the function and purpose of our bodies. It can help us appreciate how and why our embodied minds function as they do.

There is one more implication of being embodied. We believe that the redemption of our bodies does not end with the gift of eternal salvation. This is only the beginning. This salvation frees us to be of service, to bring healing to our current existence, to restore relationships to what God intended, and to embody Christ's Spirit. Because of our embodiment, we are also very much in relationship with God's good creation—since we are very much a part of it. Therefore, Christians should care about their earthly existence and the impact of hunger, poverty, disease, and injustice on bodies and relationships. People are Christ's hands and feet in this world, and he expects his followers to get moving and not waste their bodies for themselves. As Christian psychologists, we are not particularly interested in *just* saving individual souls. We are interested in saving and restoring the *whole person*—body, mind, relationships—and bringing a person into the whole body of Christ. We can thank the Lord that he had the wisdom to fashion these rather unappealing bits of flesh and bone into a collection of creatures who beautifully reflect his image.

DISCUSSION QUESTIONS

1. What are some specific physical experiences (e.g., hunger, pain) or qualities (e.g., chronic anxiety) that have influenced how you have thought or felt?

2. How have relationships been influenced by your physical life, and how have relationships impacted who and what you are physically today?

3. What would you say to someone who says that "curing" almost any life problem involves becoming more spiritual and connecting more with God?

$$4$$

Who Is in Control?

Consciousness

▶ SUMMARY: Consciousness is our most familiar experience, but because it is private to each of us, it is difficult to study. What is clear, however, is that much of our behavior is not under our direct conscious control or monitoring. In this chapter, we discuss the implications of unconscious and conscious thought, the relationship of both to behavior, and what they indicate about humans as responsible limited agents. We explore how thought and behavior, shaped by deep desires that come with seeking meaning, are influenced by conscious and unconscious thought.

> We take consciousness for granted because it is so available, so easy to use,
> so elegant in its daily disappearing and reappearing acts, and yet, when we
> think of it, scientists and nonscientists alike, we do puzzle.
>
> Antonio Damasio, *Self Comes to Mind*

Good morning! Your alarm goes off at 7:00 a.m. You wake from a dream in which you were arguing with a monkey who had stolen your new shoes. You yawn, rub your eyes, and somehow get to the bathroom to take a shower. By the end of the shower, you finally feel awake.

When a morning starts that way, where's the line between being awake and being asleep? If you are asleep, how do you hear the alarm? And how awake are you when you wake? Some days you're very aware of where you are and what day it is, but on other days you may be confused and disoriented, at least momentarily. What changed so that you feel more awake after your shower? You're more alert, but what does that mean? **Alertness** *is readiness to respond.* Yet being ready to respond is relative—we can be somewhat more or somewhat less mentally prepared to act.

Alertness falls under the umbrella of the larger subject of this chapter, **consciousness**, *which is a person's subjective, firsthand experience of reality and their own thoughts.* Although each individual's consciousness is a personal experience, not directly known by anyone else, reports of consciousness are accompanied by observable bodily responses to events, like smiling in response to a joke. If you were to record a person's brain activity, there would also be characteristic patterns of neural responses that correspond with their report of being conscious. Yet observable bodily movements can occur without consciousness or awareness of that movement. We do many things without conscious awareness, such as staring too long at someone who is attractive or saying "um" when thinking of what to say next (which is probably more likely when staring at someone attractive!).

Consciousness = Wakefulness + Awareness

Private experiences of our surroundings and our own thoughts, including our thoughts about our experiences, are deeply human. Some psychologists say that this characteristic of consciousness "is essential to what it means to be human."[1] Simple wakefulness (being alert) is seen in animals who show sleep and wake cycles; animals awaken from sleep if there is a loud noise or "alarm." What may be unique to human consciousness is the awareness of our own **subjective reality**: *what we each feel and experience from our own point of view.* This dimension of consciousness is more than just knowing that something is happening—demonstrating wakefulness by being able to respond; it's a self-awareness of our own thoughts and perceptions.

These two dimensions—wakefulness and awareness—are the basic properties of consciousness and have been shown to be separable from each other. Our own experiences, like differences in how we feel from one day to another when waking up in the morning, show us that wakefulness and awareness fluctuate. Neuropsychological research confirms these variations.[2] If both wakefulness and awareness are very low, a person will experience a **coma**; if both are high, the experience is **conscious wakefulness**. They can also vary independently of each other. During a **vivid dream**, awareness is high but wakefulness is low.

1. Schacter et al., *Psychology*, 172.
2. Laureys, "Eyes Open, Brain Shut," further describes the dimensions of wakefulness and awareness, showing how the relative strength of each of these contributes to various states of consciousness.

Conversely, in a **vegetative state**, a person can appear to be awake (with eyes open), but that person lacks awareness.

If awareness or general alertness can vary so much, how can embodied persons with limited agency responsibly live out their beliefs (themes 3 and 4)? How can Christians who believe that they must follow the Bible in their daily lives live faithfully if they are not fully alert and aware in every situation? Or is it possible that self-awareness and awareness of God aren't completely necessary or even sufficient for faithful living? We'll explore these issues in the remainder of this chapter.

Limited Consciousness, Limited Agency

We want to emphasize that consciousness alone (including self-consciousness) can't get people to always live out what they believe. From a Christian perspective, people fail to follow through on God's commands because humans are sinful (theme 2). People sin even when aware of their own sinfulness and desiring to avoid sin. As the apostle Paul says in Romans, "I do not understand what I do. For what I want to do I do not do, but what I hate I do" (7:15). In this passage, although Paul really wants to stop his own sinning—sinning of which he is well aware—he still sins. Trying really hard didn't fix it because humans don't just make errors; people are in a state of sin. Nevertheless, Paul certainly gives directives to the churches he addresses,[3] obviously expecting that people have sufficient awareness to check what they are doing against what they ought to be doing and to make changes as needed.

Not surprisingly, psychology doesn't set out to address humanity's state of sin. It can, however, provide insight into understanding how self-awareness helps us check whether our behavior follows our beliefs. To use consciousness in this way, it seems that we would want to maintain high levels of awareness when we're awake. Unconscious behaviors might best be avoided altogether because they're not consciously supervised. Yet psychological science and our own personal experiences show that we can't constantly check ourselves; much of our behavior is unconscious. Unrelenting, full awareness simply doesn't happen. Wakefulness varies throughout the day,[4] and awareness fluctuates when our minds wander as we daydream.[5]

---

3. Among the passages in which Paul gives instruction in Christian living are Eph. 4–5 and Col. 3–4.

4. Kerkhoff, "Inter-Individual Differences," provides a thorough review of how people differ from each other in terms of circadian rhythms throughout the day, also known as morningness versus eveningness.

5. Psychologists call this mind wandering. Mason et al., "Wandering Minds," provides information on the neural basis of our mental excursions while awake.

Unconsciousness

What is unconsciousness? When today's psychologists refer to the uncon-scious, they typically don't mean the sort of unconscious Sigmund Freud had in mind, with its underlying desires (drives or energies) seeking to be satisfied when a person is unconscious (i.e., dreams) or "released" during consciousness in indirect ways. Freud viewed human behavior as determined by unconscious processes, leaving people without responsibility for their actions. Freud's de-piction of humans, however, was both unscientific[6] and contrary to a biblical view of human nature in this case (see chap. 13 for a more extensive critique).

When psychologists today discuss unconscious processes, they primarily point to aspects of the **cognitive unconscious**: *mental processing that is not directly experienced yet contributes to each person's thoughts, decisions, perceptions, emotions, and behaviors.* This includes both processes that can't be brought to conscious-ness no matter how much we try (like how we detect light or configure parts of an image to determine that it's a face) and processes that are currently outside of awareness but that we could bring to awareness (like paying attention to the fact that we're saying "um" in conversation). This aspect of the unconscious works in ways that are more efficient and manageable than if such processes were consciously processed. Therefore, "simple" processes like dividing sounds into words or perceiving the color blue don't reach consciousness due to how the brain processes information, not because such thoughts are repressed, as Freud suggested. Processes that don't require conscious monitoring proceed unconsciously, while those that need more careful monitoring occur consciously. That's using our limited resources efficiently![7]

Limitations of Consciousness

The limits of consciousness are such that we can think about only a few items at once, and often only one (see chap. 5 on the limitations of attention). Much of our thinking must be unconscious for us to accomplish anything at all. Consider the ratio of conscious to unconscious thought needed in the fol-lowing situation. You're walking down a street where you live, and a person lying on the sidewalk holding their ankle yells, "Help!" What should you do?

6. Most introductory psychology textbooks outline the scientific shortcomings of Freud's theo-rizing about the unconscious. Scientific theories "must have specific implications for observable events in the natural world," as Keith E. Stanovich writes (*How to Think Straight about Psychology*, 9). Freud's theory doesn't make clear predictions; it merely explains human behavior after behavior occurs. Science is interested in prediction.

7. Psychologist Timothy D. Wilson outlines this more fully in *Strangers to Ourselves*, 8–9: "The mind is a well-designed system that is able to accomplish a great deal in parallel, by analyzing and thinking about the world outside of awareness while consciously thinking about something else."

You need to evaluate lots of information and answer many questions about the person (Is the person serious? Is it someone I know?), the situation (Is anyone else around? Is there danger?), and yourself (Am I equipped to help? Do I feel like helping?). And you need to do it fast! Most questions are evaluated unconsciously without awareness. There's no time to go through all these questions one at a time before making a decision. The conscious thought "They need help; I need to stop" may occur, but such a conclusion follows from and occurs alongside lots of unconscious processing that strongly informed it (using System 1 processes[8] as described in chap. 8 on thinking). Even a response of "How can I help you?" includes unconscious processes that result in the tone of voice you use, ensuring you use both a noun and a verb, and even your choice of which particular words to use. In the case of speech, "each and every conscious process is accompanied by (or is a residual of) unconscious processing."[9]

Free Will and Unconscious Thought

What does this picture of conscious relative to unconscious processing tell us about responsible limited agency (theme 4)? Psychologists have a variety of answers, in part because they disagree about how conscious and unconscious processing work together. A particularly disputed issue is how one type of processing might control or influence the other.

No Freedom

Some, such as psychologist John Bargh, view conscious processing as pointless. He states that the "feeling of free will is very real, just as real for those scientists who argue against its actual existence as for everyone else, but this strong feeling is an illusion."[10] This perspective reasons that although the experience of awareness is caused by the brain, this sense of awareness impacts neither the brain nor behavior—that is, being "aware" doesn't change what people actually do, so a sense of awareness doesn't matter, and it certainly doesn't make us more responsible.[11]

Supporters of this view may point to research on perceptions of self-control when people make a simple, voluntary movement. In some well-known experiments by Benjamin Libet and his colleagues, research participants were told to move their index finger whenever they wanted while the timing of three

8. Kahneman, *Thinking, Fast and Slow*, 20.
9. Dijksterhuis and Aarts, "Goals, Attention and (Un)Consciousness," 471.
10. Bargh, "Free Will Is Un-Natural," 148.
11. This is the notion that consciousness is an epiphenomenon.

events was measured: (1) when brain activity related to making a finger movement occurs, (2) when the person was aware of making a conscious decision
to move, and (3) when the actual finger movement occurred.[12] Using electrical
sensors placed on a participant's scalp for measurement of brain activity, the
experimenters found that electrical activity related to planning a move began
about a half second before the finger began to move, as measured by sensors
measuring muscle movement in fingers. That makes sense—the brain first made
a plan, then carried it out. But what about the feeling of having decided to
move? To measure this, participants watched a dot move around the face of
a clock to note the moment at which the action was consciously willed. Such
studies showed that the conscious decision to act was experienced only about
one-fifth of a second before the actual movement. The brain's planning of the
action, however, began before participants reported being consciously aware of
deciding to move—so the brain was active *before* participants even consciously
thought of the action!

This research finding is echoed in daily experiences. Often, our thoughts
about an action occur only *after* an action has been completed. If you greet
someone and a friend asks you, "Why did you say hi to her?" you are likely to
give a reason such as, "Because she lives next door to me." But prior to your
greeting, did you actually have the conscious thought, "She lives next door to
me. I will say hello"? You probably just said "Hello." We often act *without* experiencing any conscious awareness of governing our behavior, in which case
we can't claim that a behavior was caused by conscious thought. The thought
never happened! This fact that many of our behaviors aren't the result of careful, well-reasoned thought should lead us to greater humility about the wisdom
of our own behavior—and to greater grace in responding to the behavior of
others.

Such findings and examples lead some psychologists to conclude that even
when we have the sense of consciously being in charge of our brains and bodies, that may not be what is happening. Some take this as strong evidence that
humans have no agency; free choice is an illusion.

The Role of Free Will

At this point in this chapter (maybe even earlier), your conscious mind may
be yelling something like, "What do these people mean I don't choose? I do
what I want because I have free will!" But is there any place in psychological
science for free will? Some psychologists, including Roy Baumeister, argue that

---

12. Benjamin Libet has conducted several experiments on this topic, including Libet et al.,
"Time of Conscious Intention to Act"; and Libet, "Unconscious Cerebral Initiative."

those who dismiss free will should reevaluate what studies of consciousness show. Critiquing the research on sequencing brain and movement events, Baumeister says that this work focuses on "slicing behavior into milliseconds," but doing so may "conceal the important role of conscious choice, which is mainly seen at the macro level."[13] Baumeister argues that consciousness is limited, so it makes sense that it would be used sparingly, only where it's necessary. Conscious planning and oversight should be saved for big-picture behaviors (macro level), where they are needed, rather than being wasted on monitoring endless, tiny details (happening over tiny fractions of a second). For example, free will may have more to do with deciding to walk to a particular destination than diligently monitoring each footstep on the trip.[14] Although we can make ourselves aware of each footstep (or in the case of Libet's experiments, each finger movement), Baumeister argues that free will is more involved in deciding *whether* to walk somewhere (or in the case of Libet's experiments, *whether* to follow the experiment's directions) than in planning each movement. In addition, a simple, highly practiced behavior like moving a finger may require little awareness to be carried out.

This "argument" about free will shows how evidence is evaluated through interpretive lenses—those worldviews that make up a fundamental orientation regarding human nature. As we have seen, psychologists are able to study experiences of conscious will, but they can't conclude that thought (which is internal and unseen) *causes* action. Remember that in psychological science, all causes must be physical to count as scientifically valid. Daniel Wegner, a consciousness and willpower researcher, writes, "The experience of will is based on interpreting one's thought as causing one's action."[15] The experience of having caused our own behavior varies with how we interpret our situation and isn't necessarily due to thought actually causing action.

Those on both sides of the free-will debate acknowledge that the existence of free will is ultimately a question for philosophy and theology more than psychology.[16] However, psychological science informs this debate. Research findings help us better understand conditions in which humans are more likely to feel or act in ways that correspond with showing agency as well as situations in which people are less likely to do so. As we described in regard to theme 4,

13. Baumeister, "Free Will in Scientific Psychology," 15.

14. Baumeister, "Free Will in Scientific Psychology," 15. Baumeister follows the logic of Gollwitzer, arguing to separate deciding from initiating. "Implementation Intentions," 494.

15. Wegner, "Who Is the Controller?," 32.

16. E.g., Baumeister, "Free Will in Scientific Psychology," 15, and Wegner, "Who Is the Controller?," 19–23, argue the two sides regarding free will and recognize that science cannot answer the free will question. Gazzaniga's *Who's in Charge?* is largely devoted to the question of whether we have free will.

we believe that the Bible shows that we have a degree of free will—limited agency—and that we are to use that ability in responsible ways.

Goals and Desire

We are also relational persons (theme 1); wanting to be in relationship is a commitment or desire held by all people. Sin, however, distorts relational desires to be with God, others, and creation, so we look for other ways to fill that longing. That longing, Christians believe, is fulfilled in God. Christian philosopher James K. A. Smith, in his book *Desiring the Kingdom*, asserts that humans are fundamentally driven by what they love or desire, whether they are aware of it or not. Smith says that in addition to reasoned thoughts (relatively easily brought to conscious awareness) and a set of beliefs (of which we are likely less aware), unconscious processing is pervasive. As he writes, "We don't go around all day *thinking* about how to get to the classroom or *thinking* about how to brush our teeth or *perceiving* our friends. Most of the day, we are simply involved in the world."[17]

Smith says that we act out *all* our loves—our desires—through our actions. Being embodied, we enact our desires and meaning making in physical ways. We're not just talking about sex here. When we go to a classroom, brush our teeth, or meet with friends, we are aiming our desires toward some larger end. In these examples, the behaviors may aim toward greater social acceptance in one way or another, whether by education, hygiene, or companionship. Repeated behaviors eventually become unconscious, automatic behaviors that can then take on a life of their own[18] as habits sparked by cues in the environment. **Goals**—*our desired outcomes in a situation*—can be consciously set or automatically activated by our surroundings. For instance, most students in a course have conscious goals such as (at minimum) earning a passing grade. Students act in ways to meet that goal, and with practice, that goal can operate unconsciously.[19] People act as a student without even planning to do so.[20] Sometimes that goal gets altered—seeing a person we are attracted to can do that, as social and relationship goals might then become active. In fact, multiple goals may be active, and the student might now be advocating the formation of a study group (student plus social goals), or the student may forget about the course

17. J. Smith, *Desiring the Kingdom*, 50.
18. See Bargh and Chartrand, "Unbearable Automaticity of Being," 465–73, for a good accounting of how repeated behaviors can become automatic.
19. Dijksterhuis and Aarts, "Goals, Attention and (Un)Consciousness," offers a thorough discussion of the relationship between unconscious processing and goals.
20. Perhaps always sitting quietly in the same spot in a classroom.

altogether and go straight to asking that person out on a date. Here we see action, yet it may not include full, conscious awareness of why one is doing the action. Studying may no longer be a priority in the action, although the student may still think or say it's the basis of the action.

Regarding goals, it's important to note that some goals are to "do," while others are to "don't do." Some may have the stereotype that Christianity is just a big list of don'ts. The Bible certainly tells us there are things not to do: "For the grace of God has appeared that offers salvation to all people. It teaches us to say 'No' to ungodliness and worldly passions, and to live self-controlled, upright and godly lives in this present age" (Titus 2:11–12). The "no" is clear, but in the second part of this verse, a "do" follows the "don't." Scripture advocates that behavior can be changed by redirection of the heart—one's inner desires—and that will align goals, even if they are unconscious.

God and Desire

One other thing to notice from the Bible verse quoted in the previous paragraph: it's *not* saying that believers can "live self-controlled, upright and godly lives" on their own power. God's grace, through the Holy Spirit, enables people to desire God. Jesus, speaking to his closest followers, said, "Whoever wants to be my disciple must deny themselves and take up their cross daily and follow me. For whoever wants to save their life will lose it, but whoever loses their life for me will save it" (Luke 9:23–24). It's easy to focus on "deny" and "lose"—giving up desires—and then sin should be gone. But just giving up desires won't work. If, as Smith asserts, we are fundamentally lovers[21]—at our core, creatures who do things according to our desires—then we can't just give up desires! Christ says to give up, but then "take up [our] cross daily and follow [him]." Desire continues to exist; the Christian life is one not of suppression but of redirection to fulfillment in Christ. As theologian Saint Augustine so eloquently described the human relationship to God, "You have made us for yourself, and our hearts are restless until they rest in you."[22] As meaning seekers (theme 5), we desire a deity, and this desire for God comes from God. Yet in human sinfulness, desires are easily directed toward other things, including ourselves. Through the Holy Spirit's work, however, desires can be positively directed toward God.

21. J. Smith, *Desiring the Kingdom*, 51.
22. Augustine, *Confessions*, 1.1.1. James K. A. Smith uses this quotation from Augustine as well, building the case that humans have a deep restlessness whereby we end up trying to fulfill this desire for God by chasing idols. *Desiring the Kingdom*, 77.

A characteristic perhaps unique to humans is our desire to be a better person. This comes about from **self-consciousness**: *the ability to draw attention to oneself as a thing that can be examined.* The biblical call from the book of Lamentations to "examine our ways and test them" (3:40) is echoed in psychological research that suggests that each of us has the "tendency to evaluate [ourselves] and notice [our] shortcomings."[23] Self-consciousness allows us to think about what we are like and what we can be. This self-consciousness, however, varies between people and with levels of alertness. Substances like alcohol, tobacco, heroin, and other psychoactive drugs can also alter how we respond. For example, alcohol reduces self-awareness,[24] and this is likely an effect of other drugs as well. Thinking back to the case of Ethan from the introduction, his adult alcohol-use problems are likely exacerbated by alterations in brain functioning, reducing his self-consciousness. These changes impact his ability to exercise responsibly his limited agency. He has a reduced ability to modify his desires.

Redirecting Desire

Psychologists have explored how behavior might be altered by influencing desires. Desires need to be replaced with new desires, and conscious decisions can aid in redirecting them (not just suppressing them).[25] Desires operate largely unconsciously, but unconscious behavior can be redirected toward other goals. Psychologist Peter Gollwitzer has emphasized that it's important to direct behavior at the outset—deciding what is important to do—and then, as Baumeister has emphasized, many of the small details (the automatic behaviors) occur without intention.[26] The Bible confirms that redirected actions change desires: "Those who live according to the flesh have their minds set on what the flesh desires; but those who live in accordance with the Spirit have their minds set on what the Spirit desires" (Rom. 8:5).

When calling his disciples, Jesus bids them to "follow me."[27] If the disciples didn't know it immediately, "follow me" meant more than a change in lifestyle; it was a total change in the trajectory of their desires. Jesus told Simon Peter and Andrew, two fishermen, that they would "fish for people" (Matt. 4:19).

23. Schacter et al., *Psychology*, 178–79, includes a discussion of self-consciousness in humans and animals.
24. Hull, "Self-Awareness Model."
25. This is what recent research on desires by Hofman and Van Dillen shows: desires need direction ("Desire," 318–20). Conscious decisions can aid in redirecting desires, and that is a way of showing self-control.
26. Baumeister, "Free Will in Scientific Psychology"; Gollwitzer, "Implementation Intentions."
27. E.g., Matt. 4:19, when Jesus calls Simon Peter and Andrew.

Life's primary fulfillments would now come not by filling nets and selling fish but by bringing people to a saving love of Christ.

Applications

Christ calls his followers to align their will with God's will. When Christ taught his disciples to pray, in what we now call the Lord's Prayer, "your kingdom come, your will be done,"[28] he was telling his followers to set their desires on God's desires, to let their desires be taken up into God's desires. Theologian N. T. Wright has said that when Christians are praying this, "We are praying, as Jesus was praying and acting, for the redemption of the world; for the radical defeat and uprooting of evil; and for heaven and earth to be married at last, for God to be all in all. And if we pray this way, we must of course be prepared to live this way."[29]

How can conscious thought influence desires toward God? We, the authors, have a friend named Gord who begins each day by leaning up against a wall while stretching before exercise and praying, "Good morning, Father; it's your servant Gord again, reporting for duty." Gord tells us that "then I remind him that he will have to put up with all my weaknesses and idiosyncrasies but that I really do want to serve him." He continues in prayer and reading Scripture during his exercise routine. Gord sets the tone for each day—reaffirming and reminding himself of the big decision to follow Christ that puts in line both his conscious and his unconscious, unmonitored decisions for the day. Gord in effect is saying, "I want to be aware of you, God—use me." He sets a tone for the practice of spiritual awareness by giving over his will to God and acting on his decision to the extent he can.

——— DISCUSSION QUESTIONS ———

1. In what ways do you feel burdened by your conscious awareness?
2. Think of a behavior you explained after you did it (e.g., why you went somewhere or talked with someone). Was your explanation true to what you were thinking during the behavior? How would you know?
3. What percentage of your own behavior do you think results from unconscious processing? What evidence do you have for the remainder of your behavior being under conscious control?

28. The Lord's Prayer is recorded in Matt. 6 and Luke 11.
29. N. Wright, *Lord and His Prayer*, 31.

4. Is sin offensive to God if a person didn't make a conscious decision to commit the sin—that is, can a habit be a sin? Explain.

5. Psychologist Carl Rogers (and also Nathaniel Branden, who was instrumental in highlighting the importance of self-esteem) emphasized that humans need to bring to consciousness all their behavior and act out of their natural core desires. How might that be problematic both scientifically and from a Christian perspective?

6. In the anecdote regarding Gord, we emphasize that his statement is an initial decision that can help put into play unconscious behaviors that may follow. Think of an example of how turning on a movie or opening an internet connection (or some other behavior with a distinct beginning) also sets in motion a set of automatic behaviors and responses.

5

Making Sense of Your Surroundings

Sensation, Perception, and Attention

SUMMARY: Our abilities to sense, perceive, and pay attention are astounding, allowing us to navigate our environment and interact with each other. These abilities are so common to us and require so little of our conscious awareness that they go largely unnoticed. Our embodied sensation limits our ability to take in everything in our environment and also partially determines what we notice and find meaningful. In fact, meaning making appears to be what perception and attention are all about. This combination of great ability and marked limitation shapes the contours of our limited agency and has significant implications for relationality. This chapter explores how the limited but meaning seeking nature of our perceptual systems ultimately serves our ability to maintain relationship with God, the world, and one another.

> The question is not what you look at, but what you see.
>
> Henry David Thoreau, *Journal*, August 5, 1851

For those of us with normal sight and hearing, sensory abilities are so effortless that they are easy to ignore. We simply open our eyes and look; to hear, we just listen. Yet what we ultimately notice and how our senses serve us are anything but simple, and our responses to these sensations are profound. We have choices in how we sense and perceive what's around us, but there are also definite limitations, as we outline below. Limited agency is clear in our interactions with the environment. Our sensory systems are our entry point for interaction, so they're critical for relationships—those with other people and with God. That also makes them part of the fundamental meaning seeking of humans, shaping not only what we perceive but also what we pay attention to.

Sensation to Perception

To understand how sensory processes ultimately result in how we experience our environment, we need to examine how we take in that environment. When you experience a taste or smell, bits of the actual substance get on your tongue or in your nose so that a chemical reaction can occur to convert physical information into neural signals. You might (or might not) want to keep that in mind the next time you smell rotting garbage! In fact, to experience sound, vision, and touch, you need physical stimuli (sound waves, light, and pressure, respectively)[1] so that you—your sensory systems—can experience a **sensation**: *a physical input that is converted into a code that the nervous system can interpret.* Such processes eventually result in a **perception**: *a mental representation that is your sense of reality.* Perception, like sensation, is an embodied process dependent on our physical structure (theme 3). Sensory systems so shape our perception that when sensory stimuli[2] are present, our perceptions are quite predictable, even lawful.[3] While some stimuli are impossible to miss (e.g., bright sunshine), others are impossible to perceive (e.g., a dim light at a great distance). Sensory system constraints mean that we don't sense or perceive everything equally and that some things don't register at all.

Together, sensation and perception connect us to each other and to creation. They are fundamental to our relationality (theme 1). Several of Jesus's miracles involved healing sensory processes (e.g., Matt. 9:27–30; John 9:1–12). Folks who were healed didn't just experience restored physical capabilities; they were freed to engage society more fully. These miracles reveal Jesus's power and his compassion. A full and fulfilling life can be lived with some sensory loss, but if we had no sensory interaction with the world (no taste, touch, smell, vision, or hearing), our isolation from others would be complete and unimaginable. In

1. Unlike with taste and smell, vision and audition do not respond to particles of the actual object being sensed for us to see or hear it.
2. *Stimulus* is a broad term for any environmental energy that a sensory system might detect.
3. Relationships between the strength of a sensation and the intensity of a perception are so predictable that they are described as lawful, such as in Weber's law, which quantifies how much change in a physical stimulus is needed to bring about a change in perception.

addition, God is described, in many stories in the Bible, as having direct impact on humans through physical, perceptual processes, from sending food (manna) to the Israelites wandering the desert to Jesus's physical embodiment, which included him audibly speaking, physically touching, and being visibly present.[4]

The Bible also depicts people as having the possibility of **spiritual perception**: *a response to realities that go beyond physical sensations.* God acts through nonphysical means, bringing about changes that then can be perceived by people. God can have direct spiritual impact, for instance, through the action of the Holy Spirit. In one case that the apostle Paul describes, "God's love has been poured out into our hearts through the Holy Spirit" (Rom. 5:5). Accounts of God working through visions and dreams and giving general direction by the Holy Spirit all show that God works in people's lives in ways outside physical means.[5] While the consequences of such interactions may be scientifically measurable, the source of them is not, as science quantifies only natural phenomena. Nevertheless, humans are impacted physically as people change their interactions with God and the rest of creation.

If sensation and perception work in very specifiable ways, ways that even God engages, do they dictate how we necessarily interact with others? Do perceptual processes force us to perceive the world in only one way?

Perception: Making Meaning of Sensation

When sensations are interpreted through psychological processes, we have perceptions. So while your eardrum may vibrate in a specific way due to the characteristics of a particular sound wave (sensation), you *interpret* that as the sound of a dog barking (perception). Such interpretation of the world is what makes perception central to making meaning (theme 5).

Our sensory systems don't just record what is around us; perceptual processes prioritize and interpret our environment. Loud sounds startle us more than quiet ones; bitter is more noticeable than bland. Perceptual processes even result in us "seeing" things that may not be completely accurate relative to reality. For example, have you ever noticed that you rarely realize when you blink? Blinking makes the lights go out; there is no light for your visual system to respond to. Anytime you blink, you should perceive momentary darkness

---

4. Jesus reassured his disciples following his resurrection from death by encouraging them to "look at my hands and my feet. It is I myself! Touch me and see; a ghost does not have flesh and bones, as you see I have" (Luke 24:39).

5. E.g., God gives Jacob a vision in Gen. 46:2, appears in a dream to Joseph in Matt. 2:19, and works through the Holy Spirit, as attested in Rom. 8.

because the sensory input of light is interrupted. However, you usually don't "see" a blink because your visual system tells you a bit of a fib about what you're actually "seeing." You usually have the perception of *not* blinking when you blink. Since the average person blinks ten to fifteen times a minute, that's helpful.[6] If you noticed every blink, the constant interruption of normal vision by little blips of blackness could get rather annoying. Your brain controls your blinking (albeit usually unconsciously), so "seeing" a blink wouldn't give you any information you didn't already have—you don't *need* to consciously know about your blinks because part of your brain *already* does.[7] "Seeing" the blackness of a blink is less important than perceiving ongoing reality, so the blink is ignored. Perceptual processes don't just let sensations be; sensation is interpreted. Clearly, some things (e.g., delicious food or a slap to the face) are likely to impact us more than other things (e.g., a tree in the distance or a gentle breeze) and should be prioritized differently. In the case of blinking, perceptual processes don't really deceive; they prioritize.

Yet a sensation—even one that is prioritized—doesn't necessarily lead to the same perception for all. Consider the little squiggles you're currently looking at and experiencing as letters and words: you experience them as such because you know the language and can read; without those abilities, they would just be meaningless shapes. While our embodiment limits our sensory agency (our freedom to sense anything and everything that might exist), we show greater agency with our perception. In order for us to figure out what to process, meaning is imposed on sensory input. If you are a keen observer of grammar, you might have noticed the passive construction in the previous sentence. We're implying that you make meaning *regardless* of whether you consciously intend to make meaning. You can simply take in information and respond in the way you automatically respond.

Interpreting Reality: Agency and Meaning

Imagine this situation: a glass of cold milk spills on you and what you're reading. You immediately notice that things look different, and you feel wetness and cold. That sort of **bottom-up processing** *occurs when initial sensory activity determines perception without being modified; sensation drives perception.* Sensory systems are wired to respond most vigorously to change, sending lots of nerve impulses to the brain to automatically let us know that the environment has something new.[8] As the white milk covers black letters, you're now processing

6. Burr, "Vision," 554.
7. Burr, "Vision," 554.
8. Sensory systems respond maximally (highest rate of neuron firing) to contrast or difference. Contrast occurs by changes in time, space, or space and time together (motion).

more reflected light; cold milk contacts your skin, and receptors that respond to temperature signal a difference. The "decision" to detect what happened in the environment occurs due to nonconscious sensory processes. The limited agency of humans is vividly apparent in this perception.

Yet we do have some agency in how we *interpret* sensations. **Top-down processing** *is higher-level processing that may change our interpretation of a sensation based on expectations and prior knowledge.* Our goals and our context influence our interpretation—that is, we reinterpret the sensory information, perhaps modifying the perception. Meaning making results from more than just increased sensory neuron responses to the environment. We're not simple machines that react to only what's loudest and brightest. Back to the cold milk example, you quickly go from the immediate sensations of visual and temperature change to an overall picture of the situation using higher-level interpretation that may result in crying over spilled milk or perhaps laughing out loud. Did you or someone else cause the milk to spill? If someone else spilled the milk, was it someone you consider a friend or a foe? Were you expecting the spilled milk, or was it a surprise? Answers to such questions will affect your judgment of the significance of the change you've experienced. That, in turn, shapes your emotional response and the physical actions you might or might not take. In the end, your response isn't determined by bottom-up processing alone; it's modified by a variety of factors, including how you *choose* to respond. (Decision processes are further explored in chap. 8.) You can interpret different meanings from the same situation.

Nevertheless, characteristics of our embodiment—how our sensory systems respond to the environment—leave us predisposed to respond to what's new more than to what's been present for some time. Your physical experiences are a part of you, significantly impacting how you relate to others and the environment. The experience of being a relational person is profoundly physical! In addition, the initial sensations from the milk spill can't be ignored, even if it was expected. Change has priority over sameness, so change is more meaningful than sameness.[9]

Making Meaning Comes from the Bottom and the Top

Perception's bottom-up default to respond more to some things than to others is modified by prior experience and expectations. Think again about the

9. Your sensory/perceptual systems also impact determining when you no longer need to notice something. Receptor cells respond most when first exposed to a stimulus. Following that, responding declines, even if the stimulus remains the same strength, allowing us to adjust to our surroundings and monitor for what is new. For example, if you enter a kitchen with freshly baked cookies, the scent is obvious. Soon, however, the scent seems less intense.

black squiggles you are looking at right now. We understand them to be letters that, due to our imposing meaning on these squiggles, in certain combinations make meaningful messages. As meaning seekers, humans have devised ways of communication (writing) that depend on little marks that look nothing like what they stand for (e.g., the word *dog* in no way resembles an actual dog). Through lots of practice that began with learning the alphabet, then learning how letters form sounds and words, and finally being able to read whole sentences and passages of text,[10] we're able to impose meaning top-down and see these black marks as words, not just shapes.

Experience with letter combinations also allows us to read words and even to form expectations about what we will later read in a passage. In fact, language researchers have described text comprehension as a "search (or effort) after meaning" that arises out of expectations.[11] A drive to understand pushes reading. Here's an example of how our knowledge of the way words work can influence comprehension for those who read English:

Yuo cna porbalby raed tihs esaliy desptie teh msispeillgns.[12]

Although the letters are scrambled in this sentence, we're so familiar with how words work that we can relatively easily impose an interpretation on the misspellings that allows us to understand the message.

Attention's Balancing Act

We have discussed how automatic perception and interpretation of perception are altered by our experiences and expectations. However, far more information than we can process (or than might even be useful to process) impacts our sensory systems. Whenever you look at anything, your retinas respond to all of it. Yet much of what you see isn't important to you when you have limited resources for dealing with your environment. For example, when you're trying to read, and you really want to understand what you're reading, other activities around you simply distract. Unless, of course, what surrounds you is more important than what you are reading.

10. Kuhl, "Language, Mind, and Brain," provides a nice overview of how experience alters perception.

11. Graesser, Singer, and Trabasso, "Constructing Inferences," 371.

12. Here's what that sentence says: "You can probably read this easily despite the misspellings." The website of the Cognition and Brain Sciences Unit in Cambridge, UK, explains how people can read scrambled words and the limits of our ability to comprehend them: http://www.mrc-cbu.cam .ac.uk/people/matt.davis/cmabridge/. Use this website to make more readable, scrambled-letter sentences: http://www.glassgiant.com/text_scrambler/.

Attention *is the process by which you determine what incoming information is perceived*; it helps you deal with the fact that you have too much information by limiting what of that information receives detailed mental activity. Your attention system balances continuing to deal with what you're currently attending to with being able to respond to new, important events in your environment. As attention researchers Nancy Kanwisher and Paul Downing write, "Seeing the world around you is like drinking from a firehose. The flood of information that enters the eyes could easily overwhelm the capacity of the visual system," so the attention system allows "selective processing of the information relevant to current goals."[13] The limitations that come from being embodied are such that you need to make sense of only what's important in the environment, not every little detail. If you noticed everything in your surroundings, your perceptual systems would drown in information.

The settings of our attention are tremendously important because they determine what we will perceive (and not perceive) in the environment. As psychologist Bert Hodges has written, the limits of our perceptual abilities have consequences for humans: "They must be selective. And choices always mean tradeoffs."[14] Choosing to attend to something requires *not* attending to a whole bunch of other things. Giving attention to one event at the expense of not giving attention to another event is well documented. For example, **inattentional blindness** *occurs when, by paying attention to some events in a scene, we fail to notice when an unexpected but completely visible object appears.*[15] Attention is influenced by our goals in a situation, so if we're watching a movie, trying to figure out where a main character is going, we might miss changes in the character's clothing from one scene to another.[16]

Yet as attention researchers Daniel Simons and Daniel Levin emphasize, if we look at how successfully humans interact with the environment, we can see that we don't seem to need all the information out there. They write, "A system that is too precise in tracking visual details would, in the words of William James, present a 'blooming, buzzing confusion.'"[17] Attention reduces the flood

13. Kanwisher and Downing, "Separating the Wheat from the Chaff," 57.

14. Hodges, "Perception, Relativity," 68.

15. In one of the more famous examples of inattentional or change blindness, Simons and Chabris, "Gorillas in Our Midst," had participants count the number of times members of a group of people passed a basketball. Shortly after the video began, a person in a gorilla suit passed through the scene, remaining there for five seconds. A startling 46 percent of participants failed to notice the gorilla. More demonstrations of this research can be found on the Invisible Gorilla website: http://www.theinvisiblegorilla.com/videos.html.

16. These are known as movie continuity errors or mistakes. Many can be found by an internet search.

17. Simons and Levin, "Change Blindness," 267.

of incoming information to what's important, giving the gist or basic meaning of perceptual experience across time, helping us make sense of the world in a manageable way. Deriving the basic story of what is going on in a situation through attention is similar to the way memory works (see chap. 7). Nevertheless, if needed, our flexible attention systems can focus and give a more detailed perceptual experience at a single moment, such as when we are searching for a particular item, like a set of keys.

Getting Attention under Control

Human agency has a role in how attention functions to limit and then define what of the environment we will further process. Attention is automatically drawn to some events in the environment (such as strong sensory experiences or changes and important items like faces), but we are also able to *decide* about attending to much in our environment. Attentional choices matter. For example, research has demonstrated negative influences of viewing aggression and watching sexual content in childhood and adolescence. What we watch affects our relationships with others, even if we don't think so.[18] In addition, what we attend to is what we're likely to recall.

The Bible also asserts that what we see and think about have important consequences for relationships. The apostle Paul advised the followers of Christ at Philippi, "Finally, brothers and sisters, whatever is true, whatever is noble, whatever is right, whatever is pure, whatever is lovely, whatever is admirable— if anything is excellent or praiseworthy—think about such things. Whatever you have learned or received or heard from me, or seen in me—put it into practice. And the God of peace will be with you" (Phil. 4:8–9). Paul affirms that people can make choices regarding what they pay attention to. He also emphasizes that our general outlook and our general nature shape attention and perception. The human propensity toward sin (theme 2) influences how we see the world, our meaning making, and ultimately our desires. In these verses, Paul also stresses the notion that our attention isn't fully under our control, but in an additional way to that suggested by psychology. God's Holy Spirit acts within his followers to redirect desires: "Those who live according to the flesh have their minds set on what the flesh desires; but those who live in accordance with the Spirit have their minds set on what the Spirit desires.

18. The famous "Bobo doll" experiments by Albert Bandura (Bandura, Ross, and Ross, "Transmission of Aggression") have shown that watching aggressive acts increases the likelihood of acting aggressively. O'Hara et al. ("Greater Exposure") suggest that early exposure to sexual content in movies promotes sexual risk-taking and earlier age for initial sexual activity.

The mind governed by the flesh is death, but the mind governed by the Spirit is life and peace" (Rom. 8:5–6).[19]

Both Scripture and psychology propose that what we attend to can have a lasting impact on living. While we have responsibility for how we use our attention, much of what we attend to and perceive is governed unconsciously, fitting with our embodiment and limited agency. How then can we influence what we attend to?

It may help to begin by understanding that attention is always "on." Attention is restless—it seeks out something to do.[20] Research on **mind wandering**—*when attention drifts from an external task to internal memories and thoughts*—shows that when we're not interested in what we're doing, attention shifts to something else, quite on its own.[21] This is common when working on automated, repetitive tasks or on tasks so difficult that we can't even follow what's going on. If the current information or task doesn't fully occupy our attention—it's boring or not compelling—we easily respond to other things in the environment[22] and/or we "look" to our internal world, as the research on mind wandering shows.

This implies that we'll always pay attention to *something*. What is around us "gets in." Information around us can become an experience that changes us, even if we have no intention for that to happen. Stimuli containing movement and change are most likely to grab attention. Pornography is a particularly attention-grabbing stimulus. When people view pornography, normal sexual responses occur, reinforcing the viewing. Such responses are, from a biblical view of persons, misdirected because they're not within the context of a committed relationship; persons are instead depicted as sexual objects. Nevertheless, pornography grabs one's attention.[23] Repeatedly viewing pornography easily results in a habit that's difficult to break, with the porn industry doing all it can to reinforce that habit. Avoiding opportunities to view pornography can be an important, albeit potentially difficult way to influence attention that subsequently influences desires and behavior. As we mentioned in chapter 4, repeated behavior becomes automated—"habitual"—so behaviors can be set into motion by just perceiving relevant items in the environment—again, regardless of what someone intended to do. People show similar habits with smoking and compulsive spending, to name just

19. Paul, when referring to "the flesh" here, is commenting on sinful desires, not the physical body itself.

20. If you ever ask someone what they are thinking about and they answer, "Nothing," feel free to point and shout, "Liar!" Attention is occupied because attention is always occupied.

21. One study on mind wandering is Smallwood and Schooler, "Restless Mind."

22. Lavie, "Distracted and Confused?," reviews the literature on distractibility.

23. For a good discussion of pornography and its effects, see Struthers, *Wired for Intimacy*.

two more examples. Because we are embodied, our limited agency is necessarily impacted by our situation.

This example regarding pornography suggests a clear way to influence attention in the long term: modifying your environment. Consider the impact of factors such as where you live, organizations you join, even where you shop and go for a walk. Your situation greatly influences what you'll pay attention to and perceive. You simply can't perceive or attend to things that aren't around: out of sight, out of mind. We each physically live where we live and may not be able to change that for many reasons, yet we all have influence over *what we do* where we live—what we attend to or bring into our environment. We're always perceiving and always attending, so it's important to seek situations worth attending to and avoid those that aren't.

For Christians, following God's call to care for people in need is impossible if they are never around folks in need. Jesus lived among and sought out those who were poor and sick—in both a physical sense and a spiritual sense—and ministered to them. When asked why he was eating with sinners, Jesus said, "It is not the healthy who need a doctor, but the sick. I have not come to call the righteous, but sinners" (Mark 2:17). Actively serving in the world requires Christians to be aware of the world. Christians can't sequester themselves from the world's needs if they are going to serve God and be Christ followers. They need to know what is happening in the news and be involved in addressing concerns of their communities.

Finally, active involvement in a church where prayers for others are regularly offered and God is worshiped can make these be things to which a Christian regularly pays attention. A Christian community where people have meaningful, interconnected relationships can provide mutual support to make changes that alter attention. As the writer of Hebrews instructs Christians, "And let us consider how we may spur one another on toward love and good deeds, not giving up meeting together, as some are in the habit of doing, but encouraging one another" (10:24–25). Note that the writer doesn't say "you"; the writer says "we." New Testament books and letters were written to churches more often than to individuals. Christians are in this together.

--- **DISCUSSION QUESTIONS** ---

1. How might one's perception of living be affected by embracing the apostle Paul's claim: "I can do all this through him who gives me strength" (Phil. 4:13)?

2. Our sensory systems prioritize change and difference. How might this make it difficult to effectively notice areas of weakness in your life?

3. Are we responsible for our behaviors that we don't even notice?

4. Philippians 4:8 reads, "Whatever is true, whatever is noble, whatever is right, whatever is pure, whatever is lovely, whatever is admirable—if anything is excellent or praiseworthy—think about such things." Can Christians do that and still work among "sinners"?

6

Change from the Heart

Learning

▶ SUMMARY: Learning theories and research in the early days of psychology—namely, classical and operant conditioning studies—appeared to show that animals and humans alike learn in a mechanical and passive way. In other words, we are just like glorified robots, programmed by the environment. These ideas have presented challenges to notions of free will, responsibility, and our meaning seeking nature. This chapter focuses on ways to rethink these basic mechanisms of learning and shows that the research poses much less of a challenge to free will and responsibility than is commonly assumed. At the same time, these research findings also remind us that our free choices are limited by the conditions in our environment, that we learn as embodied creatures, and that we are not quite as unique from the rest of creation as we like to think.

Any fool can know. The point is to understand.

attributed to Albert Einstein

[Kids] don't remember what you try to teach them. They remember what you are.

Jim Henson, *It's Not Easy Being Green*

Let us discern for ourselves what is right;
let us learn together what is good.

Job 34:4

S everal years ago, a young boy named Jarod had to drink castor oil (a very nasty substance) over several days in preparation for some medical tests.[1] To help him tolerate the oil, his mother mixed it with an orange-flavored soft drink. Until he was in his thirties, he could not stand the taste of any orange-flavored drinks. This hatred of orange flavoring appeared to develop outside his conscious awareness because for some time he couldn't remember why he didn't like orange-flavored drinks—until his mother reminded him of his childhood tests. This story illustrates some simple but disturbing things about learning. It appears that humans, like animals, learn by making simple associations between events. These associations can influence our behavior in powerful ways, and they appear to happen at an unconscious level.

Most readers will be acquainted with the research and theories associated with classical and operant conditioning. The well-known stories about Ivan Pavlov's salivating dogs and B. F. Skinner's key-pecking pigeons are told in every introductory psychology textbook. The story above illustrates some of the principles of classical conditioning. Just as a tuning fork (Conditioned Stimulus or CS) being associated with food (Unconditioned Stimulus or UCS) causes a dog to salivate (Conditioned Response or CR) to the tuning fork, so a soft drink (CS) associated with castor oil (UCS) causes someone to feel nauseated (CR) when tasting the soft drink. If you need an example of operant conditioning, the explanations given by the school psychologist for Ethan's behavior described in the introduction illustrate a common application of this type of conditioning. The psychologist suggests that simple rewards and punishments have "made" Ethan behave a certain way.

But why should we care if dogs can salivate to bells or pigeons can do tricks? The answer lies not only in the important contributions of these learning discoveries to all areas of psychology but also in the deeper explanation for how these situations promote learning. Many early researchers in these areas of study embraced behaviorism, which promoted a set of theories about learning mechanisms but also represented a worldview about human nature. This worldview had a profound effect on psychology as well as on popular notions about why humans act the way they do.

The "Challenge" of Behaviorism

Behaviorists such as John Watson were very excited and optimistic about the discovery of classical and operant conditioning because they were certain they had uncovered the building blocks for all learning. They also felt that psycholo-

---

1. A true story—but names have been changed to protect the nauseated.

gists could use their discoveries to uncover all the laws of learning, which would allow us to "cure" individual problems (e.g., learning difficulties, annoying personalities) as well as social ills (e.g., crime, poverty). At the level of theory, they were convinced that learning involves simple connections between events—such as between a CS and a CR in **classical conditioning**, or between a stimulus and a response when followed by a reward in **operant conditioning**. These connections were likened to a switch that is flipped, closing an electrical circuit in the brain when two simple events happen close in time. Behaviorists believed that these connections occur passively; we don't analyze, contemplate, or emotionally evaluate these events—they simply occur *to us* when the environmental conditions are right. Sometimes these notions were referred to as connectionism or reflexology because it was assumed that the connections create a new reflex, just like a simple knee jerk in response to a doctor's rubber hammer on the knee. These connections then cause us to behave differently in the future, just as updated computer software responds differently to new input. More complex behaviors are produced by simply adding a string of connections together to produce complex sequences of behavior. So in their view, all learning is passive and mechanical and happens at an unconscious level. To paraphrase and summarize B. F. Skinner's position, "We do not think; we simply respond."[2]

In addition to these basic "connectionist" ideas, behaviorists believed that the learning processes for animals and humans are fundamentally the same. Humans may have greater capacity to form more and better connections, but the laws that govern the processes were viewed as identical. Not only were animals and humans considered to be governed by the same laws of learning, but behaviorists believed that we shared the same basic motivational goals: to avoid pain and to seek pleasure. Behaviorists suggested that this motivation, along with the associated learning mechanisms, was designed to help us survive in an ever-changing environment. Biological evolution helps species change over a long period of time, but survival motives and learned connections allow us to adapt to rapidly changing conditions. This view also implies that learning and all behavior follow prescribed laws, just as there are laws that govern the physical universe, and that these laws will one day be fully understood and used to change behavior in whatever way the "controller" wishes.

But behaviorists went beyond studying the laws of learning; many of them also characterized aspects of human nature. To many behaviorists, humans are like blank slates waiting to be passively altered by experience (i.e., we are not meaning seeking individuals; theme 5). This behaviorist view also implies that behavior is ultimately determined by the environment (i.e., there is no

2. Skinner, "Why I Am Not a Cognitive Psychologist."

free will; theme 4), that we are not special or unique in relation to animals (i.e., we are not created in God's image; theme 1), that human nature is neutral (i.e., not inherently good or inherently evil; theme 2), and—if carried to the logical extreme—that humans have no ultimate personal responsibility (i.e., we are not responsible agents; theme 4). You can see why the simple concepts of classical and operant conditioning, and the behaviorist views that followed, created such a seismic shift in basic worldviews that goes beyond salivating dogs and clever pigeons.

Despite the fact that these behaviorist ideas appear to challenge several of our human nature themes, classical and operant conditioning principles have been applied very successfully to many behavioral problems. While the optimism of the early behaviorists has been diminished in recent years because their techniques haven't cured all individual or social ills, there nevertheless have been countless successful applications to humans, bringing improvements to child-rearing practices, training for persons with developmental disabilities, classroom teaching, treatment of emotional disorders, and many other areas. So should we conclude that the behaviorists were correct and that perhaps we are not willful, responsible, unique, relational beings?

Responses to Behaviorism

Christian psychologists have approached this potential conflict in a variety of ways. Some have raised the possibility that a biblical perspective is compatible with a deterministic view since it's possible that God decided our lifelong fate before the beginning of time and that he accomplished his plan through natural events. Skinner himself once suggested that he believed his position to be compatible with the theological views of the Calvinist theologian Jonathan Edwards,[3] who placed a strong emphasis on our sinful nature and our complete dependence on a sovereign God (i.e., a form of divine or spiritual determinism). Some individuals have also argued that the Bible is full of examples of God punishing and rewarding people for their sinful or righteous acts, respectively, which suggests to them that using these basic survival motives to change behaviors has a scriptural basis.[4]

Another approach of Christian psychologists is to suggest that while classical and operant conditioning may work much as these behaviorists suggest, it is only at a "low level" of human, bodily functioning. In other words, in this view, the nonmaterial mind can transcend or overrule the mechanistic and passive

3. Moxley, "Skinner."
4. See Bufford, *Human Reflex*.

influence of conditioning that occurs in the "simpler" parts of the brain/mind.[5] However, one problem with this view, as discussed in chapter 3, is that the findings of modern neuroscience, psychology, and even theology have made it harder to separate mind, body, and soul. Since it is harder to conceive of separate components of the mind from both a theological perspective and a psychological perspective, this dual-level view of learning or willfulness seems less plausible.

We do believe that the views and responses of Christians described above are certainly worthy of consideration and discussion. However, we think there may be a simpler way to solve the apparent dilemma. Research over the past fifty years has consistently demonstrated that a connectionist view of conditioning is grossly oversimplified or just plain wrong. Therefore, the behaviorist worldview has not unraveled by way of religious challenges but has been the victim of its own successful campaign to do rigorous scientific research on both animal learning and human learning. A complete review of this vast body of literature is impossible here, but we do provide a small sample of these research findings.

The Cognitive Reinterpretation

Consider the classical conditioning example presented at the beginning of the chapter—but now with some additional twists to illustrate how classical conditioning has been reinterpreted. One new twist mimics a series of experiments called blocking studies. Let's assume that Jarod, after having established a strong association between the orange soda (CS) and the nausea-producing castor oil (UCS), had to repeat the process a few weeks later. But now imagine that Jarod's mom added a piece of candy that Jarod took at the same time he drank the soda–castor oil mix. According to Pavlov, because the candy is presented close in time with the castor oil, Jarod should "connect" the candy and the castor oil and develop a conditioned response of nausea in response to the candy just like he did with the orange soda. In other words, taking the candy by itself would also make him feel nauseated. However, studies on situations like this show that if this process were followed, Jarod wouldn't develop a conditioned response to the candy, but he would still maintain a horrible dislike for the orange soda. Why doesn't he associate the candy with the castor oil and nausea?

According to research coming from cognitive psychology (see chap. 8), the reason Jarod doesn't associate the candy with the nausea-producing castor oil is that it adds no new information to the situation; he *already knows* when the

5. See Cosgrove, *Essence of Human Nature*.

nausea is coming—it always comes ten minutes after the orange soda! So the first signal (the beverage) *blocks out* the association of the second signal (the candy) with the nausea because the second signal involves redundant or irrelevant information. This outcome suggests that even though the candy is paired with the castor oil, Jarod doesn't make an automatic connection.

However, if the above situation were slightly different, the associations would change drastically. Imagine that each time Jarod's mom added candy to the mix, he also got a bigger dose of castor oil and experienced greater nausea. *In this new situation,* he would in fact form a strong dislike for the candy. The reason he forms an association between the candy and the castor oil is that the candy *now adds new information;* it signals to him that he can expect even worse nausea. Studies like this show that we don't automatically form associations; rather, we learn about relationships between events based on the information they tell us about the environment. Using past events to predict future events was an idea the behaviorists rejected because mentally predicting seemed too "mentalistic" and not directly observable, but it appears this is exactly what happens. Since the original blocking studies[6] were done on animals (using things such as tones, lights, and mild shocks), we can't conclude that this type of learning is always conscious or even completely willful, but they do suggest that forming associations is more complicated than was assumed by many behaviorists.

Consider another study with human subjects, done some years ago, that paired various tones with a mild electric shock.[7] In experiments of this type, participants eventually show a learned or conditioned response to the tone—meaning that they show a measurable emotional response whenever the tone is given. Researchers told half the participants at the beginning of the experiment that "the intelligent thing is to become conditioned," but they told the other half that "the intelligent thing is *not* to become conditioned." We should mention that the task they had to do was very easy, so actual intelligence should have had no influence whatsoever. However, giving these instructions presumably influenced the *attitude* of the participants about conditioning. In the end, the first group (told that conditioning was the intelligent thing to do) showed much faster learning and much stronger responses than the second group. The researcher concluded that the instructions made the first group *want* to be conditioned, so as to appear intelligent, and made the second group *resist* conditioning because otherwise they would look unintelligent. It appears that people are not inevitably conditioned against their will by passively produced connections in their brains and that *we* control our learning destinies.

6. See Hulse, Fowler, and Honig, *Cognitive Processes in Animal Behavior.*
7. Dawson and Reardon, "Effects of Facilitory and Inhibitory Sets," 462.

One last example involving operant conditioning (i.e., using rewards) is a phenomenon called the overjustification effect.[8] Consider two children who both receive rewards, such as money, for completing their homework assignments, but one gets a much larger reward than the other. If the parents eventually quit giving the reward, which child will continue to faithfully do their homework for several weeks? A typical behaviorist explanation assumes that the larger the reward, the stronger the connection between the situation and the response. Thus the child with the larger reward should continue doing homework longer than the other child. As it turns out, the opposite is true; large rewards often work against continued performance. Why would this be? The common explanation is that humans often look for justification for why they do things. For example, I might ask myself when doing homework, "Why am I doing this tiring task?" If I am receiving a very small reward, I may conclude that doing homework must be something I value—why else would I do it? If I am receiving a large reward, I conclude that I am working only for the reward—in other words, I have too much *external* justification and no *internal* justification for doing it. It appears that large rewards can diminish our *intrinsic* motivation for a task. This result suggests that even though rewards and punishments do change behavior, we are much more thoughtful in analyzing our basic motives than has been suggested by the behaviorists.

Based on examples like these, the predominant perspective in psychology over the past thirty years has come to stress a more "cognitive" understanding of learning as opposed to the behaviorist perspective. Learning theorist Jeanne Ormrod summarizes these cognitive principles, which we paraphrase in table 1 and contrast to the older behaviorist view.[9]

Learning, from the cognitive perspective, can involve both a top-down analysis (using existing knowledge to shape and form new experiences) and a bottom-up process (in which completely new experiences can be organized according to basic learning mechanisms). The cognitive perspective also stresses that the *process* of learning may be lawful, but the knowledge structure we ultimately form and the way we actually behave are not *determined* by the immediate environment.

So hopefully you can see from this list that the newer cognitive view of learning has much greater consistency with the themes we have outlined for this book. As we have argued, we are embodied persons (theme 3) with features similar to those of animals—yet we are special. We stressed in chapter 2, on

8. This effect was coined in a different study by Lepper, Greene, and Nisbett, "Undermining Children's Intrinsic Interest."

9. See Ormrod, *Human Learning*, 168–70.

TABLE 1

Issue	Behaviorist View	Cognitive View
Animals versus humans	Animals and humans share the same basic learning mechanisms.	Some learning processes may be unique to humans (even though some aspects of learning are common to both).
Learning research	Only objective observation is allowed; we cannot make guesses about things we can't see.	While psychologists should use objective observation to study learning, we can make inferences about internal mental processes.
Passive versus active	Learning is a passive process.	Individuals are actively involved in the learning process.
Learning versus performance	Learning equals behavior (if you haven't made the right connections, you don't behave correctly).	Learning involves the formation of mental associations that are not necessarily reflected in actual behavior.
Knowledge representation	We can't speak of knowledge, only sequences of connections.	Knowledge is organized. We form structures or knowledge schemas.
Complex knowledge	Learning involves making new connections; previous experience has very little influence.	Learning is a process of relating new information to previously learned information.

research methods, that systematic observation is the best way to study behavior, but we also argued that we routinely interpret the information and make inferences about the results. We have argued that we are responsible limited agents (theme 4), which is consistent with the notions that we are actively involved in learning and that sometimes when we learn we don't necessarily act on that learning. So there are many elements about current psychological thinking and the biblical view of persons that appear to be very compatible.

This does not mean, however, that all elements of current cognitive perspectives are entirely consistent with the themes we have proposed. For one thing, while cognitive theorists rarely talk about determinism, most would still argue that if we knew all the things that go on "inside" our heads, we could predict behavior perfectly and would see that our behavior is still determined. Two other major differences between current cognitive views and a biblical worldview are that cognitive views pay very little attention to our relational nature (theme 1) and that they give relatively little consideration to our being meaning seekers (theme 5).

The way in which relationality influences learning will be addressed in later chapters, but we can say at this point that learning typically involves some form of social and interpersonal context. The issue of meaning seeking (theme 5) is a consistent theme in Scripture. One example of this idea, as it relates to learning, is illustrated in Proverbs 24:30–34:

> I went past the field of a sluggard,
>> past the vineyard of someone who has no sense;
> thorns had come up everywhere,
>> the ground was covered with weeds,
>> and the stone wall was in ruins.
> I applied my heart to what I observed
>> and learned a lesson from what I saw:
> A little sleep, a little slumber,
>> a little folding of the hands to rest—
> and poverty will come on you like a thief
>> and scarcity like an armed man.

The phrase "I applied my heart to what I observed" is intriguing. It appears that the observer (notice the "empirical" observation) not only analyzes the situation in terms of previous knowledge structures (as cognitive theorists like to talk about) but also *actively* applies all that he is. Biblical writers used the term *heart* whenever they wanted to talk about our deepest motives and emotions, our core tendencies, or our deepest thoughts—in other words, all that we are. So the observer is trying not only to form a new knowledge structure from this experience but also to find the deeper meaning by drawing from his emotions, motives, tendencies, and thoughts. Therefore, whenever we come to any new learning situation—be it simple or complex and whether we are fully aware of it or not—we bring our biases, worldviews, past experiences, moral perspectives, sins, relationships, and all that we are to the situation. Learning does have systematic and even lawful properties, and the process can be studied. Yet our learning does more than follow simple laws; it follows our hearts and can end up with wrong (i.e., sinful) conclusions about reality or with correct (i.e., consistent with God's desire) views about reality.

Implications and Applications

What are the practical implications of these perspectives for the application of basic classical and operant conditioning procedures? First, they suggest that we should be able to scientifically study the laws that govern the learning *process*, even if we will never be able to determine the final knowledge structure that an individual will create or the way that an individual will ultimately behave.

This helps to avoid the confusion that newcomers to psychology often have, wondering how psychology can be scientific without treating people as being determined by physical forces (just glorified robots).

Second, we believe that it is certainly permissible for a Christian parent, educator, or therapist to use these learning techniques to influence the behavior of humans, since doing so in no way implies that we are determining some other person's internal thought process against their will. The person will shape the experience according to what they already know, feel, and do—so even if the external behavior is manipulated, the recipient of these techniques ultimately determines the outcome of their own learning structure.

Third, while we believe that people should be careful about the overuse of simple motives and associations, these techniques have worked very well on children, on developmentally delayed adults, and in some other limited situations. The techniques work in these situations because they present simple relationships to the learner that require less complex knowledge structures, and they create simple ways to learn when more complex ways overwhelm us. However, we need to be careful in their use because we ultimately want to change more than an outward behavior; we want to change the person's heart. As Psalm 32:9 suggests, "Do not be like the horse or the mule, which have no understanding but must be controlled by bit and bridle or they will not come to you." Rewards and punishments may alter behavior, but parents, educators, and therapists should ultimately work to change understanding. In addition, while we gain understanding mostly by experiencing things in the environment, we also learn by examples from others. A child who experiences nothing but punishment from a parent—even if the punishment is effective in stopping incorrect behaviors—learns that punishment is the way to "get things done." These children may become adults who use punishment as their first option when dealing with their relationships, with potentially devastating consequences.[10] So we need to pay attention to the whole learning process and to the whole person.

In conclusion, we have tried to show that the learning procedures that are called classical and operant conditioning do not pose any essential threat or direct challenge to a biblical view of persons. We have also tried to suggest that learning ultimately involves more than passive connections; it involves the entire person. The beliefs they possess, how they have acted in the past, and the knowledge structures they have formed all shape their learning in the future.

Learning *involves using all these elements to further form our knowledge and thought structure*, but wisdom takes this one step further. **Wisdom** *involves learning with great insight, but it also involves conforming one's learning, emotions, and*

---

10. See Kaufman and Zigler, "Intergenerational Transmission of Abuse."

behaviors to God's desires. As the apostle Paul suggests in Ephesians 1:16–18, "I have not stopped giving thanks for you, remembering you in my prayers. I keep asking that the God of our Lord Jesus Christ, the glorious Father, may give you the Spirit of wisdom and revelation, so that you may know him better. I pray that the eyes of your heart may be enlightened in order that you may know the hope to which he has called you, the riches of his glorious inheritance in his holy people."

DISCUSSION QUESTIONS

1. Can you think of ways that you have been influenced by subtle rewards or punishments that come through everyday experiences? In those situations, did it feel to you as though you were the passive victim of influences that worked against your will, or were you in some ways allowing or shaping the process?

2. How has modeling from others influenced how you behave? How might the examples of your own behavior influence how others learn or behave?

3. Can you think of situations in which you came to a deeper understanding of some issue or problem through relationality—in other words, in the context of community or social interaction?

4. Think of concrete ways in which the "direction of your heart" might have influenced what you learned or how you understood what you learned.

7

Remember Me?

Memory

SUMMARY: Memory and remembering are mentioned many times in the Bible—not usually in terms of how to memorize or how memory works but in the context of relationships. Being relational persons requires memory—shared experiences and shared knowledge give a common basis for interacting. While it's important to remember where you have placed your jacket on a cold day, imagine the hollowness of a life in which you are not remembered by anyone else. Psychology benefits a Christian understanding of relationality by indicating the various memory types and showing how each handles different kinds of information. In this chapter, we discuss how these forms of memory (and their strengths and weaknesses) impact relationships with others and God as well as with ourselves, as embodied meaning seekers. In addition, we explore the notion of God's forgetting, as described in the Bible, contrasted with human forgetting.

> Remember, LORD, your great mercy and love,
>   for they are from of old.
> Do not remember the sins of my youth
>   and my rebellious ways;
> according to your love remember me,
>   for you, LORD, are good.
>
> Psalm 25:6–7

Memory connects us to each other. When you reconnect with a classmate from elementary school, it's the shared memories of long ago that tie you together. You may not even talk about the past, but a common history provides the foundation necessary to treat each other in a substantially different way than someone you've never met. Such connections become obvious when sharing a memory of the boy everyone knew as "Stinky" who went on to a career in modeling.

Memory also connects us to ourselves. Your sense of who you are is absolutely memory dependent. This includes knowledge as simple and well-practiced as your own name or your list of personal likes and dislikes. That sort of knowledge helps you increase your happiness and decrease your misery. If experience tells you that broccoli tastes good to you, you may feel free to indulge; if you despise it, you move on to something else and don't have to suffer the disappointment of broccoli each time you taste it.

Memory's importance is obvious, and people tend to think about memory a lot like they think about money: more is good, less is bad. Booksellers like Amazon have thousands of titles available on how to improve memory or to avoid memory loss.[1] In addition, seminars, drugs, and training programs are aimed at boosting memory and escaping its loss.

We also dislike and even fear being forgotten by others. Sure, there are exceptions, like when you did something embarrassing in the past and people forget that *you* are the answer to the question "Who was that kid who wet his pants in first grade?"[2] Yet if someone forgets your name or important details about you, it's understandable to feel at least a little unimportant. Our significance within relationships is based on what we mean to each other. One of the most disturbing consequences of memory loss, as occurs in the memory-destroying disorder Alzheimer's disease, is when relationships are lost in a fog of forgetting. Heartbreaking stories of when "Mom didn't know who I was" or "I need to see Dad one more time while he can still recognize me" make painfully clear that memory is what gives each of us our sense of identity.

Memory in Scripture and Psychology

In chapter 1 we made the case that being relational persons (theme 1) is at the center of a biblical view of human nature—the heart of being made in the image of God. Relating to others requires memory: through knowing and loving characteristics of others, we understand how to respond and can potentially embrace each other's personhood.[3] Scripture emphasizes the role and purpose

1. In 2023 there were over five thousand self-help book titles under the category "memory improvement" on Amazon.

2. Okay, that's one of the authors speaking from personal experience. We won't say which one.

3. Yannaras, *Freedom of Morality*, 23.

of memory within the context of relationships, particularly in relationship with God.

Scripture's Emphasis

The Bible refers to memory a lot. The word *remember* appears over two hundred times across the Old and New Testaments, and the words *forget* and *forgot* each show up about fifty times.[4] Only a few passages directly instruct people how to remember, including this passage from Deuteronomy, after the Ten Commandments were given to Israel: "Fix these words of mine in your hearts and minds; tie them as symbols on your hands and bind them on your foreheads. Teach them to your children, talking about them when you sit at home and when you walk along the road, when you lie down and when you get up. Write them on the doorframes of your houses and on your gates" (11:18–20). These recommendations for remembering God's laws involve the use of repetition (teaching, talking in all times and places) and constant physical reminders (writing on doorframes and gates).

The Bible's more common emphasis regarding memory comes just prior to these instructions on *how* to memorize: God gives his people the reason *why* they should memorize. God's people were entering the new land he had promised. God says, "Be careful, or you will be enticed to turn away and worship other gods and bow down to them" (Deut. 11:16). God reminds his people that he is with them and is calling them into a relationship once again—a relationship in which God is faithful to the creatures he has created. Remembering is about maintaining a relationship with God and not "taking up" with other gods that humans easily find enticing. As we stated with theme 5, humans are meaning seekers who desire a deity.

The Bible consists of stories of God's interactions with humans—and how humans relate to God, creation, and each other—and it speaks of memory as to how we are creatures made in God's image, crafted to be in relationships. The Bible urges God's people to remember who God is[5] and to remember each other.[6] The human need for relationship with God is apparent in human pleas

---

4. In the NIV, the word *remember* is used 231 times (https://www.biblegateway.com/quick search/?quicksearch=remember&qs_version=NIV).

5. E.g., Deut. 7:18, as God calls Israel to recall being rescued out of Egypt. Many other similar calls are given throughout the Old Testament to recall who God is. Even the birth of Jesus is a reminder of God's relationship with humans, as "all this took place to fulfill what the Lord had said through the prophet," that a virgin will have a child who will be called Immanuel, meaning "God with us" (Matt. 1:22–23).

6. E.g., Gen. 40:14, where Joseph, in prison in Egypt, interprets a dream and asks to be remembered for this deed.

for God to remember his people (particularly in the book of Psalms).[7] In all these cases, remembering means nurturing a relationship.

Psychology's Emphasis

Psychological science is most interested in the how and why of memory—how it's stored, organized, and retrieved, and why it fails. Scripture, on the other hand, simply doesn't address questions of how memory functions. However, psychological research on memory can potentially help us in how we interrelate by enhancing our understanding of ourselves and others. The topic of memory is an excellent example of how the Bible isn't a psychology textbook and how psychological science can provide information that helps us better understand God's creation (including ourselves) and perhaps even God, as he shows his nature in creation.[8]

A key finding from psychology is that memory isn't just one thing; there are several subtypes or subsystems. Perhaps the most familiar memories are those of shared experiences that happen in relationships. These are **episodic memories**[9]: *memories of the events or "episodes" of our lives*, like weddings and first days of school as well as typically less-momentous occasions like last evening's dinner. These memories of personal events include a representation of ourselves in the memories[10]—"I sat by a friend at the wedding" or "I was nervous on my first day of college." When talking with others who also have a memory for the same events, it is those shared memories that bring a connection. Most of the Bible's references to memory relate to episodic memories that provide the basis for relationality, including remembering God's acts in relation to humans. In fact, Christian research psychologist Warren S. Brown mentions episodic memory as one of the critical capacities that humans possess that make them relational persons.[11]

Episodic memory is one of the most obvious forms of memory to come to mind because such memories *can* come to mind. It's one of two forms of **declarative memory**: *a memory that we can consciously recall and retrieve*. Another form of memory, **semantic memory**, *includes facts and general knowledge that do not depend on recalling a particular time or situation* (such as knowing what a book is without having to remember the last time you saw a book). Semantic

---

7. E.g., Ps. 106:4. Examples outside the Psalms include Moses asking God to remember that Israel is God's people (Exod. 33:13) and the thief on the cross next to Jesus at his crucifixion saying, "Jesus, remember me when you come into your kingdom" (Luke 23:42).

8. Worthington, *Coming to Peace with Psychology*, 142.

9. This term was first coined by Endel Tulving in "Episodic and Semantic Memory," 386.

10. See discussion in Kihlstrom, "Consciousness and Me-ness."

11. Brown, "Cognitive Contributions to Soul," 103.

memories provide a shared understanding that doesn't require shared experiences. This allows people to decipher each other's words, perceive reality accurately, and draw proper conclusions. Within relationships, there is a communal nature to memory that builds on both the shared ability to communicate[12] and shared experience. This shared understanding helps relationships form and, once formed, continue to work.

Memory in Practice

Not all our knowledge about events or our actions relies on these conscious, verbal systems. **Nondeclarative memory** *consists of information we have learned without conscious awareness or control; it's also called implicit memory*. The word *remember* doesn't really apply to nondeclarative memory because this system doesn't rely on or access our conscious awareness. This means that our behavior is influenced in ways and for reasons we are not aware of. In addition, we can't verbally describe the contents of a retrieved nondeclarative memory.[13] There are several distinct forms of nondeclarative memory, each involving a different brain area.[14] Let's look at how just one of these systems[15]—procedural memory—contributes to our being relational persons.

Procedural memory *is a nondeclarative type of memory that includes skill learning and habits*. Riding a bicycle requires procedural memory (so do typing, walking, and knitting). The key skill in biking is maintaining balance to remain vertical on two skinny tires. The declarative memory around the concept of balancing a bike would include the words *steady* or *upright*. But verbal instructions to "balance" are almost useless when learning how to ride a bike. The nondeclarative information of how you need to slightly lean one direction or another to maintain an upright position *isn't* learned verbally—it takes experience. Sensory feedback from feeling as though you're going to fall prompts changes in body position that you can't really verbalize. The only way to learn how to ride a bike is by *trying* to ride a bike. While it's possible to say that you know how to ride a bike (semantic memory) and you may be able to talk about when you last rode a bike (episodic memory), words don't adequately describe what you needed to learn to make your body able to ride a bike (procedural memory).

12. If there is a language barrier between people, sometimes gesture or pantomime works to convey fairly universal messages, such as a need to eat or drink.
13. Reisberg, *Cognition*, 239–74, has a helpful discussion of these systems.
14. Kandel, Kupfermann, and Iverson ("Learning and Memory") break down declarative and nondeclarative memory types and indicate how they depend on different brain regions.
15. We restrict the number of examples due to space limitations, but all the nondeclarative memory systems (conditioning, sensitization, habituation, etc.) affect how people respond to others.

While procedural memory is nonverbal, it can still be relational. In the Bible, there are calls for God's people to actively worship and serve. These activities involve physically enacted, procedural memories. For example, Matthew 6 records Jesus's instructions to his disciples regarding the practices of giving to the needy, prayer, and fasting. Jesus's teaching shows important things about the relational aspects of memory. These practices are to be done regularly[16] and have repeatable physical components that will activate habits, and habits are based in procedural memory.

We use the word *practices* here because they are physical behaviors, conducted by embodied creatures (theme 3). Our practices form us, as philosopher James K. A. Smith writes,[17] and psychological research shows that these habits become less accessible to conscious awareness.[18] Through practice, repeated behaviors bring unique changes in cognitive and neural systems of procedural memory, distinct from declarative memory systems.[19] Habitual tasks like getting dressed are learned through practice (you're faster at putting on clothes than a less-practiced child), but procedural tasks aren't completely "mindless." Dressing includes habits and rituals (e.g., which arm or leg you start with), but it also involves active *choices* about what to wear. Behaviors based on procedural memory can be directed by free will at times, where we exercise our limited agency. Giving, praying, and fasting also involve decisions about whom to give to, what to pray about, and when and for how long to fast.

Religious behaviors can become ingrained and accessed almost unconsciously. When fragile episodic memories fail us, rituals—stemming from habits—can anchor us. When facing difficulties, a prayerful stance, memorized words from Scripture or songs, or deeply formed religious behavior can bring comfort and re-grounding in a way that trying to develop a new behavior may not. These impact human relationships with God, others, and even oneself.

Another type of nondeclarative memory is **priming**, *where thoughts and behaviors come to mind more easily in the future simply because they were encountered in the past.* Priming can impact interrelatedness in unexpected ways because merely being exposed to ideas, objects, or behaviors changes how quickly and how positively or negatively we respond to them later. For example, we tend to more positively evaluate things that we've seen before, including people. The **mere-exposure effect** *is a variety of priming in which people prefer an item they've*

16. In Jesus's instructions in Matt. 6:2–7, he begins by saying "when" you do these things rather than "if."

17. J. Smith, *Desiring the Kingdom*, 55–62.

18. Wood and Rünger, "Psychology of Habit," 306–7.

19. Wood and Rünger, "Psychology of Habit," 290, 294–95.

seen before, even if they don't remember seeing it previously.[20] In one experiment,[21] Chinese characters were briefly presented, and later in the experiment, participants were presented with characters that had been shown before as well as other, similar characters that had not. Although participants were unable to tell which characters had been presented before and which were new (no reliable conscious, episodic memory), they tended to prefer the old characters more than the new ones. Simply seeing something, without necessarily even being able to consciously recall it, alters our relationship with that "something." If a participant in the experiment were asked to explain why they preferred one Chinese character more than another, the reasoning given would be a conscious attempt to explain an unconsciously influenced preference! The true answer, "Because I saw it before," wouldn't be said because the person wouldn't be aware of that previous experience. In chapter 4 we further discussed how such unconscious processing influences relationality as well as implications for free will and responsibility (theme 4).

Psychology's research on nondeclarative memory shows that what we do and what we expose ourselves to may bring about changes that influence future behavior in ways we're not even aware of. This certainly happens with habits and priming. Christians might well consider how exposure to God and notions of faith could impact how they and others respond to Christianity. Clearly, psychological science findings about priming effects have implications for our understanding of a biblical view of human nature.

Meaning Makers Making Memories

Information that gets represented or encoded in memory is stored in an organized way, helping us make sense of our surroundings. Several factors influence what we do and what we don't remember. Some are biological predispositions, like our drive for self-preservation; others depend on how well the new information fits what is already stored (things we already know). This organization often comes as an effortless by-product of having an experience. For example, you've learned that it hurts to touch a hot pan just out of the oven. You don't need to think, "I'll need to remember this in the future: pans out of a hot oven burn my skin," and consciously try to rehearse that idea several times, quizzing yourself again later to make sure you know it. Such learning is immediate and allows memory to happen without using our limited cognitive resources (and without taxing our limited agency). Other times, deliberate strategies can

20. Zajonc, "Mere Exposure," 224.
21. Monahan, Murphy, and Zajonc, "Subliminal Mere Exposure."

be used, such as organizing information under a heading (like the category "themes of human nature in the Bible").[22] Such organization shows that as meaning seekers (theme 5), we make meaning of our experiences, sometimes by our own choices of how to do that but also simply as a consequence of how thinking is organized.

Organization allows thinking about one idea to activate related ideas so that those ideas come to mind more quickly than others.[23] This is useful in conversation. If a friend is talking about their dog, it's good that ideas about your friend, their dog, and other dogs, as well as other relevant (meaningfully related) ideas, come to mind quickly rather than unrelated ideas like bricks or the United Nations. Recalling and activating related ideas make the conversation go forward sensibly: responding to your friend's question "Have I shown you how my dog can play fetch?" with "I like bananas" makes for difficult interaction. The process of ideas automatically activating related ideas improves interactions. But note something else here: if you're able to share ideas held by other persons, this means you both have similar ways of representing ideas and meaning. There is great uniformity in how memory works for people. Yet there are individual differences in what we each particularly remember and what we hold as sufficiently important to recall, because each person has had their own life experiences. Nevertheless, shared memories—shared representations—make us interrelated, relational persons.

Active Meaning Seeking

Meaning is also made in more active ways. When it comes to our conscious (declarative) memories, we're hardly exact recorders of information; instead, we're more like storytellers attempting to make sense of the world around us. When dealing with the world, we don't take in all information equally. Instead, we prioritize information that is important to our situation, and we disregard the rest.[24] In addition, due to limited capacity, we don't store exact copies of events as they occur.[25] Instead, we primarily store snippets and highlights— what psychologists call the "gist" of the event. If you're someone who likes to quote movie dialogue, have you ever rewatched a movie and learned that you were saying one of your favorite lines slightly wrong? Or maybe you've caught a friend making such an error? Obviously, the original quote wasn't remembered

22. Bower et al., "Hierarchical Retrieval Schemes," published in 1969, is one of the earliest research examples showing this effect.

23. McNamara, *Semantic Priming*, 3.

24. See chap. 5 (on perception and attention) regarding events that are important or that fit with what we already think.

25. This long-standing notion dates back at least to 1932 with Bartlett's *Remembering*.

in its entirety. During recall, it's reconstructed, and people add information to fill in gaps.

We also do this when we tell the story of ourselves. **Autobiographical memory**—*knowledge of ourselves and the episodes of our own lives*—is a significant area in memory research,[26] but it isn't strongly emphasized in the Bible. Autobiographical memories are famous for their inaccuracies, as they "may be altered, distorted, even fabricated, to support current aspects of the self."[27] As a person fashions the story of their own life, they strive for coherence, trying to make memory consistent with their "current goals, self-images, and self-beliefs."[28] We may show **self-serving bias**, *a tendency to perceive our world in a way that fits beliefs we already have.*[29] We easily misremember events and retell history in a way that leaves us looking correct.[30] Therefore, as Everett Worthington writes, "we need to remain humble about whatever we think we remember clearly," as "we are liable to make errors in directions that justify our beliefs and perceptions."[31] In this way, even our memory systems can show our brokenness and need for redemption (theme 2).

Can Memory Be Trusted?

Memory is fallible, but the errors mentioned in the previous section don't just show that people forget—we make up stuff! What we recall differs from the actual event we're describing, sometimes leading to tragic consequences, such as when individuals are convicted of crimes due to erroneous eyewitness testimony.[32] When recollecting, we add to the limited memory stored—the gist—which lacks full detail. We include information about what we *believe* is most likely to have been the case, even if we don't recall that exact detail. In addition, when recounting an event to others, we vary our retelling based on the audience. We tell the "same" story differently to a grandparent than to a close friend. This is good because we consider the other person's past experiences and knowledge as well as our shared relationship. Researchers believe we modify interactions in such ways for relational purposes. We're trying to create a "shared

---

26. Conway, "Memory and the Self," 595.
27. Conway, "Memory and the Self," 595.
28. Conway, "Memory and the Self," 595.
29. Worthington, *Coming to Peace with Psychology*, 177.
30. Note the research included in most introductory psychology textbooks on false memory and memory construction, such as Loftus and Loftus, "On the Permanence."
31. Worthington, *Coming to Peace with Psychology*, 178.
32. Brandon Garrett, in his book *Convicting the Innocent*, reports that such errors are common in false convictions: 76 percent were due to errors in eyewitness testimonies (9).

reality" in a conversation[33]—that is, we're striving for two things in conversations: (1) to create a shared meaning and (2) to deepen our relationality with others.[34] Therefore, our ways of recalling reflect both our individuality (the way we shape a specific story to a specific person) and our shared nature as relational persons making meaning—echoing two of the fundamental themes of human nature emphasized throughout this book (themes 1 and 5) and also showing the organization of memory discussed in the previous section of this chapter.

There is a potential downside to how we tell stories, however: the process of telling the story changes the story. When we're telling a story, the telling itself can become integrated with our memory of the original events of the story. As one researcher has described it, "If you remember something in the context of a new environment and time, or if you are even in a different mood, your memories might integrate the new information."[35] Positively, this shows memory's flexibility, but it also means that the process of recall adds error to our memory of the original event—an event we didn't even remember with complete accuracy to begin with!

With so many errors, will our memories become completely unhinged from reality? They usually don't. When we talk about the past with friends, we likely agree on the general events that occurred, even if we may have some differences regarding details. When we talk with others about events or ideas, we create a shared or collective memory, which can provide some checks and balances (although it's also open to errors). We talk with each other about shared memories and understandings all the time. In such conversation, people influence each other's memory, reaching a mutually agreed-upon understanding of the past. As a pair of memory researchers writes, "This possibility suggests that the usual characterization of memory implantation or forgetting as flaws or 'sins' of memory may not be entirely accurate. . . . Given the sociality of humans—and the possible critical role collective memories might play in undergirding this sociality—one can see why the malleability and unreliability of memory"[36] have important survival value by building up relationships through shared understanding.

Memories consisting of incomplete (gist) information also allow for great creativity. Memory researcher Daniel Schacter says that the way we store and recall memories allows us to flexibly imagine the future.[37] We have the capacity to combine pieces and parts of past experiences in imaginative new ways—ways

---

33. Hirst and Echterhoff, "Remembering in Conversations," 70–71.
34. Hirst and Echterhoff, "Remembering in Conversations," 70–71.
35. Paul, "Your Memory Is Like the Telephone Game."
36. Hirst and Echterhoff, "Remembering in Conversations," 73.
37. Schacter, "Adaptive Constructive Processes."

that might not be possible if each memory were an absolute, complete narrative. We're able to think about what might happen if we do one course of action versus another, allowing us to "try out" different possibilities for how our own actions might play out. We can flexibly and creatively think through possibilities internally, using *episodic* information, "extracting and recombining stored information in a simulation of a novel event."[38] When we think about options for an evening, we can look back on past, related experiences (e.g., we've always had fun hanging out with a certain friend, but our last evening with a different friend was boring). Thinking through possibilities is a lot easier and safer than experimenting with every option (which isn't even possible because we can spend an evening in only one way, not simultaneously in another as well). Some of those estimations may be correct, while others may not be, showing some of our human limitations. However, this ability to imagine possibilities is one of the great cognitive capacities of humans that allows for relationality.[39]

In the end, the way that humans recall memories is influenced both by brokenness (our self-serving ways of inaccurately recalling the past) and by our limited processing abilities (leading to incomplete memories that are open to distortion). These limited abilities, however, foster relationships through forming shared memories and allow us to be creative meaning makers as we think about our past and imagine a future.

Human Forgetting, God's Forgetting

On the whole, memory functions very well for us, but forgetting is a reality. Memory—particularly declarative memory—lets us down.[40] While episodic memory is more prone to failure than semantic memory (we often forget where an item is; we only occasionally forget the name of an item), we experience some degree of failure with all types of memory.

Memory is our connection to ourselves and to others. While that is the case for everyone, profound losses of declarative memory can leave a person adrift, such as occurs in patients with Alzheimer's disease.[41] As Christian psychologist Glenn Weaver writes, such disruptions also affect relationships with God,

---

38. Schacter, "Adaptive Constructive Processes," 606.

39. Brown, "Cognitive Contributions to Soul," 113–16. We're not, however, always accurate in our projections about what will make us happy, and psychologist Daniel Gilbert wrote an entire book on this notion: *Stumbling on Happiness*.

40. Nondeclarative memory failure also can happen—priming doesn't always occur, and we can forget well-practiced behavior (although people usually don't forget how to ride a bike).

41. See Weaver, "Embodied Spirituality," for further description and personal consequences of the disease.

impairing the ability to study Scripture or attend to verbal components of worship, such as sermons.[42] However, Alzheimer's spares much of nondeclarative memory—the habits and practices one has had throughout life. Weaver writes, "The episodes of greatest spiritual assurance for Alzheimer's patients seem to arise in regular opportunities to relive very familiar *practices* that witness to the spiritual meaning of a person's life."[43] For Christians with Alzheimer's, repeated actions and behaviors (such as reciting liturgies and singing hymns), particularly receiving the Lord's Supper, become "a means of grace grounded in procedural memory which can engage dementia patients late into their disease."[44] The community surrounding those with Alzheimer's can play an important role in helping those patients enter into shared practices of faith, both spoken and physical. In this case, as is always the case for memory, the experience of being a person relies on relationships being sustained by the memory of others and of God.

Regarding God, several places in Scripture describe God as "forgetting" something. How could God possibly *forget*? God is *omniscient*.[45] The language used here is anthropomorphic, like the notion of "walking with God." God's "forgetting" says something about a relationship with him. God's "memory lapses" make sense if we understand memory in the way the Bible emphasizes—it's fundamentally about relationships. When God no longer "remembers" (e.g., Isa. 43), it's about fixing the relationship between God and his people. Christianity teaches that humans are stuck in their own sin (theme 2), unable to get out of that situation on their own. God freely chose to bring about salvation—forgiveness of sins—through Jesus Christ. Christ's sacrificial death repaired the relationship between God and his people, which no humans could do on their own (Rom. 3:21–26). Christian psychologist Harold Faw, in his book on memory in the Bible, describes this situation well: "It is through Christ's once-and-for-all sacrifice that the new covenant is established, and God chooses not to remember our sins."[46]

How fundamentally different from human forgetting! According to the Bible, God *chose* to bring about salvation and *chooses* what he will forget. God's forgetting is a willful change in relationship, not a human limitation in the abilities to take in, store, and retrieve information. It is our forgetting—due to failures in the processes just mentioned as well as the sinful human willingness to worship things other than God—that makes working at remembering God so critical.

---

42. Weaver, "Embodied Spirituality," 88.
43. Weaver, "Embodied Spirituality," 100 (emphasis added).
44. Weaver, "Embodied Spirituality," 100.
45. *Omniscience* is a biblically based notion that God knows everything, including the future. See Matt. 10:30 and 1 John 3:20.
46. Faw, *Sharing Our Stories*, 151.

Perhaps this is why the Bible contains so many references to remembering God and remembering that he is faithful to his people.

Implications and Applications

The multiple types of memory discussed in this chapter imply multiple ways that people are affected by and have an influence on their surroundings. Memory is organized so that ideas spur additional related ideas. Christian symbols and practices may spur further thought and ingrained action. In addition, they may more easily be recalled or acted on in times of stress, crisis, or incapacitation. Although many people steer clear of rituals and memorized prayers, such practices may merit greater use.

Research on episodic and semantic memory suggests that humans need to study the Bible if they wish to be faithful followers of God. Remembering God's faithfulness is subject to human memory weaknesses such as remembering only the gist and not the entirety. Clearer knowledge of Christ comes through Scripture: "I want you to recall the words spoken in the past by the holy prophets and the command given by our Lord and Savior through your apostles" (2 Pet. 3:2). Christians believe that the Holy Spirit, working within the broad body of Christ (the church), can guide believers in their understanding of Scripture, which is why many church traditions include a prayer for illumination (shining God's light of understanding on a text) prior to reading Scripture.[47] Recalling what God has done is a way for people to receive God's grace to live faithfully and resist incorrect perceptions of God that come from the world: "be on your guard so that you may not be carried away by the error of the lawless and fall from your secure position. But grow in the grace and knowledge of our Lord and Savior Jesus Christ" (3:17–18). Scripture reading and Bible knowledge can redirect current misperceptions and act to form people to be Christ followers.

DISCUSSION QUESTIONS

1. Researchers have found ways of altering memory through the use of drugs, both to help people remember and to aid them in selective forgetting (i.e., in patients with post-traumatic stress disorder). What are

---

47. Ephesians 1:17 includes the apostle Paul's words asking God to give the Ephesians "the Spirit of wisdom and revelation, so that you may know him better."

possible positives and negatives of this? How might chemically altering one's memory impact relationality, positively or negatively?

2. How does the Lord's Supper (also known as communion or the Eucharist) utilize declarative and nondeclarative memory? Look particularly to 1 Corinthians 11:17–34 for the apostle Paul's instructions for how to conduct this meal among believers.

3. Give some examples of worship or family rituals that bind Christians or families together, giving a shared church or family memory.

4. In addition to talking over past events with other people, how do our memories stay grounded in reality, keeping them trustworthy?

5. Differentiate God's forgiveness and forgetting from that of humans. Must they differ, based on how humans differ from God?

6. In Isaiah 49:16, speaking to Israel, God says, "I have engraved you on the palms of my hands." What does such striking language say about God's memory and his commitment to his people?

8

Think about It

Decision Making and Reasoning

▶ SUMMARY: Our thinking impacts our relationships as we make judgments about others, the world, and God. In this chapter, we explore how people show amazing reasoning ability yet also make silly misjudgments. Researchers specializing in the study of human thinking, or cognition, which includes decision making, problem solving, and intelligence, consistently point to two types of human reasoning: one that is automatic and quick, and a second that is effortful and slow. The need for these two types and when each is used are profoundly shaped by the embodied nature of being human. These different ways of thinking affect how we go about making meaning and when we can exercise our limited agency.

What a piece of work is a man, how noble in reason, how infinite in faculties, in form and moving how express and admirable, in action how like an angel, in apprehension how like a god!

William Shakespeare, *Hamlet*, act 2, scene 2

Two things are infinite: the universe and human stupidity; and I'm not sure about the universe.

attributed to (but probably not actually said by) Albert Einstein

W hich of the previous quotations is true? A reasonable answer might be that it depends on whom you're talking about because people differ in their intellectual abilities. Yet consider this: given some time, many people can accurately solve a multistep multiplication problem (say 27 × 86), but in an instant they'll rate an item costing $2.99 as significantly less expensive than one costing $3.00—a difference of one cent![1] Maybe the question isn't *which* quotation applies but *when* each applies. The highs and lows of human reasoning are all around us and in us.

Why Think?

Before delving into variations in thinking, let's think about the purpose of thinking: to interact successfully with the environment. **Cognitive psychology** *studies how we perceive, think about, know, remember, and use information.*[2] Cognitive processes involve internal mental states that plan and supervise our actions according to goals. For example, if you want to sit on a chair, you need to perceive where you are relative to the chair, plan how to get to the chair (e.g., walking), and recognize and avoid obstacles (e.g., is there a lamp in your way?), all while remembering your ultimate goal of sitting. Throughout these processes, you need internal mental activity that represents the environment usefully. Thinking has important implications in a Christian understanding of persons. As Christian psychologist Warren Brown states, these abilities allow us to be in relationship with others, creation, and God because we can communicate, remember each other and past experiences, and decide how to act.[3] In other words, our cognitive abilities make possible our relationality (theme 1).

Representations—*internal mental states that represent reality*—allow us to make meaning of the world (theme 5). We make conclusions about happenings based on evidence, prior expectations, and knowledge. We draw inferences based on what we see and believe, and we use those to make new beliefs that go beyond the original information. Representations allow us to modify our thoughts, making us able to solve problems and use memory to appropriately

---

1. Thomas and Morwitz, "Penny Wise and Pound Foolish," showed that when the leftmost digits of the prices differ, the prices are perceived as different; this does not usually occur for a difference such as $3.09 versus $3.10. This is a good explanation for stores using prices ending in 0.99 rather than rounding up to the next dollar.

2. One of the founders of cognitive psychology, Ulric Neisser, defined cognition as "all processes by which the sensory input is transformed, reduced, elaborated, stored, recovered, and used." *Cognitive Psychology*, 4.

3. Brown, "Cognitive Contributions to Soul," 101–2.

apply representations to new situations. Representing reality well and using that representation in a situation are the heart of intelligence.

Creativity

Intelligence includes **creativity**, *having ideas that are both novel and valuable.*[4] Leading researchers on creativity have described it as "one of the key factors that drive civilization forward."[5] Indeed, Christians believe that acting creatively in God's world (creation) is very much in line with being bearers of God's image. Caring for each other and all of creation as relational persons was part of what God tasked humans to do (Gen. 2:15)—to be God's workers and "co-workers for his kingdom."[6] As Christian writer Madeline L'Engle has noted, the creative work of humans is consequential and not neutral: "Everything that we do either draws the Kingdom of love closer, or pushes it further off."[7] The freedom to be creative—our creative agency—carries with it significant responsibility (theme 4), as humans can work toward God's desires or at cross-purposes to his will. And while being "smart" or creative may vary between people based on previous learning and ability, as L'Engle writes, "No one is too unimportant" to join in what she calls "co-creation" with God in being his stewards on earth.[8] Each person has gifts and knowledge and a place to use them. Gifts used by a person doing plumbing differ from those used by a mathematician, but in both cases (and many more), using one's abilities in one's circumstances can have importance in God's kingdom.

Thinking, Right and Wrong

Creativity is just one remarkable aspect of our impressive thinking abilities. As the authors of a cognitive psychology textbook claim, human cognitive processes are consistently "remarkably efficient and accurate."[9] For example, if asked to get a guest a drink of water, most of us succeed. The request seems simple, but fulfilling it is amazing, considering how many processes are involved and how little information we're working with. We need to understand language; see, hear, and move accurately; and draw proper conclusions to

4. Hennessey and Amabile, "Creativity," 572.
5. Hennessey and Amabile, "Creativity," 570.
6. *Catechism of the Catholic Church*, 81.
7. L'Engle, *And It Was Good*, 19.
8. L'Engle, *And It Was Good*, 19. By "co-creation," L'Engle is referencing the idea that God intends for his kingdom to be restored and that humans play a role in this consummation of creation. She also encourages believers: "If we accept that God is within each of us, then God will give us, within us, the courage to accept the responsibility of being co-creators" (19).
9. Matlin and Farmer, *Cognition*, 27.

execute the task based on just a few sounds made by another person. In addition, for one person to fulfill another person's request, both people need to have the same idea in mind. This shared understanding of a representation brings interrelationship between persons. It's obvious but important to note that thoughts or representations can also be incorrect (relative to reality around us), causing us to draw wrong conclusions about our world and others with whom we share it. When that representation isn't quite the same between people, miscommunication results. For example, a son of one of the authors, warm from playing, asked for water. His father got a glassful of water and brought it to him. But the father's representation of his son's desire didn't match that of his son. When handed the glass, the son responded, "No, pour it on my head—I'm so hot!" Shared language and culture allow shared understanding, but individuals have their own thoughts. As soon as his son spoke, the dad knew exactly what he meant.

Easy and Hard Thinking

Individual thoughts can obviously differ between people. The way people think, however, shows striking similarities between people. Humans consistently show two broad ways of thinking. Those two patterns and what they imply regarding basic characteristics of human nature and how they might be influenced are the focus of this section.

Decision-making researcher Wim De Neys writes, "One of the clearest characteristics of people's mental life is that some thought processes are easy and others are hard."[10] This differentiation has been popularized by Nobel Prize–winning psychologist Daniel Kahneman in his book *Thinking, Fast and Slow*. Kahneman differentiates two kinds of thinking: System 1 and System 2.[11] **System 1** *is fast, efficient, and intuitive*. It's great for making snap judgments. In terms of the themes of this book, it's a quick meaning maker but has little agency. On the other hand, **System 2** *is slow, requires effort, and involves deliberation*. It relies on past knowledge and experience to make reasoned judgments. In terms of our book's themes, this kind of thinking involves experiences of agency and choice in which an individual feels they are thinking deliberately and actively making sense or meaning of information.

10. De Neys, "On Dual- and Single-Process Models of Thinking," 1.

11. This general type of distinction was first outlined in Stanovich and West, "Individual Differences in Reasoning," 658. Jonathan St. B. T. Evans and Keith E. Stanovich have further differentiated Type 1 and Type 2 processes, which correspond to the distinction between intuition and reflection. "Dual-Process Theories," 224.

This distinction between systems has become popular and influential,[12] but there are a couple important caveats regarding this differentiation. First, it's important to note that these "systems" are just two patterns of thinking—System 1 and System 2 are *not* specific areas of the brain.[13] Second, System 1 and System 2 are likely not completely different ways of thinking. Instead, it might be more helpful to think of the systems as representing two ends of a spectrum: there are ways of thinking that have more System 1 characteristics and other ways that have more System 2 characteristics.[14] We'll focus here primarily on how thinking varies in terms of how much we are directing our thinking. We'll use the terms *System 1* and *System 2* as anchor points, distinguishing ends of a continuum between intuitive and deliberative thought.

General differences between these systems are seen in their use. Dealing with the environment often doesn't require the reflective thought of System 2, so System 1 processes are at work. System 1 uses a variety of sources to draw conclusions: inborn abilities (such as recognizing objects and preferences or avoiding pain and loss), practiced abilities (such as reading and understanding social situations), and even culturally held knowledge (such as stereotypes about gender roles). Such thinking happens with little conscious intention or mental effort. For example, in the price judgment mentioned earlier ($2.99 versus $3.00), intuitive thinking keys in on the leftmost number, draws a quick conclusion by "noticing" a 2 versus a 3, and decrees that one price is a lot less than the other.[15] Once you decide what something costs (and that $2.99 is considerably less than $3.00), action is likely to follow. System 1 judgments can provide the basis for complex, multistep behaviors that eventually require slower reasoning, such as when you actually make a purchase. Kahneman concludes that "most of what you (your System 2) think and do originates in your System 1, but System 2 takes over when things get difficult, and it normally has the last word"[16] in drawing a conclusion.

When System 1 processing fails to generate a quick answer, System 2 processes tend to kick in. When we are surprised, we can't figure out what something is, or a conclusion just doesn't come to mind right away, we tend to "think" more. In the multiplication problem mentioned earlier, most of us can't answer it from memory: we know 2 × 2 without mental calculation; 27 × 86 takes System 2 effort. But here's the twist: What if you ask a friend to calculate

12. Melnikof and Bargh, "Mythical Number Two," 280.

13. This point is also emphasized in J. Evans and Stanovich, "Dual-Process Theories," 224.

14. De Neys, "On Dual- and Single-Process Models of Thinking," argues throughout his paper that there is no strong evidence that these two ways of processing are separate from each other.

15. Thomas and Morwitz, "Penny Wise and Pound Foolish," 55.

16. Kahneman, *Thinking, Fast and Slow*, 25.

27 × 86, but they say, "That's too hard" and do no math at all? How does that fit with System 1 versus System 2 thinking? Perhaps your friend deliberated about whether to take on the problem and decided to give a math-less answer. Or they may have started a little math and found it too hard and quit, then gave their "That's too hard" response. To what degree did your friend use agency in giving an answer? It's hard to tell; the line between System 1 and System 2 gets blurry as we see active use of agency come and go.

Negotiating Intuition and Reflection

While the line between these two types of thinking is certainly under debate, the interplay between these two systems has been investigated by many.[17] Here's Kahneman's view of how these two systems operate together. He argues that System 1 continuously generates information and conclusions based on intuition. If those suggestions are unquestioned by more reflective, System 2 processing, then "impressions and intuitions turn into beliefs, and impulses turn into voluntary actions. When all goes smoothly, which is most of the time, System 2 adopts the suggestions of System 1 with little or no modification. You generally believe your impressions and act on your desires, and that is fine—usually."[18]

As we said above, our focus in discussing these two varieties of thinking is to concentrate on agency and meaning. In the quotation from Kahneman above, notice how meaningful conclusions, even beliefs, result from thinking. System 1 does it intuitively, making simple, effortless associations; System 2 does it in a more orderly and slow way. If further reasoning or analysis is needed, System 2 often uses System 1 conclusions (meaning or beliefs produced by it). For example, if you quickly conclude that a voice sounds angry, you may develop a plan to deal with that "hostile" person. System 2 may not have fully checked to see if the other person actually is hostile—the first impression and broad conclusions developed by System 1's snap judgment were simply adopted. Kahneman states that this is what usually happens, unless the conclusions of System 1 don't work. For example, if the angry voice is followed by laughter (it was all just a joke!), you reevaluate your judgment that the other person is hostile, perhaps concluding that there's nothing to fear.

Together, our two systems tend to interplay efficiently and effectively, with System 1 minimizing effort, saving resources for situations requiring System 2 functions. Just as our resources for paying attention are limited, so too are our resources for conducting effortful, deliberative thought. System 2 is also too slow and inefficient to use all the time. Imagine using as much mental effort

17. De Neys, "On Dual- and Single-Process Models of Thinking," 1–2.
18. Kahneman, Thinking, Fast and Slow, 24.

and attention to walk across the room as to solve the math problem 27 × 86. Fortunately, System 1's low requirements for supervision result in effortless walking, which allows simultaneous walking and talking. Yet when System 2 is more fully involved in a task, that processing can interrupt System 1's control of routine tasks. Walking and solving 27 × 86 at the same time is too much for most people: they stop walking to solve the multiplication problem.[19] This also shows some of the fluid back-and-forth between intuitive and deliberative thought.

Both varieties of thinking have great strengths, but each is limited in important ways. That's to be expected based on the general human limitations we've emphasized throughout this book. Intuitive thinking involves many shortcuts, avoiding most conscious deliberation. System 2 thinking, while long on deliberation, can still result in a bad decision.[20] This can particularly be the case when we think about ourselves. For example, **false justification** *involves justifying a behavior (often an impulsive behavior) through rationalization, even if that rationalization might not be correct.* When we look at our own behavior, we may tell ourselves a story regarding why we did something, creating a narrative that shows ourselves in a better light than the light of reality. We have a hard time seeing such a bias in ourselves (although we may be quick to point it out in others!), and this affects our self-understanding.[21] Errors, of course, also occur with more "objective" information, such as making an error during a math problem or failing to consider some important details when carefully planning a vacation.

Agency Even in System 1

Despite the possibility of the occasional error, deliberative thought is incredibly powerful. System 2's power comes at a price, however: it's a resource hog, and we have limited cognitive resources. As a result, we rely on the low-conscious involvement and efficiency of System 1 for many of our judgments and decisions—in fact, likely most of them. System 1 thinking, which tends to occur unintentionally, seems to profoundly limit human agency or free will. Can you exercise free will when you neither plan nor monitor much of your behavior? Yes! You have exercised agency over a lifetime of developing System 1. Your automated beliefs, reasoning, and behaviors come out of your embodiment and your experiences—all of which are completely yours. Who you are in terms of your social and intellectual history as well as your individual genetic makeup

19. Kahneman, *Thinking, Fast and Slow*, 39.
20. De Neys notes that System 2 doesn't guarantee the kind of critical thinking that would result in error-free reasoning. "On Dual- and Single-Process Models of Thinking," 13.
21. Pronin, Gilovich, and Ross, "Objectivity."

influences your System 1 responses. We each have choices regarding many of these influences and how we use our genetic makeup. Past choices regarding friendships, going to college or not, practicing a skill or leaving it behind—all such decisions and many more—set us on pathways that establish System 1 thinking.

This means that, for each of us, trajectories we choose set us in certain directions, even if these directions are ones over which we now have little choice. We can be responsible for our behavior despite limited agency (theme 4).[22]

Shortcuts, Categories, and Stereotypes

If agency is limited, why give up any of it? Wouldn't it be best to use System 2 as much as possible to maximize free will, deciding your own future in each moment rather than letting it automatically occur? Let's explore that question by imagining this situation: You're to be an usher at a friend's wedding. Driving to the ceremony, you check yourself in the rearview mirror and discover a mess. Your teeth are blue. You check your breath—it could gag a skunk. Perhaps eating a basket of onion rings followed by blueberry pie wasn't a good idea! Already ten minutes late for the ceremony, you still have your image to consider. Needing a toothbrush and toothpaste, you stop at the first grocery store you see, a huge building you've never previously entered. Hurrying down the first aisle of the store, you see a woman wearing a shirt with the store's logo. There's also a smiling man wearing a T-shirt that reads "Ford Trucks." Without a second thought, you ask the person wearing the shirt with the store logo, "Miss, could you tell me where the toothpaste is?" She immediately points you to the dental hygiene supplies, and within minutes, you're out of the store. Although this sort of shortcut doesn't guarantee success (e.g., this person may have bought the store-logo shirt at a used clothing shop), it does save the time of a methodical System 2 search, as you systematically walk up and down each aisle (assuming the aisles are not labeled) or search for a customer service counter staffed with employees. System 2 processing of this situation would make you even later for the wedding. Score one for System 1 efficiency.

System 1 efficiency, however, comes from jumping to all sorts of unexamined conclusions through instantly categorizing people in terms of gender, occupation, and perceived knowledge based on how much a person's characteristics are judged to represent a group.[23] *Representativeness and other shortcuts in reasoning*

22. Thanks to Laird Edman for insights regarding agency and history in this paragraph (personal communication, July 16, 2013).

23. This is known as **representativeness**: *judging the likelihood that someone belongs to a group based on similarities to that group.*

are called **heuristics**. You efficiently used multiple, loosely informed biases based on a logo to draw intuitive, unconscious conclusions. Consulting someone who looks like a store employee clearly makes more sense than asking someone who, based on the same reasoning, might work for Ford. It's highly unlikely that you would have had the conscious thoughts, "She's a woman, she's a store employee, and she'll know where toothpaste is." Quick, logical shortcuts in the form of heuristics allow you to get on with your life by not thinking too much. In fact, for successful daily living, people *need* to avoid thinking too much. (When have you ever read a line like that in an academic book?)

Categorization and Stereotypes

We categorize intuitively by System 1, or more systematically with System 2, and sometimes we use a mix of intuition and deliberation (e.g., that person's wearing a T-shirt with writing on it; might it be a store logo?). We categorize to interact with the environment. We constantly fit objects into our preexisting categories (such as when we recognize a new object as a chair and use it as such by taking a seat). When we do this with people, we're using social categorization by way of a **stereotype**: *the identification of someone as part of a group and the judgments made about their potential behaviors.* The shopping example contained several stereotypes about occupation and interests of people. Social categorization impacts relating to others as persons because such categories impose meaning on interactions with others. Categorization sets the tone for beginning a conversation or avoiding one, depending on the implications of such categorization.

Stereotypes have a reputation for being bad—a reputation that's well deserved in many situations. First, at a practical level, stereotypes are a problem when they are inaccurate. Perhaps the person wearing the store's shirt in the example above was simply a fan of the store, like the "Ford Trucks" fellow may have been a Ford enthusiast. That sort of mistake would be relatively harmless, even if it led to an incorrect conclusion. Wrongly assuming that someone is a store employee with particular knowledge of store items doesn't debase that person, as hopefully you would be courteous to someone you believe to be a store employee. So we agree with Kahneman's assertion that social categorization is a "neutral" activity.[24]

A second, more problematic effect is **causal stereotyping**:[25] *the application of a group stereotype to an individual rather than remembering that it best applies*

24. Kahneman says that social categories consist of norms and prototypical exemplars. *Thinking, Fast and Slow*, 168.
25. Kahneman, *Thinking, Fast and Slow*, 167.

to the group (and in that case, only if the stereotype is accurate). For example, one school may have lower average reading scores than other schools. You would be using a causal stereotype if you believed that Liam, a particular student from that school, must certainly have low reading achievement. This could lead to prejudice in how you respond to Liam, perhaps treating him as if he were unable to read. Characteristics of a group don't necessarily apply to the individual (as we discussed in chap. 2).

Negative stereotyping as a whole—whether accurate or inaccurate—can have significant relational implications. It can limit the expression of the image of God in others by reducing others' humanity. If you have experienced or witnessed racism or sexism, you may have seen how such categorization imposed on other humans can fracture relationships in a way that categorizing inanimate objects never can. Judging another's likelihood to be intelligent or trustworthy based on a single piece of information from physical appearance (e.g., skin color, clothing style) undercuts the expression of God's image in that person. Such stereotyping concludes that another is less worthy of being engaged in a relationship. This devalues that person's personhood.

Not "Us versus Them"

The Bible also has a stereotype of humans, and it's simple: everyone is God's creation, made in his image (theme 1). Jesuit priest Gregory Boyle,[26] who helps former gang members and convicted felons transform their lives through employment in Los Angeles, acts from this Christian worldview of humans. These people, Boyle says, are the "them" that people have in mind when they think of "us versus them." Yet he bases his interaction with others on the foundation that each person, regardless of criminal past, is "so much more than the worst thing that [they] have done." That's his System 1 setting for interaction. Rather than judging others through a stereotype like "threatening criminal," Boyle begins with God's perspective about each person. "God is compassionate, loving kindness. All we're asked to do is to be in the world who God is. Certainly compassion was the wallpaper of Jesus' soul, the contour of his heart, it was who he was.'"[27] Boyle writes that this intuitive assumption about compassion "isn't just about feeling the pain of others; it's about bringing them in toward yourself. If we love what God loves, then, in compassion, margins get erased. 'Be compassionate as God is compassionate,' means the dismantling of barriers that exclude."[28]

26. Boyle is a Catholic priest working in Los Angeles, where he founded Homeboy Industries, which employs otherwise unemployable former gang members.
27. Boyle, *Tattoos on the Heart*, 62.
28. Boyle, *Tattoos on the Heart*, 75.

Boyle emphasizes an intuitive component—start with compassion—but also includes deliberative thinking and action to dismantle barriers that exclude. Boyle's book *Tattoos on the Heart*, in which he relates stories of lives transformed during his decades of work, shows that he too notices the usual categories— differences in race and gender, whether someone looks scary, angry, or just a mess. But his overarching causal stereotype goes beyond these superficial characteristics to see the foundational truth that everyone needs and is worthy of God's love. In Jesus's prayer for future believers in him, recorded in John 17, the first thing he prays is "that all of them may be one, Father, just as you are in me and I am in you. May they also be in us so that the world may believe that you have sent me" (17:21). Being "one" isn't about joining forces against others. It's not about creating an "us" to be against "them." Being united in Christ is part of how people are meant to be—the fundamental unity with God for which people are made and that embodies God's love for all to see. Because we are relational persons, the need to belong is in our very being. When people try to fill that relational need apart from God, divisions often result because such groups can't provide ultimate reconciliation. The "us versus them" so common in groups may stem from brokenness in need of redemption, emphasized in theme 2, when people try to achieve wholeness on their own.

Becoming Faithfully Impulsive

What can be done when System 1 responses are incorrect or even work to degrade the image of God in others? System 1 may tell us to exclude people or ignore situations in which care for others is needed. In effect, System 1 conclusions can foster excluding "them" from "us." Impulsive System 1–based actions are largely outside of our limited agency. System 2 may be able to help. Negative stereotyping isn't inevitable.[29] Kahneman writes, "One of the tasks of System 2 is to overcome the impulses of System 1. In other words, System 2 is in charge of self-control."[30]

Perhaps you have some larger goals that require self-control, like doing well in a class. However, habitual behaviors other than studying may get in the way of your academic goals. Would you rather watch videos than study? Which do you consistently choose to do?[31] Psychologists have shown that you can employ strategies to make lifestyle changes to redirect System 1. Overcoming some

29. Kawakami et al., "Just Say No (to Stereotyping)."
30. Kahneman, *Thinking, Fast and Slow*, 26.
31. Such conflicts are very common, as shown in Hofman, Vohs, and Baumeister, "What People Desire."

cognitive biases can begin by simply raising your awareness of other possible ways of thinking or living.[32] Asking a question like "How do successful students live differently than I do?" leads to better thinking and decision making. Looking for differences in this way gets around System 1's **confirmation bias**: *the seeking out of information and examples that confirm what you already believe or do*, such as looking to others who don't study as examples for how to succeed as a student![33]

On the other hand, impulses may be good as they are. If a first impulse is to care for the needs of others, without thought for oneself, that's an impulse to be supported and nurtured. Help in discerning good from bad impulses can come from a healthy Christian community attending to the leading of God, where believers are building each other up through encouragement as well as correction. Practicing habits such as reading the Bible can also open one's eyes to seeing the nature of impulses that may be largely automatic. As Psalm 1 begins, people prosper by avoiding wicked and mocking ways and instead meditating on God's Word (1:1–2). This is particularly the case when done with other believers who are also seeking the Holy Spirit's guidance in understanding the Bible.

When real change is needed, it goes beyond just thinking. Thinking alone doesn't necessarily lead to better behavior. We focus on this much more in chapter 12, where we explore how attitude may or may not relate to action. It's clear that Scripture points to the importance of action as well as thought. The apostle Paul urges the church in Ephesus to "live a life worthy of the calling you have received" (Eph. 4:1). Rather than living impulsively, "tossed back and forth by the waves, and blown here and there by every wind of teaching and by the cunning and craftiness of people" (4:14), Christians should speak truth to each other in love. Similarly, asking questions such as "Would an intelligent, faithful person disagree with what I'm doing?" can help derail the confirmation bias.

This fits well with Kahneman's suggestions to override errors that originate in System 1.[34] Yet Kahneman also says that constantly second-guessing our thinking would take forever. So when should System 2 be used? "The best we can do is a compromise: learn to recognize situations in which mistakes are likely and try harder to avoid significant mistakes when the stakes are high."[35]

But what is "significant"? Psychology isn't a lot of help in answering this. Recall from chapter 2 that psychological science is simply descriptive, not

32. Roese and Vohs, "Hindsight Bias," 418, discuss the hindsight bias, in which people overestimate the degree to which they believe they "knew all along" that an outcome was likely to occur. They show that if people consider other points of view, they reduce this bias.

33. Kahneman, *Thinking, Fast and Slow*, 81.

34. Kahneman writes, "The way to block errors that originate in System 1 is simple in principle: recognize the signs that you are in a cognitive minefield, slow down, and ask for reinforcement from System 2." *Thinking, Fast and Slow*, 417.

35. Kahneman, *Thinking, Fast and Slow*, 28.

prescriptive of how to better live life. This is particularly clear in research on decision making. "Good" decisions are defined in terms of the decision maker's own criteria—that is, if you set out rules for what counts as a "good" decision, the only way you can make a "bad" decision is if you don't follow your own rules. By this logic, if you decide that having the most fun possible is your goal for a Saturday evening, but you make a decision that doesn't follow that rule (e.g., you spend the evening talking with a troubled friend), you have made a bad decision. **Irrationality** *is when you go against your own values or criteria; this may often lead you to make bad decisions.* In this way, psychology's stance regarding decision making is completely relativistic, depending entirely on one's own rules.

Christians believe that God's plan for living is better than what they devise on their own, so they have a different set of priorities than "I should always do what I want to do." For Christians, examining how well one is following Christ would be a priority worth System 2 effort. The Bible says that, in figuring out how to live and acting on that belief, Christians aren't left to their own devices to live as Christ followers. As the apostle Paul wrote to the church in Philippi, "For it is God who works in you to will and to act in order to fulfill his good purpose" (Phil. 2:13). God works in the fellowship of believers (the church) through God's Word and the empowerment of the Holy Spirit. As a result, Christians can employ their limited agency to live increasingly Christlike lives, following God's will.[36]

DISCUSSION QUESTIONS

1. Gregory Boyle writes, "How much greater is the God we have than the one we think we have."[37] In what ways do you stereotype God? What are the consequences of that?

2. How can belief bias (the tendency to accept conclusions based on how believable those conclusions are rather than on whether they are logically valid) be influenced by others? How could a Christian community establish or possibly overturn such beliefs? Is there a role for being relational persons here?

3. Is knowledge different from belief? If so, what are the differences?

4. We've emphasized that fellow Christians can be helpful guides for Christians who want to change biases and behaviors. What are some necessary conditions for this to work well? Perhaps consult an introductory psychology textbook regarding common biases and heuristics.

36. See Rom. 6 for the apostle Paul's explanation of how God acts through the lives of Christians.
37. Boyle, *Tattoos on the Heart*, 38.

9

Moving toward a Goal

Developmental Psychology

▷ SUMMARY: The pattern of human development shows certain goals and tasks that are almost universal across persons, yet each of us is differently shaped by our experiences and our genetics. In this chapter we explore developmental psychology's questions of how much and in what ways people change as well as the relative roles of environment and genetics in making that pattern of change different for each person. In doing so, we address issues of embodiment and responsible limited agency. Finally, we explore how the propensity toward meaning seeking is apparent in developmental psychology theories and compare the goals, or *telos*, of those theories with a Christian understanding of the direction of development.

> The great thing about growing older is that you don't lose all the other ages you've been.
>
> Madeleine L'Engle, *New York Times*, April 25, 1985

Development is ideal for exploring the relationship between Christian faith and psychology, as all the themes of this book seem particularly relevant for the topic. We will first focus on whether developmental psychology has anything to say about the basic condition of humans being broken, in need of redemption (theme 2). At the beginning of this book, we raised the question of whether persons are inherently good or bad (using Ethan

117

as an example). Can research on children provide insight into this question? After all, newborns have yet to experience a full dose of the good, bad, or in-between effects of parents, friends, and broader culture,[1] so their original essence of humanity—their human nature—should be evident. Although babies can't tell us their experiences, philosophers, theologians, and psychologists have all speculated on the essential core of human nature observed in infants.

A decidedly positive view of human nature was taken by philosophers such as Jean-Jacques Rousseau[2] and humanistic psychologists such as Carl Rogers,[3] who saw each individual as complete and saw the core of each person as good. Some developmental psychologists have concluded, based on observations of children's unprompted helping and sharing, that "young children are naturally helpful, generous,"[4] and willing to share beneficial information with others. Children act this way before even being taught, so one may conclude that being nice is natural.

Another position, outlined by philosopher John Locke,[5] is that the environ-ment entirely shapes a child (and adult). In that view, also held by psychologists such as John Watson, children have no predisposition toward goodness or badness; their only real predisposition is that they can be influenced by what surrounds them.

Christians believe that humans sin, live in a world that's broken, and need redemption. But is this brokenness evident in infants and children? Over the centuries, Christians have debated whether sinfulness is apparent in the behav-ior of young children or if they are morally innocent, unable to choose to sin until later in life.[6] Debates continue over whether the behavior of babies shows their selfishness or their innocence and trusting nature. Christian theology also addresses the question of goodness at a spiritual level and concludes that humans always fall short of that goodness without the reconciling work of Christ.[7] This more eternal sense of "goodness" or "badness" and the related topic of culpability for sin are theological issues, however, and aren't our pri-mary focus here.

---

1. This is *mostly* true, but the experiences in the womb have been shown to be correlated with later health, such as in Whitaker and Dietz, "Role of the Prenatal Environment," as well as preferences for the language of their mother at just two days after birth, presumably due to their experience with hearing their mother's language prior to birth, as in Moon, Cooper, and Fifer, "Two-Day-Olds Prefer Their Native Language."

2. Rousseau, *Emile*, 5.

3. Rogers, "Notes on Rollo May," 8.

4. Warneken and Tomasello, "Varieties of Altruism," 400.

5. Locke, *Some Thoughts concerning Education*, 74.

6. Bakke, *When Children Became People*, 56–109, discusses a variety of views held by early Christians.

7. Romans 3:23: "For all have sinned and fall short of the glory of God."

Moral Babies

Psychological science isn't equipped to determine whether infants are born "good" or "bad" in the eternal sense. But psychology can give insight into what conditions make a behavior more or less likely to occur. Science can tell us which conditions promote culturally agreed-upon positive outcomes, such as school success or marital satisfaction, and can suggest whether those behaviors are learned or natural. Deciding whether such behaviors are right or wrong, however, is a question for ethics and the law. While such moral judgments vary across culture and historical time, there is broad agreement about foundational moral principles that include behaviors and attitudes such as fairness, cooperation, and being helpful.

Therefore, psychology has much to say about the development of universally identified moral behaviors and attitudes, including the tendencies of babies to act in ways that are either selfless or self-serving. Research suggests that babies show **morality**, *the ability to distinguish right from wrong.* Their moral code appears to be based on cooperation and includes showing degrees of empathy as well as prosocial behaviors like sharing. Infants demonstrate this as soon as they have the physical skills to give objects to others.[8] As early as two days after birth, babies show a form of empathy through simple emotional reactions to others' suffering by crying when other infants cry.[9] Young babies also make judgments that indicate they have a moral sense and judge whether others' actions are good or bad, deserving reward or punishment. Infants indicate these preferences by more often reaching for toys that had "acted" in morally desirable and cooperative ways than for toys that had not.[10] After watching an animal puppet that had earlier helped another puppet achieve a goal, babies prefer to look at (by three months of age) or reach for (by six months of age) the helpful puppet rather than a similar puppet that hindered another puppet from achieving a goal. Further, puppets that harmed those that previously hindered or blocked the goal of another puppet were preferred by infants as young as five months[11]—that is, babies like "helpful" puppets, but they also like puppets that punish "bad" puppets. Infants appear to develop this moral code or moral sense without instruction. While the content of what people consider moral or immoral is certainly learned and shaped by others, it appears that we are "intrinsically moral creatures."[12] Christians would assert that this is because people "bear the image of God."[13]

8. Hamlin, "Moral Judgment and Action," 187.
9. Sagi and Hoffman, "Empathic Distress in the Newborn," 175.
10. Hamlin, "Moral Judgment and Action," 187–88.
11. Hamlin, "Moral Judgment and Action," 187.
12. Worthington, *Coming to Peace with Psychology,* 245.
13. Worthington, *Coming to Peace with Psychology,* 245.

While direct observation of infants may not tell us about the innate goodness of a child, infant and childhood development research confirms that embodied humans are naturally relational meaning seekers (themes 1, 3, and 5). We will explore what developmental psychology says about these themes in the following sections.

Babies Are Relational Persons

Babies are born prepared for social connection. Inborn abilities and genetically predisposed preferences drive babies into relationships from birth. For example, newborns prefer looking at human faces more than any other tested objects.[14] This inborn preference draws other human beings into the beginning of a relationship with infants. If you ever observe adults interact with infants, you will notice that adults light up when a baby's gaze meets their own—parents love seeing their babies look at them. In addition, the burst-pause pattern of feeding, present in newborns, allows social interaction virtually every moment while infants are feeding. Babies take a few drinks and pause, at which time the feeder usually jiggles, pats, or talks to the infant.[15] After receiving social interaction, the baby resumes feeding. Babies are also born with several types of cries that most adults can successfully interpret to mean hunger or pain.[16] Furthermore, babies begin intentionally smiling at human faces when they are between one and two months old; it's their first intentional act. Taken together, these and other abilities bring babies into close contact with other humans who care for and comfort them. Embodied relationships meet physical needs (human infants cannot care for themselves), so these relationships are critical for survival. Growing through childhood into adulthood and later life, we desire relationships with others, as those connections also feed some of our deepest emotional needs as relational persons (theme 1).

To get a sense of how foundational relationships are, think back to your childhood. Did you ever believe there were monsters under your bed or lurking in your closet, ready to pounce when the lights went out at night? Even if your bedroom was monster-free, at some time you probably woke up in the middle of the night, scared by a sound or nightmare or sick from an illness. To whom did you go? That person (or maybe several persons, if the monster was big!) was among those to whom you had formed an **attachment**: a *"lasting psychological connectedness between human beings."*[17] As child psychologist John

14. Valenza et al., "Face Preference at Birth."
15. Kaye, *Mental and Social Life of Babies*, 36–40.
16. Zeskind, Klein, and Marshall, "Adults' Perceptions."
17. Bowlby, *Attachment and Loss*, 194 (emphasis added).

Bowlby claims, infants are born with behaviors that are the building blocks of these strong emotional ties to a caregiver, and behaviors promote the baby's survival.[18] Attachment "can be observed throughout the life cycle, especially in emergencies,"[19] as it provides a "home base," providing psychological support and often even physical aid to people. Parents and caregivers play this role in childhood. In adulthood, we go to friends or family when difficulty arises. As psychologists Roy Baumeister and Mark Leary state, "Human beings are fundamentally and pervasively motivated by a need to belong, that is, by a strong desire to form and maintain enduring interpersonal attachments."[20]

In addition to relationships with other people, the Bible also stresses that humans need relationship with God. Psychological research confirms this biblical emphasis. A leading researcher on attachment and religion states, "Much research in the psychology of religion supports the idea that religion, and particularly a perceived relationship with God, serves both the haven of safety and the secure base functions of attachment."[21] Researchers have shown that people who report feeling attachment to God continue that attachment over long periods of time and that the likelihood to turn to God in times of need was related to a person's level of attachment.[22]

Babies Are Meaning Seekers

Along with showing predispositions toward relationships with others, infants and children also demonstrate predispositions to make meaning and, as we will discuss, even to worship. Humans try to understand and adapt to whatever situation they find themselves in. The biblical theme that humans are meaning seekers can be seen in psychological research on infant preferences and childhood beliefs.

Perceiving Patterns and Making Meaning

Children, even infants, work hard at trying to figure out their world. They take cues from their caregivers to determine how to investigate the world. Babies also "think, draw conclusions, make predictions, look for explanations, and even do experiments," write the developmental psychologist authors of *The Scientist in the Crib*.[23] Babies and children don't stop there. Developmental

18. Bowlby, *Attachment and Loss*, 223.
19. Bowlby, *Attachment and Loss*, 669.
20. Baumeister and Leary, "Need to Belong," 522.
21. Kirkpatrick, "God as a Substitute Attachment Figure," 962.
22. Kirkpatrick, "God as a Substitute Attachment Figure," 969–70.
23. Gopnik, Meltzoff, and Kuhl, *Scientist in the Crib*, viii.

psychologist Alison Gopnik writes, "We can learn about our environment, we can imagine different environments, and we can turn those imagined environments into reality."[24] As they act and react, children transform themselves and the world around them.

These transformations begin with humans' fundamental meaning seeking search for knowledge and understanding—the drive to figure out the situations in which we find ourselves. The beginnings of such abilities are apparent in infants. Unconstrained by social rules, such as "It's rude to stare," babies look at what interests them, staring until they are no longer interested. Measuring time spent looking and other behaviors,[25] researchers have concluded that babies understand a lot. For example, babies as early as four months demonstrate that they categorize objects by looking longer at members of one category than another (e.g., cats versus horses).[26] Six-month-olds make conclusions about cause and effect from scenes they observe.[27] Such abilities provide the foundation for children (and adults) to infer deeper conclusions about why things happen as they do.[28] They also allow them to categorize causes as good versus bad for making moral decisions. Children are meaning makers, and their predispositions lay the groundwork for continued development of that capacity.

Identifying Agents

A critically important meaning-making skill of infants is their ability to spot an agent and differentiate it from mere objects. An **agent** *is a possible cause that can bring about an effect—someone or something that can get things done.* As cognitive psychologist Justin L. Barrett demonstrates in his book *Born Believers*, children can think about agency because they know about cause and effect. "Children are born with minds ready to make sense of the world around them."[29]

Children distinguish agents from other objects early in life. When one of the author's sons was three or four years old, he told his dad that a favorite toy train engine was his friend and helped him do things, an imaginative display of attributing agency when agency obviously was not possible for the object. Children experience a sense of comfort and security snuggling with a favorite

24. Gopnik, *Philosophical Baby*, 7–8.
25. Oakes, "Using Habituation of Looking," 255–59.
26. Madole and Oakes, "Making Sense of Infant Categorization," 279.
27. Alan M. Leslie and Stephanie Keeble showed that babies looked longer at events that included an apparently causal sequence than they did at identical events without such a sequence included. "Do Six-Month-Old Infants Perceive Causality?," 278.
28. Gelman, *Essential Child*, explores categorization and provides one view of how it develops in children.
29. Barrett, *Born Believers*, 41.

stuffed toy.[30] Yet when push comes to shove, children know what is and is not possible for an object. That son never asked his train to get him a sandwich; he asked a parent for food. This same child once called out from his room in the middle of the night, "I'm lonely"—this despite having his favorite stuffed turtle, Swimmy, in bed with him. Half asleep (wanting to be fully asleep), his dad replied, "Just hug Swimmy." He yelled back, "But he doesn't work. I need you." While the stuffed toy was cozy and snuggly, it didn't hug back.

As we have already mentioned, attachment is important for survival, but so is an understanding of agency, which is a form of meaning making. When it comes to identifying agents, Barrett says that agents "represent both our greatest threat and our promise for survival and fulfillment."[31] He continues, "So it is little surprising that infants show signs of knowing the difference between agents and inanimate objects and that they show a great sensitivity to the possible presence of agents around them."[32]

Desiring a Deity

In that search for agents, we include the possibility of agents that are unseen and not human. Barrett[33] and evolutionary psychologists including Jesse Bering[34] and Paul Bloom[35] suggest that we are born to believe in a deity or deities. These psychologists point to research suggesting that children may be "intuitive theists"[36] or "born believers"[37] and that "religion is natural."[38] Barrett shows that children have a predisposition to think about deities because they tend to see purpose and recognize that purpose and order come from beings that have minds, and this "makes children likely to see natural phenomena as intentionally created. Who is this creator? Children know people are not good candidates (e.g., humans did not create the Rocky Mountains or pumas). It must have been God."[39]

The interpretation of why children show religious beliefs reflects on one's worldview. If one takes a purely evolutionary view of religion's development,

30. Harlow and Zimmerman, "Affectional Responses in the Infant Monkey," famously showed the importance of physical contact, even with an inanimate object, resulting in an emotional response in monkeys.
31. Barrett, *Born Believers*, 41.
32. Barrett, *Born Believers*, 41.
33. Barrett, *Born Believers*, 41.
34. Bering, *Belief Instinct*.
35. P. Bloom, "Is God an Accident?"
36. Keleman, "Are Children 'Intuitive Theists'?," 295.
37. Barrett, *Born Believers*.
38. P. Bloom, "Religion Is Natural," 147.
39. Barrett, *Born Believers*, 135–36.

as Bloom does, one may conclude that religious beliefs exist as a by-product of a more useful predisposition to look for causes of events and to make conclusions about how the environment works.[40] In that view, the mechanism that looks for causes gets, in essence, carried away, and when obvious causes can't be found, it resorts to an unseen agent—a god.

If one takes a Christian view, as Barrett does, the desire for God can be seen to arise because God has created us such that we are born to seek him out. People search for a god because humans bear God's image and are made to be in relationship with him. God has made us with a deep desire for him,[41] being made by God and for God. Although that desire is easily misdirected by sin, a longing for God remains. In the end, both Christian and non-Christian psychologists agree that children have a predisposition to look for a god, but the two groups differ regarding why that predisposition exists.

Development throughout Life

Studying infants has shown us several basic characteristics of human nature. Developmental psychology, however, focuses on more than just babies. People continue to grow and change throughout their lives, and psychologists are interested in understanding the pattern of that change and the factors that impact that pattern from conception to death. In their work, developmental psychologists have identified several basic issues or questions that cut across all the topics of their field.[42] Perhaps the most basic but most debated is the interaction between **nature**, *a person's genetic inheritance*, and **nurture**, *a person's experience with their environment*. Exploring how development is lived out physically, shaped by both genes and environment, relates to theme 3, being embodied. The fact that we are relational (theme 1) means that as we develop, we are impacted by the people and things around us.

The nature-versus-nurture debate pits two deterministic extremes—genes and environment—against each other. If you say a person is shaped entirely by their genes (e.g., temperament), then biology—embodiment—dictates who that person becomes. If you say that environment—relational factors—makes a child who they become as an adult, then parents and surroundings are the determining factors. Chapters about development in introductory psychology textbooks usually point out that neither of these extremes is correct, saying that development is always a product of nature and nurture working together.

---

40. Bering, *Belief Instinct*, 80; P. Bloom, *Descartes' Baby*, 210. See also discussion of evolution in the appendix to this book.
41. See further discussion in chap. 4 on consciousness.
42. Santrock, *Life-Span Development*, 18–19.

As one textbook states, "All that people are and all that people become is the product of an interaction between nature and nurture."[43] This more nuanced view, however, is still deterministic. Although scientifically more accurate, this position misses the important emphasis on responsible limited agency in a biblical perspective. Theme 4 acknowledges that humans have constraints on their choices, but it also points out that they are responsible agents. We have a role in shaping ourselves to the degree each of us is able. Beginning in childhood, each person has a role in developing self-regulation, leaving them able to shape their own actions, thoughts, and even ways of living. As creatures made in God's image, we are stewards of creation *and* ourselves. If a psychology of human development is to meaningfully take up a biblical view of human nature, it must recognize agency and responsibility for choices made.

Focusing solely on the physical environment and human genes also misses some of God's activity in bringing about personal spiritual change. The Bible teaches that God formed humans and continues to act in the lives of people,[44] thus working through nature and nurture as well as supernaturally through the Holy Spirit. As the apostle Paul wrote to the Corinthians, those who are in Christ "are being transformed into his image with ever-increasing glory, which comes from the Lord, who is the Spirit" (2 Cor. 3:18). Paul also wrote that believers are being built up spiritually, "being strengthened with all power according to his glorious might so that you may have great endurance and patience" (Col. 1:11). God works in creation and in the lives of people living out their faith responsibly in both physical ways and spiritual ways. These are not mutually exclusive of each other.

Development toward a Goal: *Telos*

Reflecting on the shaping effects of environment, genetics, and each person's choices raises a larger question always present in development: What are we developing *toward*? The most obvious path of development goes from the womb and eventually ends at a tomb—hopefully with some interesting stops in between. Individual theories have ideas about the best path for development of a person as a whole or of a particular aspect of a person, such as social development or intelligence.

Consider Sarah E. Hamson's research[45] exploring how childhood personality traits impact adulthood. The goal studied in this research is adult well-being, which develops over one's life. Hamson's studies define well-being as consisting

---

43. Ciccarelli and White, *Psychology*, 313.
44. Isaiah 64:8 describes God as the potter and humans as the clay.
45. Hamson, "Mechanisms."

of "good physical and emotional health, satisfying interpersonal relationships, and mastery in chosen fields"[46] and identify processes by which people attain it. While the components of well-being included by this researcher may not fit everyone's definition of functioning well (e.g., a sense of having a meaningful existence is not directly included), outlining any set of characteristics as "well-being" implies that these are developmental goals and that reaching and sustaining them are in some sense better than not doing so.

Developmental psychologist James Fowler writes that developmental theorists often provide a standard or norm for the "*telos or goals of human life.*"[47] The word *telos* comes from the Greek word for *purpose* or *end*.[48] Theories of development sometimes overtly, sometimes subtly, imply what counts as "good" development despite science's attempts to be objective.

Christian philosopher James K. A. Smith says that much of our action is not "'pushed' by ideas or conclusions; rather, it grows out of our character and is in a sense 'pulled' out of us by our attraction to a *telos.*"[49] In the example above regarding the development of well-being, the researchers are referring not just to ideas but also to behaviors. Those behaviors that aim toward well-being also promote the goal of well-being. We are actively involved in the goals toward which we aim, and this involvement changes us and forms us toward that *telos*.[50]

To see where a developmental theory is "going," Christian psychologist Ken Bussema has suggested we "turn developmental theories upside down."[51] The final stage or end point of a theory indicates the overall goal of development from that theorist's perspective. From the goal state, a theorist can "work backward, uncovering the steps along the developmental path, noting the possible disruptions, and the necessary motivation required to reach the final developmental destination."[52]

Erikson and Stages of Human Development

To further understand this *telos*, we will "turn over" the influential developmental theory of Erik Erikson.[53] His eight-stage theory of social development

46. Hamson, "Mechanisms," 264.
47. Fowler, *Becoming Adult, Becoming Christian*, 11 (emphasis added).
48. An area of philosophy known as teleology is the study of the purpose of things, including life.
49. J. Smith, *Imagining the Kingdom*, 6.
50. Here Smith is primarily arguing this in terms of the outcomes of education. J. Smith, *Imagining the Kingdom*, 7–8.
51. Bussema, "Perspectives on Developmental Psychology," 2.
52. Bussema, "Perspectives on Developmental Psychology," 2.
53. Erikson, *Identity*. Several other theories attempt to explain aspects of development over the life span, including Lawrence Kohlberg's theory of moral development. See Kohlberg, "Stage and Sequence," 376–83.

attempts to encompass the entire life span and paints a picture of successful development. The culmination of a person's development in Erikson's theory—its *telos*—is to become an independent self with meaningful relationships. Throughout life, individuals progress through a series of stages, each stage involving overcoming a critical challenge before the person goes forward to the next stage. The successful navigation of life challenges, such as achieving basic trust, leads to developing independence with good personal boundaries and is followed by developing a sense of purpose and initiative. In adulthood, cultivating a clear understanding of who one is as a person and developing the capacity for intimacy lead to a well-lived, purposeful life.[54] The more successfully a person meets these challenges that come through experiences particular to various stages in life, the likelier they are to reach a psychologically healthy state in later life.

Interrelationships between the biblical themes of relationality and meaning seeking (themes 1 and 5) are apparent throughout Erikson's theory. In the first stage of development, an infant develops a "sense of basic trust," versus a "basic mistrust,"[55] through interactions with caregivers. This is a lot like the processes of attachment, which, as we discussed earlier in this chapter, have significant implications for relationality. Tasks relating to trust continue into adolescence, as a person needs to trust adulthood and abandon childhood to develop their full personal **identity**: *who a person wants to be and where they want their life to go.*[56] Erikson also emphasizes that the development of trust "becomes the capacity for *faith*,"[57] which he views as vital. Erikson indicates that faith (or the lack of faith) flows from resolving trust versus mistrust and may be part of development from infancy.

Throughout the rest of Erikson's stages, the emphasis on successfully making meaning of one's life continues. This culminates in Erikson's depiction of aging well: "In the aging person who has taken care of things and people and has adapted himself to the triumph and disappointments of being,"[58] the positive outcomes of the previous seven stages of development can grow into what he calls integrity. A person achieves **integrity** *when they are at peace with their life and accept it without regret or the desire to have lived a different life*, while **despair** *is characterized by doubt and gloom as one looks over the past with regret, wishing it would have been profoundly different.*[59] Those who experience integrity can accept

---

54. See Bussema, "Perspectives on Developmental Psychology," 5, for a succinct summary of Erikson's theory.

55. Erikson, *Identity*, 96–97.

56. Erikson, *Identity*, 96–97.

57. Erikson, *Identity*, 106.

58. Erikson, *Identity*, 139.

59. Erikson, *Identity*, 140.

their lives, and even their impending deaths, as important and satisfying. In this integrity, there can be a drive to connect with things beyond oneself through rituals that come not only from religion but also from the arts or mythology.[60]

Much in Erikson's theory fits with a Christian view of human nature, yet in significant ways, they don't fully align. First, as we have stated, the theory focuses on the importance of being relational persons. However, Erikson's theory can be critiqued for the same shortcoming that Bussema has identified in many developmental psychology theories: they "honor the autonomy of the individual person and stress the importance of self-realization and self-determination over the importance of meeting the needs of others."[61] Erikson views human relationality in terms of the links between the individual and others but not in light of humans being God's image bearers who steward creation. Each person is on their own (although interacting with others) to develop a full sense of self and integrity. Emphasizing individual responsibility for this isn't counter to the Bible, but Erikson gives less weight to the need for relationality with and service toward God and others.

Second, Erikson's theory stresses the importance of meaning seeking in that humans must make sense of their environment and themselves. This is apparent in each person's struggle between integrity and despair, for example. Such meaning seeking "evokes 'ultimate concerns'"[62] for the purpose of one's life and potentially even an interest in God. From a biblical perspective, this emphasis isn't wrong, but it misses the mark a bit. While Christian faith does emphasize personal responsibility, it also strongly (perhaps more strongly) emphasizes relationality: persons are meant to be upheld by others within a creation actively upheld by God. For Erikson, the struggle for integrity is the work of each individual, alone.

Christian Telos

For a clearer comparison between psychological theories and a biblical view of life's goals, let's turn Christianity "upside down." If we look to the goal for Christians, it's ultimately to live forever with God. Psychology, however, necessarily focuses on this life alone, so we're overshooting its time frame of development by looking beyond the present life. In fact, it's a mistake to think that psychology could adequately address something that it never intended to address (eternity). Thinking this would make improper theological demands of a science that studies only natural phenomena (see chap. 2). In a Christian

---

60. Erikson, "Reflections on the Last Stage," 161.
61. Bussema, "Perspectives on Developmental Psychology," 5.
62. Erikson, *Identity*, 140.

worldview, *this* life's goal is to love and serve God and others. This might best be summed up in the theological term **sanctification**: *becoming holy and set apart for a special purpose,* "being conformed in disposition and behavior to the image of Christ, . . . living as God's people, both ethically and spiritually."[63] Richard J. Plantinga and his colleagues add that sanctification, while personal, also occurs "in the context of God's larger work of renovating all of created reality."[64] The **Christian *telos* for humans on earth** *is a reconnection with God, to once again be set apart for God's perfect use as God's image bearers.* This reconnection includes restored relationships with others and creation. Being made in God's image means that everyone has inherent value and is called to the Christian *telos*—called to reconnection with God and to caring for everyone's physical, emotional, and spiritual needs (Lev. 19:33–34). Christ said, "Let the little children come to me, and do not hinder them, for the kingdom of heaven belongs to such as these" (Matt. 19:14). Contradicting the culturally held perception of children that they were little more than slaves or animals, Jesus valued children.[65] Scripture stresses care for the most vulnerable in society, including the poor, widows, and orphans.[66] Ultimate goals of self-fulfillment, coming to peace with one's life, and living by one's own rules stray from the emphasis of a Christian *telos*.

If we look at the developmental path of sanctification, each person is involved in that process (Phil. 2:12–13), but people can't achieve reconnection and holiness without God. Sanctification comes about through believers joining in the work of the Holy Spirit in their lives.[67] Aiming desire toward the Christian *telos*, as Smith says, "pulls" out "action that is directed toward the kingdom of God."[68] Psychology's theories and findings can be helpful here in redirecting our actions. Insights gained through psychological research regarding such things as how to change habits, achieve forgiveness, and support and aid those with

---

63. R. Plantinga, Thompson, and Lundberg, *Introduction to Christian Theology*, 329–30 (emphasis added).

64. R. Plantinga, Thompson, and Lundberg, *Introduction to Christian Theology*, 332.

65. Bakke, *When Children Became People*, 16. At that time, women were also lumped together with slaves and animals as being without reason. Jesus acted counterculturally toward women by speaking with and teaching them (e.g., Luke 10:38–42; John 4).

66. James 1:27: care for widows and orphans.

67. The process of sanctification is described in Jenny, "Sanctification," 1166:

The sanctification of the world takes place at a personal and individual level. Those who choose to be sanctified by the Spirit must cooperate in the process (1 John 3:3; Rev. 22:11)—just as in the water purification rites of the [Old Testament]. This process removes the sin but "saves" the individual. The Spirit's role in sanctification begins before conversion with conviction (John 16:8–11), includes cleansing the believer at conversion (1 Cor. 6:11; 2 Thess. 2:13; 1 Pet. 1:1–2), continually washing him or her from sin after conversion (John 4:10–14; 7:38–39; cf. 1 John 1:7–9), through guiding him or her in righteous living (John 14:26; Rom. 8:5–13; 1 Cor. 2:9–16).

68. J. Smith, *Imagining the Kingdom*, 6.

mental illness can be harnessed toward enacting Christian goals of living a life of faithful service.

Finally, one might ask why developmental theories even have an end state, or *telos*, in mind. We all search for purpose in our lives. Trying to explain that purpose is inevitable for developmental psychologists who, like everyone, show the meaning seeking nature of being human. Just like people differ from each other, different theories will have different emphases. Although a theory such as Erikson's psychological model doesn't include theological concepts, it has some compatibility with the theological *telos* emphasized by Christians. Erikson, for example, adds important insights about when and how identity develops. Such understanding can aid us all in comprehending the pattern of change over the life span.

Born to Develop

God certainly could have made us fully developed from the moment we appeared on earth, but human persons are not born fully mature. Yet God does not leave us as infants—we have an inborn drive to become mature. We see this in universal examples of mental and physical abilities (e.g., attachment and speech) as well as in Christians' development of mature faith as God pulls humans to develop.

--- DISCUSSION QUESTIONS ---

1. Explaining behavior in terms of only nature or nurture (or a combination) leaves us with deterministic explanations. How might understanding an aspect of one's personality be informed by taking seriously the role of responsible limited agency? What about other characteristics such as gender or sexuality?

2. If babies are "born believers," what becomes of that natural belief through childhood and into adulthood? Regarding your own life, how have parents and/or communities in which you have lived influenced your notions about who or what God is or if there is a God at all?

3. Think about the *telos* of your development to this point. What future goal(s) are you striving toward? What has been your role in your *telos*?

4. What is the *telos* of other major developmental theories such as Jean Piaget's theory of cognitive development and Lawrence Kohlberg's theory of moral development? Compare it with the *telos* of Christianity.

5. What are some ways that meaning seeking has changed over the course of your life? What are the "big questions" you face now, and how do they differ from the ones you faced earlier? How do you make sense of the world and your existence now versus five or ten years ago?

10

Trust Your Feelings

Emotion

▶ SUMMARY: Emotions have had a bad reputation for two thousand years—thanks in large part to the influence of Greek and medieval philosophers, who valued reason above emotions. Christians have also downplayed emotions, and many psychologists seemed uninterested in studying emotions, since they were viewed as too "messy" to measure and too much a sign of human weakness. However, in recent years, psychologists have rediscovered how essential emotions are to our basic nature. This chapter examines the embodied nature of emotions and how they are integrated into our whole being. We also explore how emotions illustrate our image-bearing quality and how they allow us to relate to God and others in ways that go to the core of our being. Finally, we also stress that we are responsible limited agents who can engage in emotional self-regulation, despite the limitations of our situations or physical existence.

Indulging in unrestrained and immoderate laughter is a sign of intemperance, of a want of control over one's emotions, and of failure to repress the soul's frivolity by a stern use of reason.

Saint Basil, *On the Vice of Laughter*

I have a Bible study that my friends and I go to here in L.A. I go to church every Sunday. I've always been a believer. I love singing. I don't have the best voice—I just love getting my emotions out.

Kellan Lutz, interview in *Elle*

Grieve, mourn and wail. Change your laughter to mourning and your joy to gloom. Humble yourselves before the Lord, and he will lift you up.

James 4:9–10

When you were young, perhaps you sang the song "If You're Happy and You Know It." These "complex and deeply moving" lyrics go on to describe additional happy actions (e.g., "stomp your feet"). Despite its painfully simple message and annoyingly catchy tune, the song captures two profound ideas. The first idea is that one can experience emotions either consciously or unconsciously ("if you're happy *and* you know it"); the second idea is that when you experience an emotion, it is expressed in automatic body responses ("your face will surely show it") and overt actions ("clap your hands"). One other interesting element about the song is that it is always sung in a group setting. The song is sung with others because, as we believe, emotions are meant to be shared and are part of our relational nature.

But why should we have emotions at all? When we ask students in our classes about emotions, we get a large variety of answers. Some say emotions are untrustworthy, cloud judgment, hinder problem solving, make us think and act irrationally, disrupt relationships, turn us into unthinking Christians (e.g., in worship), lead us into bad or even sinful behavior (e.g., anger, jealousy, anxiety), and are a general sign of personal weakness. Other students claim that emotions are more trustworthy than rational or scientific thinking, help build relationships, motivate us, help us be more authentic people—and more authentic Christians—and are a sign of personal depth.

Even for students who value emotions, they still wonder what life would be like without emotions. Of course, such a person has never existed except in the old science fiction television series *Star Trek*. The original version of the series had a character named Mr. Spock,[1] who had few, if any, human emotions. While Mr. Spock lacked the kind of passion and courage of the spaceship's captain, he was always portrayed as the cool, rational individual who often made better decisions because of his dispassionate nature. Although the conflicting views of our students are in many ways true (i.e., that emotions have both good and bad implications), current psychological research has shown that if a person like Mr. Spock ever existed, he wouldn't live long in this world. It appears that emotions are essential to our very survival.

1. In later versions of the series, a character named Data replaced Mr. Spock as the emotionless individual.

A Brief History of Emotions

Before exploring the value of emotions, we need to understand why there are conflicting views regarding emotions. The negative view of emotions dates to ancient Greek philosophers such as Socrates and Plato, who suggested that the mind is part of a nonmaterial soul—equated with pure reason—while emotions are assigned to the body and are less noble and worthwhile. These ideas about emotions were strengthened by seventeenth-century philosopher René Descartes, who taught that the body is a mechanical entity (like a clock) but that the mind is a "nonmaterial substance" that can rule over the body. However, body and mind can also interact, in that the mind has awareness of the body and the mind can influence the body. Communication and control between the two entities happens, according to Descartes, through the pineal gland, a small structure toward the center of the brain.[2] For example, "passions" can originate in the body and might remain "in" the body and never be experienced by the nonmaterial mind, or they might create such a strong response in the body that the mind becomes aware of it. Desires of the nonmaterial mind might also translate into bodily actions and passions that influence behavior. Descartes thought that animals have passions (i.e., bodily reactions) but not emotions because emotions require a conscious experience of the mind (soul). Like the Greek understanding, Descartes's view placed a high value on reason and gave emotions a much lower level of importance in human functioning. It also suggested that we can "transcend" our bodies, as discussed in chapter 3, and with a bit of reason and self-discipline, we can easily rule over our emotions.

Christians have also downplayed emotions throughout much of church history. Being influenced by Greek philosophy, many early Christian leaders felt that emotions are associated with our "fleshly" nature. Since the "desires of the flesh"[3] are equated with sinful tendencies, it was presumed that emotions have a great potential to lead us into sin. Early Christians pointed to Bible passages that appear, at first reading, to make a direct statement about temptations that arise by way of emotions (see, e.g., Eph. 2:3; 4:26);[4] more about this issue later. Even many early psychological theories saw emotions as troublesome or as having little benefit. Sigmund Freud and later psychoanalysts saw emotions as mostly

2. N. Smith, *Current Systems in Psychology*, 36.

3. Phrases like this are often translated into English as "sinful nature" or "selfish desires" in some contemporary translations, such as the Contemporary English Version, rather than "lusts of the flesh" or "in my flesh," as in the King James Version (compare translations for Rom. 7:18, 25; Gal. 5:16; 2 Pet. 2:18).

4. Ephesians 2:3: "All of us also lived among them at one time, gratifying the cravings of our flesh and following its desires and thoughts. Like the rest, we were by nature deserving of wrath"; Eph. 4:26: "'In your anger do not sin': Do not let the sun go down while you are still angry."

destructive forces, and behaviorists such as John Watson and B. F. Skinner saw emotions as something that required restraint through proper conditioning.

However, some historical influences created positive views about emotions within psychology. Perhaps the strongest was the **humanistic psychology** perspective. This movement *stressed that emotions are equal to or perhaps more important than rational thinking.* "Getting in touch with your emotions" was a common refrain, and it was assumed that authentic relationships can happen only when we are aware of our emotions, express our emotions freely, and trust emotions more than reason.[5] Some movements within the church have also brought emotions into greater popularity among many groups of Christians. Those that emphasize the power of the Holy Spirit encourage full emotional expression to become more Spirit-filled and more authentic Christians.

The combined influences of these historical ideas have resulted in many conflicting views and perspectives about emotions—and sometimes these conflicting views are held by the same person at the same time! Thankfully, recent research and contemporary psychology—especially neuropsychology—have provided a clearer picture of emotions and their value. Contemporary research has finally rediscovered the essential role of emotions in our lives and can help us recapture a more complete and scriptural understanding of human nature.

Contemporary Views of Emotions

Let's first examine what cognitive neuroscience research has discovered about normal emotional functioning to help us understand what emotions do for us. Neurologist Antonio Damasio says that "feelings, along with the emotions they come from, are not a luxury. They serve as internal guides, and they help us communicate to others signals that can also guide them,"[6] suggesting that emotions serve an important role in relationships.

Consider the little-known emotion mirth. **Mirth** *is the distinctive emotion that is elicited when a person perceives that something is humorous.*[7] It is a subcategory of happiness and occurs in response to unexpected but pleasant outcomes as well as during times of "playfulness." But the more important question is, Why would human beings have such an emotion? Is this something that we manufactured through culture, or was it given to us at the beginning of time? If it was given to us, what possible purpose does it have? To say that the purpose of mirth is "to make us happy" is circular reasoning, since mirth is a type of

---

5. Shotter, "Getting in Touch."
6. Damasio, *Descartes' Error*, xv.
7. Martin, *Psychology of Humor*, 8.

happiness. As it turns out, mirth does much for us that helps us survive. We have learned a lot about the value of mirth by studying chimpanzees. Psychologist Rod Martin describes how young chimps engage in lots of interactive play and even tickling.[8] This play mimics adult chimp life in that it involves some aggressive actions (e.g., biting, pushing)—just as human children's play sometimes does. One benefit of mirth is that it is an internal signal to the young chimp that this activity is valuable (i.e., it provides an internal reward signal) because it teaches the young chimp how to behave as an adult. It also communicates a signal to the other chimp that this activity is playtime and not an actual act of aggression. Finally, once the second chimp sees the first one laughing (yes, chimps do have a distinctive laugh), the second chimp responds with its own internal signal telling it that the first chimp means no harm. There is another value to the entire process, driven by emotional-motivational triggers: it fosters relationship. These signals not only provide information but also draw the two chimps closer together. The intimate emotional and physical exchange allows the chimps to "read" each other, to become more emotionally attached, and to feel more comfortable with each other. When complex organisms form strong attachments like this, they also survive better.

Humor and mirth have many of the same functions for humans. While emotions such as mirth provide us with important internal signals and provide important communications to others, perhaps their most important element is to create and maintain relationships. There are many other examples of normal emotional function and the purpose of emotions, but perhaps the most compelling illustration of our need for emotions comes from cases in which emotions are disrupted because of disordered or damaged brains.

Emotions and Brain Damage

Individual case studies of emotional damage have made it clear that we don't function well without emotions. Damasio describes one such case in his highly acclaimed book *Descartes' Error: Emotion, Reason, and the Human Brain*. The book argues that the separation of reason and emotion promoted by Descartes is terribly misguided. To illustrate, Damasio tells the compelling story of Elliot, who experienced a radical change in personality because of a brain tumor. Elliot, a very healthy man in his thirties, had been a "good husband and father, had a job with a business firm, and had been a role model for younger siblings and colleagues."[9] He had attained a good deal of success in his business and personal life; he was very intelligent, was able to remember and keep track of important

8. Martin, *Psychology of Humor*, 165–67.
9. Damasio, *Descartes' Error*, 35.

details, and made good personal and business decisions. However, after surgery to remove a tumor in the middle of the frontal lobe (i.e., right behind his fore-head and above his eyes), he became a very different person. He retained his good memory, ability to talk and move effortlessly, problem-solving skills, and overall high IQ. He also remained calm and, in casual conversation, seemed socially adept. However, his personal life quickly unraveled; he now made risky and ultimately disastrous business decisions, went through two divorces, and seemed unable to stop himself from bad decisions, even when everyone in his life advised him to do otherwise.

After extensive testing, it appeared that Elliot's primary problem was that he could no longer access or appreciate his internal emotional state. He continued to experience emotions (although they were diminished), but he could not read or evaluate his own emotional response. So despite superior intellect, when making any significant decision—be it business, social, personal, or moral—he lacked the most important thing of all: a gut feeling. When most of us make bad decisions, we get feedback from others by way of facial expressions (e.g., frowns or angry looks), which activate our own bodies (e.g., arousal or anxiety), informing us that the decision was bad. This information, along with cogni-tive analysis of the situation, comes together in the middle frontal lobe area of the brain, the area affected by Elliot's tumor and surgery. We learn from these experiences that we should not repeat such actions because we not only see the consequences intellectually but also "feel" them. Damasio knows that Elliot cannot experience these feelings because his bodily response, as measured by a GSR (galvanic skin response) machine (which gauges the activity of the skin in response to emotions), showed a nearly flat response when he was confronted with events that normally create emotional reactions. Elliot simply could no lon-ger access this feeling response, and it had devastating consequences for his life.

Emotions and Autism

Brain damage from a tumor is not the only condition that can blunt emo-tions. Individuals with some forms of autism spectrum disorder also have moderate to severe difficulty with emotional and social issues. These indi-viduals range considerably in their intellectual and language abilities, but they share common difficulties in reading facial expressions and understanding the social-emotional conventions of everyday interactions. Temple Grandin[10] is one such individual. She has exceptional memory and cognitive abilities and is well known in the worlds of engineering and animal sciences for her work in the

10. See Grandin and Scariano, *Emergence*.

design of humane cattle-handling systems. However, she also has tremendous difficulty understanding the simplest of emotional cues and social rules. She told neurologist Oliver Sacks that while she could understand the feelings of animals, "It's different with people, . . . studying the people there, trying to figure out the natives." She also suggested to Sacks that trying to understand people was like being an "anthropologist from Mars" because they seemed like a foreign species to her. "I can tell if a human being is angry, . . . or if he's smiling," she stated, but she could not really understand or relate to the emotions she observed. Sacks recounts how Grandin compared her lack of ability to the ability of children: "Children, she feels, are already far advanced, by the age of three or four, along the path that she, as an autistic person, has never advanced far on. Little children, she feels, already 'understand' other human beings in a way she can never hope to."[11]

Grandin's difficulty is not that she lacks any internal emotional experience but that she doesn't have the same internal experience of emotions that others have when she sees emotions from others. Most individuals have an unconscious or inborn sense about emotions, but Grandin must "compute," as she states it, the intentions of others in order to determine their "state of mind." While she has a fulfilling career and has achieved a great deal of professional and personal success, she relayed to Sacks that it was somewhat painful to her that she never had a close, loving relationship with another person. She has friends she relates to intellectually and professionally and she feels are sometimes on the same "wavelength," but she does not experience close, loving relationships. She suggested that she had never dated because "she found such interactions completely baffling and too complex to deal with."[12] In fact, she had a hard time even articulating what love is or what loving someone might feel like. "Maybe it's like swooning," she suggested at one point. She could also describe how others act when they say they are in love, but as with reading facial expression, it was more like a scientific analysis than something deeply felt.

Individuals like Elliot and Grandin illustrate how central emotional experience and understanding are to everyday life. We already described some additional examples in chapter 3. In that chapter, we told the story about the woman known as S, who lost the ability to be angry, and we described how people form emotional attachments because of the hormone oxytocin. Emotions assist us in virtually all decisions. Emotions help us negotiate the social and interpersonal world around us, and what appears to be abundantly clear is that they make meaningful, reciprocal relationships with other people possible.

11. Sacks, *Anthropologist on Mars*, 270.
12. Sacks, *Anthropologist on Mars*, 285.

Therefore, perhaps the saddest aspect of these stories of brain and emotional dysfunction is the disruption of meaningful relationships.

Biblical Pictures of Emotions

As we have suggested throughout this book, God designed us for relationships (theme 1), and the embodied emotions (theme 3) that we possess are part of that grand design. These emotions also mirror God's character in many ways. An electronic Bible search reveals countless passages about God's emotions. God is described as angry in over two hundred passages, and that doesn't count the times he is described as "slow to anger." God, as Father or as Son, shows a wide range of emotions that humans also experience, including concern (Exod. 2:25), happiness (James 5:13), sorrow (Matt. 26:37), and jealousy (Deut. 4:24). There is also a wealth of emotional language throughout Scripture. If you want to see how emotional Scripture can be, examine 2 Corinthians 7 and count the emotion-related words (we count thirty-two). What this suggests to us is that when God created us in his image and with characteristics that allow us to have relationships, emotions were a very significant part of that creation. To have deep and meaningful relationships with other persons (including God), we need to be able to communicate (using language), represent ideas in our minds (cognitively), and understand the intentions and ideas of others (sometimes called theory of mind),[13] but we also need to be able to communicate our emotions and form emotional bonds. Therefore, emotions are an essential part of our created image and our relational nature. While this idea makes the case studies of disordered emotions all the more painful—since relationships with God and fellow humans are disrupted—Warren Brown has suggested that even when some individuals struggle in relating to God, God can still maintain that relationship with them.[14] God continues to provide us with his love and care and maintain his promises to us, even when we can't feel his love.

"Problem" Emotions?

It appears that contemporary psychological science and Scripture emphasize the essential nature of our emotional life. However, our experience tells us that emotions may sometimes create problems for us. Isn't it still the case that emotions can cloud judgment and make us do irrational things at times—or even

13. Brown, "Cognitive Contributions to Soul," 108.
14. Brown, "Cognitive Contributions to Soul," 123–24.

cause us to become superficial (i.e., nonthinking) people or Christians? Isn't it still the case that some people express too much emotion, or not enough, or don't control their emotions? Psychology and Scripture are on the same page in addressing these concerns about emotions. Both Scripture and psychological science point to the harmful impact that very extreme negative emotions can have and the need to "manage" our more powerful emotions.

Some biblical passages seem to suggest that emotions can be a vehicle for sinning. Emotions such as anger, envy, anxiety, and others appear to be condemned in some parts of Scripture. But a closer examination of many scriptural passages shows that the problem is not the emotions themselves but the way we use these emotions. After all, God shows every one of these same emotions at times, so it doesn't appear that the emotions themselves are the main problem. The cause for experiencing a particular emotion and how we act when we become emotional are the key concerns of many passages. Take worry or anxiety, for example. Several passages seem to command us not to worry or have anxiety (see Matt. 6:25–34; Phil. 4:6). But if we examine the context of most of the passages, we see that the focus is on what people are anxious about—money, clothing, and other aspects of material daily existence—not on condemning all anxiety. The point of such passages is to show that the main attention of Christians should be focused on God's kingdom, not on all these things of lesser importance. We can also contrast these ideas to passages in which there is a clear indication that some legitimate concern or worry is appropriate (such as 1 Sam. 9:5–6, where Saul is worried that his father will be concerned about his whereabouts) or that a lack of concern seems to be the greater sin (such as Prov. 6:9–11, where the lack of concern over property maintenance brings on poverty).

Much the same could be said about anger, where the problem isn't the anger itself but what the anger is directed toward and how people react when angry (1 Cor. 13:4–6; James 1:19–20). There are also clear admonitions about how long people stay angry and what they do when angry (Eph. 4:25–27). So none of the emotions we experience appear to be inherently sinful, but our own sinful tendencies can distort why we experience certain emotions and how we react when we have the emotions. There is also clear indication that how we act when we have powerful emotions can damage relationships. Therefore, Scripture clearly teaches that people need to be in control of their emotional responses and consider the impact of emotions on relationships.

In the psychological community, it is intriguing that therapists also understand that we need to exercise control over our emotions. This is a significant change from the days of Freud, who felt that unbridled "release" of problem emotions was almost always a good thing (called "catharsis" by psychoanalytic therapists), and from the humanistic psychologists, who felt that most emotions should be accepted for what they are and rarely considered good or bad. Much of current therapy practice recognizes that unregulated emotions can be destructive and that we need, and are able, to learn how to manage them. For example, a study by Kevin N. Ochsner and his colleagues showed that participants were able to cognitively "retrain" or self-regulate their emotional responses. More importantly, this retraining had profound effects on their brain activity in response to an emotional event.[15] Therefore, with an emotion like anger, the current view in psychology is that releasing it, repressing it, and expressing it whenever we want are not particularly helpful. Rather, when we experience strong emotions like anger, we need to identify the real source or situation to which we are reacting, learn to constructively deal with that issue, and learn to regulate the intensity and direction of the emotion we experience.[16]

We believe that our God-given emotions help us form meaningful relationships, but they can also be distorted by our own sinful tendencies, or they can be distorted because we live in a broken world (think of Elliot and other case studies presented). But whatever the cause of our emotional turmoil, God's desire is that we learn to understand the source of our emotions, balance our emotional responses, and learn to restore relationships damaged by emotions.

The Pursuit of Happiness?

In chapter 9 we introduced the notion of *telos*, or "end goal," suggesting that most developmental theories have unspoken ideas about what a good outcome should be. Applying this idea to emotions, what does a good emotional outcome look like from God's perspective? Most people in Western societies value happiness, and many therapists strive to bring about greater happiness in their clients, but are negative emotions always something to be avoided? Psychologist Joseph Forgas reviewed a series of studies showing that negative mood states (mostly sadness) can have positive effects on people.[17] Sadness was associated with more accurate memories of events, more polite behavior, increased sensitivity to social cues, and greater fairness in social situations. Forgas is not arguing that we should remain in these states, since there are benefits for positive moods as well, but he suggests that we should not attempt to eliminate all up and down emotional experiences, since these moods may be a response to a life situation and just what we need at that time.

15. Ochsner et al., "Rethinking Feelings," 1215–29.
16. See Tavris, *Anger*.
17. Forgas, "Don't Worry, Be Sad!"

In a very different way, author Kathryn Greene-McCreight, who writes about her own struggle with clinical depression, suggests that her lengthy bout of depression and sadness had some surprising benefits in the end. While she would never wish such struggle on anyone, she says that having gone through this struggle made her have "deeper compassion for the sick, bedridden, and homeless."[18] She had always thought that she was a compassionate person, but after she experienced moods that caused her great pain, she realized this was not true. As she asks, "How, after all, can one put oneself into the shoes of another who is suffering without having suffered personally?"[19] Deeply negative and even painful emotions can be part of a growing experience. But in her case, and in the case of many with mental illness, such negative mood states seemed ever present, robbing her of the benefits and important consequences of positive states that we also need.

Scripture also points out the value of experiencing guilt, remorse, and other negative moods from time to time.[20] While God may not desire for us to remain in painful emotional states, we often learn from the variety of emotional states that God has created for us to experience. Just as a bad taste in our mouths from spoiled food helps us learn that we should avoid such foods in the future, so a negative mood state may help us learn about our current situation and about ourselves. So we can be thankful that, by God's grace, psychological science has also pointed to ways that we can learn from our emotional experiences and learn to manage our emotions or restore some emotional balance and self-regulation to our lives.

Implications and Applications

These scriptural and psychological insights into the value and purpose of emotions don't necessarily help us in dealing with all the practical issues related to emotions, but here are a few practical applications that we believe grow out of these larger ideas.

1. Develop your God-given emotional life by nurturing relationships with God and others—which requires you to "practice" understanding emotional cues from others, using appropriate emotional expression, and en-

---

18. Greene-McCreight, *Darkness Is My Only Companion*, 156.
19. Greene-McCreight, *Darkness Is My Only Companion*, 156.
20. See the following: Ps. 32:5: "Then I acknowledged my sin to you and did not cover up my iniquity. I said, 'I will confess my transgressions to the LORD.' And you forgave the guilt of my sin"; 2 Cor. 7:8: "Even if I caused you sorrow by my letter, I do not regret it. Though I did regret it—I see that my letter hurt you, but only for a little while"; and James 4:9–10, quoted at the beginning of this chapter.

gaging in appropriate self-regulation. (It's also worth noting that Grandin nurtured these abilities through careful observation and constant practice—even though she struggled with using emotions "naturally.")

2. Be mindful and aware of your own emotional responses. Some emotions are very automatic and can occur outside of our immediate conscious awareness (being embodied as they are). Becoming aware of when and why you have strong emotional reactions is the first step in regulating your own experience and expression of emotions.

3. Evaluate the reasons for your emotions. Is the issue impacting your emotion (be it a positive or negative emotion) as important as you think? Scripture and psychological practice agree that it's very important to rethink—or as some psychologists suggest, reframe—your priorities. This reframing may cause you to realize that your emotion is inappropriate or out of proportion to the situation. For example, are you angry about a true injustice or sinful action (which is what God gets angry about), or are you angry about some rather minor issue that affects only you? Scripture admonishes us to put others first and to reduce how emotional we get about our own personal issues.

4. Determine (perhaps with insights from wise friends or professional therapists) if your emotional experience or expression is beyond your current ability to regulate by yourself. The embodied nature of our emotions and our learned tendencies that may make some emotions strong habits of the mind may limit our ability to manage our emotions on our own. Perhaps your difficulties with emotions are due to intense or long-term experiences that have had a strong impact on your ability to self-regulate (e.g., post-traumatic stress disorder, long-term depression). In the case of these more extreme examples of emotional difficulty, you may need the support and assistance of others—and perhaps medication—to help you regulate your emotional experience.

5. Finally, learn to observe the impact your emotional experience has on your relationships. If emotions were given to us to foster our relationships, then make sure that your emotional life is being used to enhance, not destroy, those very relationships that are so valuable to God.

———————— DISCUSSION QUESTIONS ————————

1. Think about how emotions influence small and large decisions you make (e.g., choosing an outfit to wear, which person to talk to, which career to

select). Identify times when these emotions influenced you in positive ways and in negative ways.

2. How have emotions been beneficial to you in your interpersonal relationships, spiritual life, or worship experiences? Would you have been diminished in each of these areas if you had not been able to feel emotion?

3. Have there been times in your life when you really "lost it" emotionally (e.g., strong anger, extreme anxiety, or intense sadness)? Were you surprised at your own response? Did you feel "out of control," and did you regret or feel embarrassed by your intense emotion?

4. How could you have "reframed" your experience in question number 3? How could you have responded more constructively?

11

We're in This Together

Social Psychology, Part 1

▶ **SUMMARY:** One theme for this book is that we are relational persons. No area of psychology exemplifies this more consistently than social psychology. This chapter focuses on the powerful influence that groups have on individuals as well as evidence that humans are motivated to seek relationships with others. Social psychology research mirrors the strong scriptural emphasis on the power of the group for good or evil. However, these influences raise significant concerns about what it means to be responsible limited agents (theme 4) when we can be easily influenced by groups.

> We are half ruined by conformity, but we should be wholly ruined without it.
>
> Charles Dudley Warner, Obstacles to Living Life Fully

> As you navigate through the rest of your life, be open to collaboration. Other people and other people's ideas are often better than your own. Find a group of people who challenge and inspire you, spend a lot of time with them, and it will change your life.
>
> Amy Poehler, Harvard University commencement address

 male college student we know once said that his dad was convinced that the "collective IQ of a group of adolescent boys dropped steadily as the group got larger." (He was quite sure the effect applied to adolescent girls as well.) No doubt this statement was based on his experience of mostly well-behaved adolescent boys doing "dumb" or bad things when they got together. Many parents have also heard their adolescent son or daughter complain that "everyone does it," with the assumption that right or wrong is determined by percentages. The standard response that one of the authors heard from his parents was "And if everyone jumped off a cliff, would you follow?"

Most people feel the effects of peer pressure most strongly during their adolescence, but people experience conformity pressure at any age. The point is if we reflect on our own actions and thoughts, we realize that we often think and act differently when we are around other people. Social psychologists have carefully documented the powerful ways that we are influenced by groups.

The Power of the Situation

The powerful influence of groups and social situations is well established in **social psychology**: *a branch of psychology that deals with social interactions, including their impact on the individual.* Many studies have documented how frightfully easy it is to alter the behavior of everyday, run-of-the-mill people (regardless of age, education, experience, etc.) simply by changing the situation. Solomon Asch demonstrated that most people will conform and give obviously wrong answers to easy questions when influenced by a group of strangers;[1] Stanley Milgram documented that a large majority of people would give very painful electric shocks to other human beings just because they were told by an "authority figure" to do so.[2] Surprisingly, participants in these types of studies are rarely aware that they are being influenced by the situation and in fact vehemently deny that other people or the circumstances altered their natural behavior. For example, in a follow-up study to Milgram's shock experiment, he had participants first watch other people (who were in fact confederates or paid actors) *refuse* to give electric shocks to a person in another room. The rate of "shock giving" in this version of the experiment, compared to his earlier experiments, went down tremendously.[3] When he asked the participants if the action of the other people had influenced their own behavior, they were certain that there was no influence; they were convinced that they had acted of their own free will. However, the evidence showed otherwise: they had been powerfully influenced by the situation. Apparently,

1. Asch, "Opinions and Social Pressure."
2. Milgram, "Behavioral Study of Obedience."
3. Bolt and Myers, *Human Connection*, 91.

we can be so caught up in a situation or with a group that we often lose ourselves.

Of course, peer pressure can also have many positive effects on people. When all your teammates keep training, you are more likely to follow suit—even when you are tired. Certainly, society would be in trouble if there were no conformity pressure. In fact, many cultures value conformity far more than Americans or Europeans because they see how important it is in encouraging correct behavior. The difficulty lies in recognizing the influences—given how easy it is to miss them—and resisting the influences when they are negative.

If you have ever visited a culture very different from your own, you can also see the powerful influence of other people or circumstances. When you see how differently people in another culture live, you begin to realize that your own behavior, attitudes, and thinking patterns have been profoundly shaped by your family, your friends, and the wider culture. Our personal identity is strongly tied to our group identity. We often assume that our behavior and the behavior of those around us is "normal" (and everyone else is "strange"), but we rarely stop to think that we might have become very different people if we had been born to a different family or lived in a different culture.

These influences are directly relevant to two of the biblical themes of human nature we identified earlier—that we are relational persons (theme 1) and that we are responsible limited agents (theme 4). As individuals, we want to believe that we are the masters of our own fate and that we consciously and purposefully direct our actions. Previous chapters have shown that our choices are more limited than we like to think because of the constraints of our genetic inheritance, bodily existence, and learned patterns. But social psychology also vividly illustrates that our choices and actions are very much a part of our social circumstances *and* that we are typically unaware of these powerful influences. This thought can be especially disturbing to people of faith because Christianity stresses that people are personally responsible and accountable for their behaviors and choices, especially moral choices. As we described earlier, Scripture is clear that all humans are accountable before God and that no one can simply blame their circumstances for bad or sinful behavior. We will also discuss in chapter 13, on personality, that we are individually defined and that we each have our own unique identity. However, we collectively bear God's image. God relates to us as persons, but as we describe, personhood inherently involves interrelationship, as God deals with us communally in families, tribes, and nations.

Yet how can we be individually accountable if we are so influenced by groups? To resist the negative effects of conformity pressure, some people of faith may suggest that we should simply exercise more willpower or perhaps rely more on the Spirit of God. The reasoning goes that through *individual* efforts, we can reduce the influence of the group and overcome our circumstances—thereby reestablishing our personal control. There are some valuable truths within this line of reasoning, as we will discuss later, but we believe that Scripture provides a more complex picture of human nature that does not easily eliminate either of these seemingly contradictory truths.

Our Relational Nature

Before exploring a scriptural understanding of the dilemma caused by individual accountability and group influence, let's examine more thoroughly what psychologists have learned about why relationships and groups are so powerful.

Christian psychologist Warren Brown says that what makes us uniquely human is our ability to have deep interpersonal relationships. He describes how human traits such as our cognitive abilities, our ability to understand others' perspectives (i.e., theory of mind), our language capabilities, and our emotional qualities (among others) collectively allow us to have deep reciprocal relationships with God and others.[4] But he also states that these qualities and abilities make having relationships an "imperative," or deep need. So we appear to be "programmed" to seek relationships with others from infancy (see chap. 9 for a full discussion).

Studies show that children have a powerful "need to belong," and when children have no close personal friends, they experience significant emotional turmoil.[5] Studies on adults show that the presence of other people—even strangers—can greatly reduce stress in a fearful situation. Research on brain activity and social relationships confirms how powerful social interaction can be. In these studies, participants watched and participated in an animated game of catch between themselves and two other cartoon figures. Whenever the participants were excluded from the game by rarely getting the ball, areas of their brains devoted to emotional distress became very active.[6] Apparently human beings have a deep-seated desire for inclusion.

Humans also seem to thrive best when they have a social network or close support group—even experiencing less heart disease in these circumstances.[7] There is evidence that people often create better solutions to complex problems and take fewer unnecessary health risks when they are part of a positive support group.

4. Brown, "Cognitive Contributions to Soul."
5. La Greca and Lopez, "Social Anxiety among Adolescents."
6. Crowley et al., "Exclusion and Micro-Rejection."
7. Lett et al., "Social Support and Coronary Heart Disease."

While it appears that we are programmed for relationships and that we find them deeply fulfilling, they can also be our greatest curse. When we think about broken friendships, family fights, or social rejection, we are reminded of how painful relationships can be. As described at the beginning of the chapter, other people can also influence us to act in ways that are stupid, cruel, or even sinful. So psychology verifies that relationships are important—even essential—but also that relationships can be painful or damaging because they are so much a part of what defines us. We simply can't think about anything in the world without thinking relationally.

The "Collective Mind"

The North American and European cultural emphasis on individual effort and individual responsibility may make it difficult for those of us from that background to appreciate how essential and even mysterious our relational nature really is. We tend to think of groups as a collection of individuals who may (or may not) influence one another—depending on the strength of the individual personalities involved. But many contemporary thinkers (coming from diverse disciplines such as theology, philosophy, and neuropsychology) suggest that the idea of an individual mind acting "alone" is an illusion. In this new way of thinking, a cohesive group can be thought of as a single, "indivisible unit." Theologian Alan Torrance, in his essay "What Is a Person?," describes a change in thinking about persons that has happened in recent years: "No longer defined as thinking subjects whose primary relationship was to the world of ideas, or as mere agents defined by their relations to impersonal objects, human beings came to be defined as essentially *persons* constituted by their relations to other persons."[8] You may recognize that this echoes our description of personhood in chapter 1.

Likewise, researcher Raymond Trevor Bradley concludes that our personal agency—our ability to choose or decide—cannot be considered apart from cooperative interaction with others: "Agency requires an active brain: a self-conscious brain that can assess the significance of and assign meaning to sensory input; . . . a brain that can establish priorities and plans; and a brain that can implement, and coordinate with others, purposeful programs of social action."[9]

Therefore, psychological research confirms that being responsible limited agents (theme 4) is not only an individual issue but also a collective issue. The minds of individuals can be "joined," as it were, into collective thought and

8. Torrance, "What Is a Person?," 202.
9. Bradley, "Values, Agency," 472.

action. Just as hydrogen and oxygen can combine to form a substance completely unlike either part, so thoughts can join to form a holistic and unique experience between individuals, with the whole being greater than the sum of the parts.

You may have experienced this "joining of minds" when working with someone on a math problem. Perhaps you both suddenly realized the answer at the same time. Or this joining can be seen when several people—all at once—get the punch line of a joke, or when you have shared emotional experiences of sorrow or joy, and the shared glances in the room are understood by all. Perhaps the best example of this joining is married couples who, after years of marriage, complete each other's sentences or anticipate each other's thoughts. This joining of the minds can continue over time with groups of people developing a "personality." A chairperson of a committee sometimes refers to the ongoing dynamic in the group, a teacher often talks about the personality of their class, and a pastor talks about the character of a congregation.

So a group of people can be thought of as acting as a single entity with its own developmental history (i.e., like infants growing into adults) and personality. When this "personality" does something good or bad, is each individual responsible, or is the group entity? This may seem like a silly question since each person is able to make an individual choice. Yet we can also see that when we are part of a whole, we are caught up within it; in other words, we are influenced by the whole as much as we contribute to it. This truth has the potential for both positive outcomes and negative ones, since we can sin or act obediently as individuals and as groups. We can develop "mindsets" coming from group membership that are obedient (e.g., desiring justice) or sinful (e.g., racial prejudice).

Social Identity

In addition to influencing our behavior and thinking, groups influence how we think about ourselves. We often define ourselves according to unique qualities (e.g., "I am short") but also according to the group or organization to which we belong (e.g., "I'm from California," "I go to church X," "My family is . . ."). Thus social identity helps answer the question "Who am I?" But these self-descriptions can begin to change who we are. One study did extensive interviews of physiology graduate students at the beginning and end of their graduate program. Most if not all the students saw the program as a stepping stone to medical school. But over time, they began to identify less and less as premed students and more and more as physiology students. They also developed value systems that were similar to those of their professors and fellow students and less like those of medical students.[10]

Perhaps you experienced this form of transformation in which, having settled on a particular academic major, you began to act and think more like people in that major. Maybe you selected one college over a rival college. Initially, the choice may have been a close call, with both schools being attractive, but after being at your selected college, you began to disparage the other. If you ever changed churches or joined new groups of friends, you may have quickly adopted the thinking patterns of those around you and began to contrast yourself to others not in your circles. Again, this implies that this social identity can have positive influences on your thinking (e.g., "My church is very involved in outreach and social justice") or can be potentially damaging (e.g., "My social media friends are really into buying lots of material goods"). If a person belongs to a group that develops very destructive thoughts (e.g., hatred toward certain groups, excessive materialism, aggressive or violent ideas), to what extent does that person bear responsibility for their own tendencies?

Covenantal Relationships in Scripture

It's fascinating that Scripture also captures many of these contradictions about groups and individuals that psychologists have studied—the good and bad influence of groups as well as the amazing, almost mystical joining of minds that can happen within a group. Scripture describes the mutual accountability in relationships and how responsibility is both individual and collective. Many Scripture passages stress the responsibility of the individual (e.g., "Choose for yourselves this day whom you will serve" [Josh. 24:15]), but just as many show the power of the group for promoting good or evil. Families, tribes, churches, and nations are often treated as a single entity and singled out for praise or blame. Certainly not all individuals within these families, tribes, churches, and nations were equally responsible for all the actions of the whole, yet all were held accountable for the actions of the whole. Many biblical scholars have pointed out the extent to which God **covenants**—*forms a reciprocal promise*—with both individuals and groups and that God works through groups in very profound ways.

The New Testament is also full of references to the fact that Christians are part of the "body of Christ." Some may think that this phrase speaks to a kind of unity of spirit, like the camaraderie you might find being part of a sports team. But careful reading of the passages reveals that this unity of the body of

10. Ashforth and Mael, "Social Identity Theory."

Christ is much richer and deeper than the fellowship a person might feel with a group of friends. For example, 1 Corinthians 12:18–20 says, "But in fact God has placed the parts in the body, every one of them, just as he wanted them to be. If they were all one part, where would the body be? As it is, there are many parts, but one body." This passage captures the uniqueness of each person but also the unity of the whole. Even though one human body is a collection of "entities," we still talk about the whole person acting; likewise, a body of believers has parts but can also be considered one whole "person." The notion of having a collective mind is captured in Philippians 2:2, which says, "Then make my joy complete by being like-minded, having the same love, being one in spirit and of one mind."

Practical Implications for the Church

There are many practical implications of social psychological findings and scriptural revelation about group membership. For one thing, North American Christians tend to focus attention on their individual sins and personal failures, but they rarely look at how they were led to sin within a family, group, or culture. Sinful tendencies of individuals can be developed and incorporated into groups to which the individual belongs, and groups in turn shape and modify these tendencies. For example, individuals who define themselves by what they own tend to find each other and become friends. Before long, the influence of the group accentuates this desire in each member of the group to the point that they may all develop excessive materialism.[11]

Can we escape the impact of the group when and if the group is leading us astray? The bottom line is that we are "embedded" creatures. We cannot fully escape the reality of our family, church, tribe, or nation. So asking how we can escape group influence is like asking how we can escape our own bodies—it simply can't be done. This is one part of the "limited" aspect of being responsible limited agents. We can't transcend our circumstances, but we can change our group membership. As Christian psychologist Martin Bolt notes, "We think the solution is found in developing greater independence; we teach our children, 'Dare to be a Daniel; dare to stand alone.'"[12] But he suggests that living as Christians is a community task and can't really be done alone: "It requires social support. Without a sustaining environment it is hard to develop and even more difficult to maintain a Christian lifestyle. Being created social

11. This tendency is sometimes called group polarization and has been demonstrated in many studies. See Myers and Lamm, "Group Polarization Phenomenon," 602.
12. Bolt and Myers, *Human Connection*, 91.

means that we need to be nourished; we must be encouraged by each other to live our commitments. It's tough to maintain one's Amish identity while living in San Francisco."[13] He goes on to say that churches often fail at this community building because "it is certainly a lot easier to 'attend church' than to 'be church.'"[14]

So social psychology and Scripture are telling us a very similar message: we humans are so relational that we cannot think of ourselves outside our situation. In fact, it makes little sense to talk about the individual outside their experience. Of course, there are key differences in the way Scripture refers to the body that is the church and the way social psychology describes group dynamics. As the well-known theologian Dietrich Bonhoeffer suggests, "Because Christian community is founded solely on Jesus Christ, it is a spiritual and not a psychic reality."[15] But he also goes on to say that the church needs to develop a greater psychic unity (i.e., become of "one mind"), so there are many ways in which Christian communities do function very much like other communities.

Problems with Christian Communities?

There is a serious and legitimate concern that may arise from being in a Christian community. Does this unity of the body mean that Christians should separate themselves from the rest of the world and live in a monastery, an Amish community (as Bolt alludes to above), or a Christian commune? While many find this a tempting scenario, we don't believe that Scripture is necessarily telling us to engage in separatism (although there may be great value in doing this for a time). In fact, there are some significant dangers in becoming an isolated community. Social psychology research on social identity (discussed earlier) and "in-group" and "out-group" bias reveals that we have a strong tendency to quickly view our group as superior and all other groups as less valuable.[16] (See chap. 8 for examples and additional descriptions.) This tendency can extend to families, schools, cultures, and races. Christians run the risk of developing an in-group bias and a sense of superiority over other communities if they separate themselves from others too much.

The cure for this dilemma is to be grounded in community but not isolated from other communities. Scripture paints a picture of Christians being involved in the Christian community and then using that foundation to be a blessing to

13. Bolt and Myers, *Human Connection*, 91.
14. Bolt and Myers, *Human Connection*, 93.
15. Bonhoeffer, *Life Together*, 21.
16. Otten and Moskowitz, "Evidence for Implicit Evaluative In-Group Bias."

others. The apostle Paul indicates in 2 Corinthians 1:12 that Christians need to be active in the world while they maintain strong relationships within the church: "Now this is our boast: Our conscience testifies that we have conducted ourselves *in the world*, and especially in our relations with you, with integrity and godly sincerity. We have done so, relying not on worldly wisdom but on God's grace" (emphasis added). In Romans 12:2, Paul also says, "Do not conform to the pattern of this world, but be transformed by the renewing of your mind. Then you will be able to test and approve what God's will is—his good, pleasing and perfect will." Christians can be transformed in community with other Christians, but this transformation needs to be put into practice beyond that community. Therefore, we can combat the potential in-group bias that can arise even in positive communities by also being active in the world.

A second serious concern about being in community is that even mostly positive communities can still influence us in harmful ways. Humans easily become blind to negative influences that can become woven into a community, including the church. Remember that participants in many social psychology experiments were not aware of how much the group influenced them, so we may miss the fact that negative group tendencies exist and that they influence us (e.g., "I'm not influenced by movies I watch"). Christians sometimes come to believe that the practices in their community are the best or only ways to behave as Christians, ignoring the fact that Christians over the centuries and across many cultures have found a variety of ways to practice their faith. Visiting a megachurch in Kenya, an underground house church in China, and a mission outpost in Honduras—even if from the same Protestant denomination—will quickly underscore the powerful effects of culture and circumstances. The fact that culture and time can create varied practices and expressions of faith across communities is not a bad thing and in many ways enhances the overall church, but Christians need to be aware of these influences. Persons in any community of people—including a Christian fellowship—need to take time for a little reflection on how the community has adopted ideas or practices that are ultimately bad for them. It's very easy for a church community to gradually adopt practices that lead to excessive individualism, materialism, or even racism without realizing the influence of the wider culture. An extreme example of negative church influence is evident in the German Lutheran Church prior to World War II when it gradually conformed to Nazi thinking—in part because of its loyalty to German culture—without noticing the subtle influences that came in small increments. German theologian and pastor Dietrich Bonhoeffer was able to resist this influence in part because of his experience with churches outside Germany but also because of his complete immersion in Scripture and fellowship with other faithful Christians.[17] So visiting other cultures, groups, or communities can be used as a mirror to examine and critique our own practices and help us identify how we have been affected—for better or worse.

Final Words on Accountability

Despite these concerns about the negative influences of groups, we would do well not to spend an excessive amount of time trying to disentangle individual responsibility from the responsibility of the group for bad behavior. While there is clearly individual responsibility for bad behavior that we must all recognize, everyday life is often rather complicated. (This complex picture has implications for understanding personality, psychological disorders, and therapy, which we will discuss more in chaps. 13, 14, and 15.)

One reason we need to be cautious about attributing blame in a given circumstance is because social psychology research shows that we tend to make the **fundamental attribution error**: *we underestimate the power of the situation and blame individuals exclusively for their failures*. On the other hand, we often attribute our own failures to the situation (e.g., "My boss is a jerk," "The train made me late"). Whether this pattern is caused by basic human sinfulness, our cognitive processes, culture, or some other psychological function—or all of these—is unclear. The truth, of course, is that we do bear the blame for our failures, but so does the group. Why do people abuse drugs? Why do people have messed-up families? Why do individuals have emotional problems? In many of these situations, we spend a lot of time dividing up blame and placing most of it on the individual, when in fact the answer lies in both the individual and the context of their circumstance. We believe, in most cases, that it is more useful simply to focus on doing what needs to be done—individually and collectively—to remedy the problem. This may sound simplistic, but it may also be more fruitful.

Responsible Limited *Groups*?

Christians debate who should care for the poor, create better families, build a better church, create a better community, and so on. Which is needed: individual action or communal responsibility? We believe that God cares little about this question and more about just getting it done; Christians must simply acknowledge that responsibilities are both individual *and* communal.

17. Marsh, *Strange Glory*.

Finally, when we study social psychology and the influence that groups have on us, our free will and responsibility are not diminished; they are enhanced. Those who are most oblivious to social influences or think that the social setting has no impact on them are more limited by their social setting, being unaware of its impact. When we understand the power of these social influences and when we see the dangers and blessings of being in community, we can most assert our agency in both individual action and collective action. Therefore, when we help shape the groups we are in, join with positive groups, and allow ourselves to be shaped positively by a group (mindful of the potential negative influences), great things can be accomplished!

DISCUSSION QUESTIONS

1. Can you think of times when group conformity pressure caused you to do something dreadfully stupid or bad? Can you think of times when social pressure had a very positive influence on your thoughts or actions?

2. Have you experienced times when you had a "coming together of minds" or became like-minded with other individuals? Did you find that the experience drew you closer to those people?

3. If you are part of a church community, can you cite examples of how your church community fosters "being a body"? Can you think of ways your church fosters individualism?

4. How do we manage to form healthy groups and positive, close relationships without forming an in-group/out-group bias?

5. If you have an annoying or bad habit that you would like to change, how could you utilize group influence or community to foster a change?

6. If you feel that a community is influencing you in a very negative way, how can you avoid or change that influence?

12

Faithful Attitude and Action

Social Psychology, Part 2

▶ SUMMARY: Chapter 11 emphasized the role of people and situations in influencing our behaviors and attitudes; this chapter explores the interplay between behaviors and attitudes and how each may shape the other. As embodied, responsible limited agents, humans reveal attitudes through behaviors, but behaviors also strongly influence attitudes. Yet the Bible clearly emphasizes the importance of a person's heart in determining their actions. In this chapter, we discuss the interplay of attitudes and behaviors in the Christian life, in which the Bible claims God is active.

> Therefore, I urge you, brothers and sisters, in view of God's mercy, to offer your bodies as a living sacrifice, holy and pleasing to God—this is your true and proper worship. Do not conform to the pattern of this world, but be transformed by the renewing of your mind. Then you will be able to test and approve what God's will is—his good, pleasing and perfect will.
>
> Romans 12:1–2

Have you ever made a New Year's resolution? If you have, chances are good that you failed to keep your pledge. About half of resolution makers fail within six months of their commitment, and as time goes forward, the percentage of those succeeding only declines.[1] Of course, failing

---

1. Norcross, Mrykalo, and Blagys, "Auld Lang Syne."

to live up to a goal isn't limited to New Year's resolutions. Everyone has fallen short of a goal, whether it was something general like being a better person or something more specific like eating five servings of vegetables a day. Behavior is often inconsistent with attitude. Psychologists define an **attitude** *as a favorable or unfavorable evaluation of people, objects, ideas*—really anything. Attitudes can also be ambivalent. Before we delve into how attitudes work, it makes sense to ask why we even make such evaluations. As Russell Fazio, a leading attitude researcher, has written, "Attitudes simplify our day-to-day existence," and although "relatively thoughtless," they promote behaviors that direct us toward what will bring pleasure or away from what will produce pain.[2] Attitudes reflect our nature as meaning seekers (theme 5) in that they help us make sense of our surroundings and give guidance for what we should do.

Attitudes have three components: (1) *affect* (a feeling of liking or disliking), (2) *behavior* (a tendency to approach or avoid the thing evaluated), and (3) *cognition* (thoughts, including knowledge and beliefs that reinforce feelings).[3] When we act, we have thoughts and feelings. It makes sense that these would line up so that the *ABCs of attitude*—affect, behavior, and cognition—all point in the same direction. We should *do* what we *feel* and *think* positively about but avoid what we negatively evaluate. Yet many times our thoughts and feelings do not match our behaviors.

Looking at the relationship among the components of the ABCs of attitude, we can better see some of the reasons for people falling short of a goal. Consider a goal that people commonly fail to achieve: exercising more. Obviously, a person claiming this goal *feels* that exercising more is positive and *thinks* that exercise is important. Affect and cognition agree: exercise is good. Now "just do it." Likely a person's affect and cognition toward exercise have been favorable for some time (few people think that exercise, in principle, is bad). Yet the feelings and thoughts haven't resulted in a change in behavior.

Three Ways Attitudes Diverge from Behaviors

Social psychologists point to at least three reasons for this incongruity.[4] First, situations may make it difficult to follow through, as discussed in chapter 11. You may lack the time to exercise, have no exercise equipment, or feel social pressure to do something other than exercise (you like to exercise but your significant other doesn't, and you don't want to complicate that situation). Sec-

2. Fazio, "Attitudes as Object Evaluations," 629.
3. Eagly and Chaiken, "Attitude Structure and Function," 271.
4. Gilovich et al., *Social Psychology*, 238–43.

ond, your attitude toward exercise may be positive, but your attitude toward something else may be *more* positive. For example, you may like sitting around watching movies more than you like to exercise, so movies win and exercise loses. Finally, exercising more requires changing habits. *Not* exercising can be a well-practiced, habitual behavior. In addition, those things you already do instead of exercising more—whether they be reading, talking with friends, or daydreaming—are well practiced too. As we discussed in chapter 4 on consciousness, we often have little self-awareness of our ways, so changing them takes work. It's as if routine behavior has a momentum of its own that needs to be recognized, restrained, and redirected (depending on whether the habit is a good one or a bad one).

In the previous paragraph, we could substitute the words *Christian practice* for *exercise* and draw basically the same conclusions for Christians. In psychology, attitude is often measured through verbal response regarding how strongly something is liked or disliked. This same sort of measure is also reported in the Bible. Many passages in Scripture discuss instances of people speaking approvingly or disapprovingly of actions, others, or even God. Yet psychology and Scripture both show that one's words may not reflect actual beliefs; expressed attitudes don't always lead to enacted behaviors. Both Scripture and the history of Christianity clearly show that believers' intentions may differ from the behaviors one might expect.

Let's now examine more fully how situational influences, the relative strength and consistency of attitudes, and habits influence the relationship between attitudes and behaviors.

Situational Influences

As relational persons (theme 1), we are influenced by our situations, and particularly the presence of others. We care what people think about us, so what we say often depends on whom we're around. For example, standing up for and doing what you believe in is easier if you're standing with others who believe the same thing. Positive talk about exercise comes easily among those who exercise. If you believe differently, you may remain silent or moderate the view you express to fit the majority's opinion. Similarly, Christians may find it easier to live out their faith among fellow believers than before nonbelievers. For a biblical example, look at the apostle Paul calling out Peter for behaving like a gentile (people who are not Jewish) when among gentiles but following Jewish laws regarding food when around Jews (Gal. 2:11–13). Peter did this despite having been told in a vision from God that such rules were no longer required following Christ's life and death (Acts 10:9–16).

Strength and Consistency of Attitudes

A second factor that influences an attitude's impact on behavior is the relative strength of that attitude.[5] Like the person who believes exercise is good but remains seated, people may claim to love Jesus but not prioritize that belief in a way that impacts how they live. Speaking of the actions of a particular church in the book of Revelation, Jesus says, "I know your deeds, that you are neither cold nor hot. I wish you were either one or the other! So, because you are lukewarm—neither hot nor cold—I am about to spit you out of my mouth" (3:15–16). God wants the attitudes and behaviors of his people to align with his desires—people should be fully committed to living out God's will.

Attitudes are also weak predictors of behaviors when components of attitudes are inconsistent. For example, one may think that following God is a really good idea (positive *cognitive* appraisal) but may feel that following God is less enjoyable than following personal desires (negative *affective* appraisal). The A and C of the ABCs of attitude are inconsistent, so the B, or behavior, is likely to vary. The result can be **hypocrisy**: *when a person's beliefs and behaviors don't align; when what a person says differs from what they do.* In that situation, it's hard to know what a person really believes (if you're just asking them to tell you).

Jesus claimed that the actions of a hypocrite show that person's true loves, or in psychology's terms, which attitude they prioritize. Jesus said a lot about the hypocrisy of the Pharisees[6] and other teachers regarding Jewish regulations. Those groups talked a lot about what was required for a person to serve God, but Jesus said that what those people actually did was often for show—they wore exaggerated signs of their religious devotion on their clothes, basked in seats of honor at special occasions, and loved being recognized as religious leaders (Matt. 23:5–7). They were religious to earn praise, admiration, and (likely) money from people. The Pharisees may have had some desire to serve and glorify God, but their greater desire (stronger attitude) was to serve and glorify themselves. This type of hypocrisy is what psychologists call **moral hypocrisy**: *when someone wants to appear moral without all the cost of acting morally.*[7] The Pharisees wanted the impression of religious devotion and being respectable that comes from publicly giving physical goods to God. But they left the deeper, less publicly visible needs, such as caring for an "unimportant" widow in poverty, unmet. Jesus wasn't a fan of this, saying to the Pharisees, "You clean the outside of the cup and dish, but inside they are full of greed and self-indulgence. Blind

---

5. Fazio, "Multiple Processes," 83.

6. The Pharisees were members of a Jewish group made up of experts in the law, emphasizing religious ritual and purity, but they were condemned by Jesus for not practicing what they preached.

7. E.g., Batson and Thompson, "Why Don't Moral People Act Morally?," 54.

Pharisee! First clean the inside of the cup and dish, and then the outside also will be clean" (Matt. 23:25–26). Their outward behaviors indicated that their sinful attitude toward self-glorification overruled any righteous attitude toward glorifying God.

Habits

A third factor in the relationship between attitudes and behaviors is **habits**: *well-learned and well-rehearsed behaviors*. Habits are apparent in what people consistently do, even if they're not aware that they do it, because habits can be automatic and unconscious. This means that unless a person is consciously monitoring a habit, they may not know that an attitude and a habitual behavior aren't in line. Limited self-monitoring means limited agency (theme 4), making change difficult. Habits can be hard to break.[8]

The Pharisees and teachers of the law were definitely people of habit. They emphasized the "right" behaviors, such as ritual hand washing done several times a day, every day. Jesus was clear that these regulations couldn't earn God's favor, so the habits were practiced for the wrong reason. Jesus called the Pharisees and teachers of the law "blind guides," concerned with public displays of righteousness but ignoring God's deeper desires for his people: "justice, mercy and faithfulness" (Matt. 23:23–24). The Pharisees guided Jews in ways that wouldn't bring them toward God, all the while likely blind to their own habitual behaviors. Jesus condemned this hypocrisy, perhaps not just because it was wrong but with the hope that highlighting this habitual blind spot might change their behaviors.

Recombining Attitudes and Behaviors

When we become aware that our behaviors and attitudes clash, we tend to do something about it. We experience **cognitive dissonance**—*a feeling of conflict when there is a gap between our attitudes and our behaviors*—and often rationalize this difference, or perhaps change either our attitudes or our behaviors.[9] We don't like it when our behaviors contradict our beliefs. As meaning seekers, we're motivated to make sense of ourselves to ourselves—we try to understand the meaning of our behaviors and make them coherent with our attitudes and beliefs. Imagine someone passing a man holding a sign saying, "Hungry and homeless. Please help." They have concern for poor people but pass him by

---

8. Wood and Rünger, "Psychology of Habit," 292.

9. Festinger, *Theory of Cognitive Dissonance*, 1–3, says that people find it emotionally unpleasant to experience inconsistency between what they believe and how they act.

without helping. How do they justify this difference between their attitude and their action? They may look to their behavior to justify their attitude ("I can ignore this poor man because I've given money to the church"). Or they may modify their attitude to justify their behavior ("I'm not giving any money to this man; he should get a job instead of standing on a corner"). Either way, they are making a sensible story of what they did, reducing cognitive dissonance. How did the Pharisees react when Jesus exposed their hypocrisy? They resolved the conflict by rejecting Jesus's authority and therefore rejecting any claims he made (e.g., Matt. 12:23–24).

Of course, we're not so different from the Pharisees. Our attitudes and behaviors can be out of sync, sometimes without us even being aware. Psychologists have developed effective measures of unconscious attitudes that may reveal our hypocrisy in subtle behaviors. Research on racism, for example, demonstrates that we physically distance ourselves from things we don't like or respond more slowly or with greater caution toward things we fear, although we may not have conscious awareness of such actions.[10] In fact, even people who say they're not racist show racist behaviors. The behavior betrays the seemingly unknown attitude. Underlying attitudes can affect our behaviors without us knowing it, even if we don't know we have the attitudes!

This seems depressing: we believe one thing but do something else—sometimes without even knowing we're doing that. Obviously, attitudes and behaviors go together much of the time, but in instances where they don't, this pattern often reflects the limited agency of humans (theme 4). Even if people take on a new attitude and give it priority, they often find it difficult to change long-standing behavior, particularly if that behavior is a habit or happens without awareness.

Attitudes Affect Behaviors, and Vice Versa

Despite all this, it's tempting to think that attitudes are what really drive our behaviors (after all, we tend to think of ourselves as in charge of our behaviors). Psychology, however, has shown that the relationship between attitudes and behaviors is a two-way street. As David Myers and C. Nathan DeWall write, "Not only can we think ourselves into action, we can act ourselves into a way of thinking."[11] Behavior clearly affects attitude, as attitude can be changed and formed by what

10. See Dovidio et al., "On the Nature of Prejudice," for one of the seminal studies on the relationship between implicit and explicit responses.

11. Myers and DeWall, *Psychology*, 472. More thorough discussions of this relationship are given in most introductory psychology textbooks as well as in chapters on behaviors and attitudes in social psychology textbooks.

people do—that is, if you're able to get someone to say or do something, they tend to have a more positive appraisal of such behavior afterward.

Role-playing, for example, may change attitudes so that what we do becomes what we believe.[12] The more we act in a certain way or say particular things, the more those behaviors and words become part of us. Thinking back on some early teaching experiences, one of us recalls taking on the role of classroom leader and authority figure, not really believing he was either. He role-played being a professor based on stereotypes he had and models he had experienced from past professors. To begin, it felt unnatural—he acted as he thought he was supposed to act. Frankly, he even felt a little like a fraud whenever he messed up. Soon, however, he became more comfortable in the classroom, coming to believe he really was a professor. Taking on the role of a professor allowed an attitude shift to occur, as "doing becomes believing."[13] As his actual belief in being a professor became part of his identity, he was then able to modify his behavior from the stilted stereotype of a professor he had when he first started teaching.

The idea that behavior influences attitude relates to at least two biblical characteristics of human nature: our embodiment and our tendency toward meaning seeking (themes 3 and 5). Physical action changes our thoughts and our future actions, showing that we're not just disembodied minds. This being the case, righteous behavior should positively impact one's attitude toward God, while sinful behavior could make one more distant from God's concerns. Paul writes to Jesus's followers in Rome, "Just as you used to offer yourselves as slaves to impurity and to ever-increasing wickedness, so now offer yourselves as slaves to righteousness leading to holiness" (Rom. 6:19). As David Myers and Malcolm Jeeves write, "Throughout the Old and New Testaments, we are told that full knowledge of God comes through actively doing the Word. Faith is nurtured by obedience."[14] James K. A. Smith, commenting on our fundamental desires, writes, "Habits are inscribed in our heart through bodily practices and rituals that train the heart, as it were, to desire certain ends."[15] Behaviors that have trained the heart for serving oneself need to be altered to move desires toward worshiping and serving God.

Implications and Applications

Interactions between attitudes and behaviors discussed in this chapter show once again the limited agency of human beings. No doubt Ethan from the

12. Kelman, "Attitudes Are Alive and Well," 314.
13. Myers and DeWall, *Psychology*, 471.
14. Myers and Jeeves, *Psychology through the Eyes of Faith*, 195.
15. J. Smith, *Desiring the Kingdom*, 58.

introduction wanted his life to work out differently than it did. Yet simply setting our minds to do something may not work as we might hope—we don't
have unlimited freedom to do whatever we want. Both psychology's findings
and the human story told in Scripture show that wanting to act in a certain way
doesn't necessarily result in acting that way.

In the remainder of this section, we will focus on Christian faith and action.
The apostle Paul's letters in the New Testament contain lengthy passages to
churches about ways that Christians fail to live out their claim that Jesus is their
Lord, and he gives instruction on how to change those behaviors.[16] Yet Paul
himself continued to struggle with sin even after one of the most spectacular
conversion experiences recorded (the man was stopped in his tracks and struck
blind!).[17] In a broken world, sin continues (theme 2) and Christians struggle
to enact their beliefs. The prescription that Paul provides in this struggle is to
depend on God and fellow believers.

How can Christians go from saying "Jesus is Lord" to acting out that belief?
It's important to note first that faith isn't something people can earn, so it's different from other kinds of beliefs studied by psychologists (Eph. 2:8–9). In
addition, when people are considering how to live faithfully, Christianity makes
a unique claim: Christians don't have to do it alone. Paul assures the Roman
Christians that they are controlled not by a sinful core or nature but by "the
Spirit, if indeed the Spirit of God lives in you" (Rom. 8:9).[18] By contrast, psychology makes no claims about the role of God's Spirit in the lives of people.

It makes sense then that, elsewhere in the Bible, Paul (after encouraging
Christians to hold strongly to their faith and follow his instructions for faithful
living) prays this: "May our Lord Jesus Christ himself and God our Father, who
loved us and by his grace gave us eternal encouragement and good hope, encourage your hearts and strengthen you in every good deed and word" (2 Thess.
2:16–17). Paul is asking for God to *sanctify* those he is praying for. Paul is praying for Christians to increase in holiness—to "work out your salvation with
fear and trembling, for it is God who works in you to will and to act in order
to fulfill his good purpose" (Phil. 2:12–13). Again, humans have responsibility
for their behavior, but God is with them to uphold and forgive them when they
fail. Paul is calling for Christians to have an attitude readjustment that will then
result in more holy behavior.

16. First Corinthians by itself addresses failings that include infighting between believers within
the church, varieties of immorality, and abuses of the Lord's Supper.
17. Paul's conversion is in Acts 9; he discusses the struggle with sin in Rom. 7.
18. The apostle Paul wrote to the church at Ephesus, "For it is by grace you have been saved,
through faith—and this is not from yourselves, it is the gift of God—not by works, so that no one
can boast" (Eph. 2:8–9).

To change an established behavior (e.g., to go from not exercising to exercising regularly), a person first must become aware of that behavior. For Christians, one of the best antidotes to hypocritical behavior or failing to follow through on beliefs is to return to the Bible for a reality check. Are beliefs matching behavior? Instructions such as these from John the Evangelist help Christians tie together what they believe about Jesus and what they do: "If we claim to be without sin, we deceive ourselves and the truth is not in us. If we confess our sins, he is faithful and just and will forgive us our sins and purify us from all unrighteousness. If we claim we have not sinned, we make him out to be a liar and his word is not in us" (1 John 1:8–10). The limited agency of humans is painfully obvious when it comes to sinful behavior and a lack of awareness of personal hypocrisy and shortcomings. Because confession follows self-examination of one's thoughts and behaviors, Scripture calls God's people to a self-awareness that comes from a clear-eyed view of their state and what to do about it.

Theologian Cornelius Plantinga Jr. says that for a Christian to do their part in self-change, that person "needs to *attach* to Christ by prayer, sacraments, and listening to the Word of God,"[19] to experience God and the church. Plantinga writes, "Anybody who has tried to lose a bad habit . . . knows that good intentions and a few New Year's resolutions seldom do the trick. Similarly, to break the power of sin, a Christian needs far more than good feelings and songs about Jesus."[20] Psychologists show that attitudes become more potent when they are brought about by actual experience.[21] To effectively enact intended attitudes, it may be helpful to practice the action that would go with the attitude, making the action habitual. For example, if you believe reading Scripture is important for your spiritual development, make doing so a habit. A helpful way of doing this is to develop intentional plans for how you will implement your belief by identifying possible situations in which your belief could most easily result in action.[22]

Changing a habit is hard; it requires self-regulation. Strategies such as avoiding cues that prompt old habits can help bring success.[23] For example, if viewing pornography is a struggle for someone, avoiding places where pornography has been viewed before or setting up an internet filter that blocks websites containing pornography may help by reducing the prompts for viewing. As relational persons, we also need to recognize how others can help in our attempts to change. Involvement within a community of believers—the church—or with a

---

19. C. Plantinga, *Engaging God's World*, 93.
20. C. Plantinga, *Engaging God's World*, 92–93.
21. Regan and Fazio, "On the Consistency between Attitudes and Behavior."
22. Gollwitzer, "Implementation Intentions."
23. Wood and Neal, "New Look at Habits," 859–60.

study group or accountability partner (someone who will ask you about your success or failure to help you keep your commitment) may be very beneficial.

Though Christians fail, they are assured of forgiveness through God's grace. God is at work on behalf of people—Christ died to free Christ's followers from the burden and penalty of sin. Humans as responsible limited agents nevertheless should humbly repent, working to overcome sin and its consequences in creation and to redirect their desires. Yet, in the end, Christians need to recall that salvation is from God, not themselves: "For it is by grace you have been saved, through faith—and this is not from yourselves, it is the gift of God" (Eph. 2:8–9).

DISCUSSION QUESTIONS

1. Think of a belief or attitude you have that you typically don't act on. Which of the three reasons for attitudes diverging from behaviors may be the cause of this (it may be more than one)?

2. Recall a time when you experienced cognitive dissonance. How did you resolve this difference between your attitude and your behavior?

3. Identify a specific hypocrisy you have (or be bold and ask someone to point one out for you). Why does your behavior go against your attitude?

4. Some people describe themselves as "spiritual but not religious" regarding their faith—that is, they have a favorable affect and cognition toward God but reject the behavior associated with or expected of organized religion. Why, as meaning seekers, might people be drawn toward this stance? What is it about being an embodied human that may make this stance difficult to maintain?

5. C. S. Lewis writes in *Mere Christianity*, "Do not waste time bothering whether you 'love' your neighbor; act as if you did."[24] How might loving one another be better thought of as an *act* than as a *feeling*? How might one's actions change one's attitudes toward others?

24. Lewis, *Mere Christianity*, 65.

13

The *Real* You

Personality

▶ **SUMMARY:** Theories of personality all have something to say—either implicitly or explicitly—about the themes we have outlined in this book. Given that many of these theories contradict basic biblical assumptions about human beings, does this mean we should reject or abandon all aspects of each theory? Is there a straightforward alternative to these theories that is correctly grounded in a biblical understanding of persons and that is completely compatible with well-established psychological research? This chapter provides a critique of personality theories based on the key themes of this book and provides some direction to Christians grappling with alternatives to the "standard" personality models in psychology.

In the progress of personality, first comes a declaration of independence, then a recognition of interdependence.

Henry Van Dyke, quoted in *Born to be Happy*

Just as a body, though one, has many parts, but all its many parts form one body, so it is with Christ.

1 Corinthians 12:12

Here is a riddle: How is personality similar to yet different from hair? It's similar because it comes in many shades; it's different because you can't have more or less of it. Personality is not something that is measured as a quantity—it's measured as a quality. Just as there are many shades of personality, so there are many shades of theories *about* personality. Because of that fact, most introductory psychology textbooks contain a chapter on personality that focuses more on the various theories of personality and less on each person's unique set of qualities. While the various views that psychologists have about personality have become more similar over the years—with most psychologists accepting elements of several views—psychologists still approach the subject in diverse ways. This diversity comes from the fact that they have differing views about what defines and distinguishes human beings.

Consider how you might think about this case study presented by Christian psychologist John McDonagh.

> Lucy was referred to me for psychotherapy by her spiritual adviser. The reason for the referral was not clear in Lucy's mind; she was incensed that anyone would tell her that she needed to see a psychologist. It soon became apparent, however, that Lucy was filled with overwhelming rage, and that this rage was ruining her life. In particular, she felt betrayed by nearly every person with whom she was intimate. Most of this rage was being directed against her husband. Lucy believed that it was he, and not she, who "needed to be straightened out," and then her life would be fine.[1]

Why is Lucy this way? Is her anger an inborn trait, or has it developed over time? Can she change this characteristic, or is she destined to be an angry person all her life? All **theories of personality** *attempt to explain how and why each person—such as Lucy—is unique compared to any other person and the extent to which that person's qualities can predict how they will act over most of their life.*[2] The explanations for these differences derive primarily from how each theory understands our biology, internal motives, mental operations, and experiences. Of course, all personality theories acknowledge that, as Henry Murray notes, "every person is in some respects (a) like *all* other persons; (b) like *some* other persons; and (c) like *no* other person,"[3] but the emphasis in personality theory is understandably on the latter two. As psychologist Gordon Allport noted many years ago about personality theorists, "We emphasize the fact that the outstanding characteristic of man is his individuality. He is a unique creation of the forces of nature. There was never a person just like him, and there never will be again."[4] This emphasis on individuality and unique qualities is one of the central notions of most theories of personality.

1. McDonagh, "Working through Resistance," 200.
2. Myers and DeWall, *Psychology*, 517.
3. Quoted in Van Leeuwen, "Personality Theorizing," 174.
4. Allport, *Patterns and Growth in Personality*, 4.

Before evaluating the major personality theories based on this book's biblical themes, we provide a summary of them here.

A Brief Overview of Theories

Roughly in order of their historical development, the major theories about personality include psychoanalytic, behavioristic,[5] trait, humanistic, and cognitive-behavioral approaches.

Psychoanalytic Approach

Sigmund Freud emphasized our biological and unconscious instincts for survival—contained within a personality component he called the id. Humans have additional mental structures called the ego, which guides conscious and rational thinking, and the superego, which regulates moral decision making. The relative "strength" of these mental structures and early developmental experiences dictate the growth of unique qualities. The largely unconscious conflicts that occur between these components and our inadequate attempts to resolve them ultimately lead to dysfunctional personalities or psychological disorders. There are more contemporary versions of psychoanalysis within the larger psychodynamic approach to personality; they differ from Freud's view in many ways, but they retain the emphasis on our unconscious motivations and our often "distorted" mental functions. From the psychoanalytic approach, Lucy's anger may be caused by repressed memories or possibly an unchecked id (i.e., underdeveloped ego or superego).

Behavioristic Approach

The behavioristic approach suggests that people have very few unique characteristics at birth, and it de-emphasizes inborn individual differences. Behaviorists such as John Watson and B. F. Skinner emphasized that our behavior follows very lawful and predictable patterns and that the social environment shapes individual differences. As outlined in chapter 6, behaviorists believe that the situational "associations" we experience and the effect of consequences (i.e., rewards and punishments) ultimately determine our personality. Over time,

---

5. Many introductory textbooks on psychology do not include the behaviorist school of thought in the list of personality theories because this approach does not give a great deal of credence to the very notion of having a stable, internally guided personality. However, we include behaviorism here because it does have something to say on the topic of personality, and it is helpful to contrast it with other approaches.

these tendencies become strong habits that can be very hard to change—at least without extensive and long-term changes in consequences. Watson once suggested that it is easier to "change a zebra's stripes" than a person's personality.[6] A key element to this view is that social and environmental influences determine a person's personality in a passive way because we are simply response-generating machines. Therefore, Lucy's anger is a product of social consequences that subtly reward her for being angry—such as successfully getting others to do what she wants whenever she is angry with them. Altering her social environment and the rewards and punishments she experiences will eventually lead to changes in her personality.

Trait Approach

The trait approach is less interested in explaining why personality characteristics develop and more interested in simply characterizing and measuring (i.e., using paper-and-pencil personality inventories) the unique traits that we have. It operates on the assumption that traits are mostly inborn or genetic or that early child experiences set traits in place for an extended period—perhaps for life. So Lucy was simply born angry; she might manage it, but she will probably always be a somewhat angry individual. By measuring her angry tendencies, she might be able to predict or manage her anger better.

Humanistic Approach

Abraham Maslow and Carl Rogers were the primary figures behind the humanistic approach. This approach opposed Freud's more negative view of human nature as well as the behaviorist emphasis on passively influenced behavior. Humanistic psychologists stressed the importance of conscious choices (i.e., free will) and the basic human goodness within each person. As the theory was further developed, a good deal of emphasis was placed on individual fulfillment and increased self-esteem as a means toward personal growth. In this view, Lucy is not an inherently angry person. Instead, negative messages, a lack of acceptance from others, and a lack of self-acceptance led to these angry tendencies. Only Lucy can decide to change, and she needs to reach inside herself to find the good person she really is.

Cognitive-Behavioral Approach

The cognitive movement stresses reasoning or thinking processes as the primary focus of personality development. Our mental schemas, or thinking

6. *Corsini Encyclopedia*, 1757.

patterns, that develop over time (by way of genes, social environment, and patterns of behavior) shape how we think about our environment, how others think about us, and how we think about ourselves. Self-improvement is possible within this view, but it is challenging because these thought patterns become ingrained, so change is difficult on our own. While cognitive psychologists disagree with the somewhat simplistic mechanisms of the behaviorists and are more likely to stress internal mental processes, most still believe that, ultimately, there are external causes for every action (i.e., actions are determined).[7] Perhaps Lucy has developed an external locus of control—a thinking pattern that suggests she cannot control her life outcomes, which can lead to a sense of helplessness. Lucy can change her angry personality if she first corrects her thinking patterns.

Critiquing Personality Theories

Christians often wonder how to respond to these theories. Do we decide based on research support alone, dismiss them all as potentially dangerous since some elements of these theories seem to contradict elements of Christian thought, or pick and choose parts of each approach based on what we do or don't like about the theory? A good starting point in grappling with these questions is to describe the primary strengths and weaknesses of all the theories in relation to the biblical themes concerning human nature. Analyzing all the theories to see how they match each theme would take several more chapters, so we have provided a concise table (see table 2) that shows how each theory does or does not emphasize a particular theme.[8]

Keep in mind that this table provides only an abbreviated summary of views, so many subtleties of these theories are lost. The column showing each theory's emphasis on relation to God is mostly focused on how that theory describes our tendency to explain aspects of the world through religious explanations, since none of the theories describe a relationship with God.

Greatest Strengths

All these theories capture important truths about human nature—or they would not have lasted so long. As table 2 shows, each theory contains some

7. Seligman et al., "Navigating into the Future," 123.

8. The column under the heading "Relational persons, relating to God" in table 2 does not actually explain how each theory describes our relationship to God but rather states the emphasis each theory places on the human need to understand a deity or some deeper religious or moral principle.

TABLE 2

	Relational persons, relating to			Broken (evil)	Embodied	Responsible agents (free will)	Meaning seekers
	God	Others	Creation				
Psychoanalytic approach[a]	moderate	low	moderate	high	moderate	very low	moderate
Behavioristic approach	none	none	high	neutral	moderate	none	none
Trait approach	none	none	high	neutral	high	none	none
Humanistic approach	moderate	moderate	low	low	low	high	high
Cognitive-behavioral approach	low	low	moderate	neutral	moderate	low	moderate
Emphasis in this book	high	high	high	high	high	moderate	high

a. The reader should keep in mind that newer psychodynamic theories differ in many ways from psychoanalytic thought—particularly as it pertains to relations with others. However, full discussion of all these differences is beyond the scope of this chapter.

agreement with scriptural themes about human nature. So we believe that Christians should not abandon these theories but should build on their strengths and work to reorient their weaknesses.

Not surprisingly, given the strong materialistic emphasis in psychology, the strongest aspect of personality theories—except for the humanistic approach—is their emphasis on our embodied nature (theme 3). As we discussed earlier, a biblical perspective emphasizes our embodied nature and the limitations that come with that existence, so Christians should be willing to embrace these perspectives. In the case of Lucy, we cannot ignore the role that her embodied traits play in her angry tendencies. In the past, some Christians favored a humanistic approach because it downplays embodiment, but we feel that this is actually a shortcoming. At the same time, we also need to recognize that other approaches have overemphasized this aspect of our being without proper consideration of our relationality, our brokenness, our responsible agency, and our desire to seek meaning.

One of the greatest strengths of the humanistic approach is its emphasis on our meaning seeking nature (theme 5). This approach has long emphasized that humans are motivated by more than a reduction of pain or a need to survive and that we seek purpose and meaning for our existence. There is also a growing trend within contemporary cognitive-behavioral approaches to emphasize this meaning seeking tendency,[9] so we feel that personality theory is moving in the right direction in this regard.

A strength of the behavioristic, trait, and cognitive-behavioral approaches is their adherence to scientific investigation. As discussed earlier, Christians need not fear scientific investigation in psychology. As Alan Tjeltveit states, "In creation, God made a relatively orderly world and gave human beings minds capable of grasping that order fairly well. Because we obtain from psychological science knowledge about human beings, about human problems, and about effective methods to resolve human problems, Christians should pay attention to science."[10] Too often Christians have been captivated by various elements of personality theories that *appeared* consistent with biblical themes but did not stand up to scientific scrutiny—and did not match biblical perspectives as well as they appeared. This is particularly true of some elements of humanistic and psychoanalytic approaches that were not well supported by contemporary research. For example, psychologist Martin Seligman and colleagues summarize the mixed outcomes for studies on psychoanalytic ideas by stating, "Even though recent experimental research has provided increasingly strong and detailed information about the importance of unconscious processes . . . , 100 years of psychoanalytic practice aimed at uncovering repressed childhood conflicts has failed to provide convincing evidence of efficacy."[11] Several researchers have likewise discredited many claims of humanistic psychologists suggesting that improving self-esteem and self-acceptance would lead to improvements in a variety of problem behaviors.[12] So Christians should be just as careful in embracing ideas that have not been well supported by science as they are in embracing ideas that are incompatible with biblical images of human nature.

Of course, Christians also need to be a prophetic voice within the discipline and speak against the extreme empiricism (i.e., science can discover all truth) and reductionism that have been prevalent in the field. Tjeltveit balances his earlier support for science by saying, "Many psychologists claim we know only through science. That reflects a certain understanding of human beings, one not derived from scientific research."[13] In other words, the assumption that we can understand people only by way of scientific research is itself a nonscientific statement and reflects a bias on the part of psychologists not to consider any

9. See discussion of recent trends in cognitive science in N. Smith, *Current Systems in Psychology*, 94.
10. Tjeltveit, "Faith, Psychotherapy, and Christian Counseling," 251.
11. Seligman et al., "Navigating into the Future," 123.
12. See Dawes, *House of Cards*, 234–51.
13. Tjeltveit, "Faith, Psychotherapy, and Christian Counseling," 253.

other sources of knowledge (i.e., Scripture, direct revelation, or guidance by the Holy Spirit).

Greatest Weaknesses

In addition to some weaknesses alluded to above, personality theories often fall short because they do not consider key aspects of human nature.

EXCESSIVE INDIVIDUALISM

A major concern, in our view, with the psychoanalytic, behavioristic, cognitive, and trait approaches is that they place so little value on the central theme of being relational persons—with others (theme 1). The humanistic approach places slightly greater emphasis on interpersonal relationships, but even here the primary focus is on internal and individual psychological processes. As Christian psychologist Paul Vitz suggests, "When [humanistic psychologist] Carl Rogers titles his well-known book *On Becoming a Person*, he is simply wrong. Instead he has written a book on becoming an individual, in particular, an autonomous, self-actualizing, independent individual. An individual is created by separating from others, by breaking, by concentrating psychological energy and effect on the self instead of on God and others."[14]

What are the consequences of this emphasis on the individual? The tendency within personality theory is to misunderstand the way in which our central characteristics are very much the product of reciprocal relationships. This overly individualistic focus may be one of modern psychology's greatest shortcomings. The corrective for this individualism, as Vitz suggests, is a renewed emphasis on a **covenant theory** of personality. Vitz contends that *when a person enters into a covenant with God and others, and then surrenders to God and others, they truly become a flourishing person and have true freedom, aligning with a biblical view of personhood* (theme 1).

> The central psychological principle here is that personality is developed into its highest form through loving others. It is through agape: through serving others—even unto death—that the Christian personality grows and reaches its highest development. The very idea of commitment, of deep caring for another, of being bonded to another, is the exact opposite of so much of today's humanistic psychology. Today nothing must hinder the growth of the ego; nothing—no one—must restrict the autonomy of the individual. Perhaps James Bond of movie fame is the best example of this ideal—a man without any bonds with anyone. He appears

14. Vitz, "Christian Theory of Personality," 207.

to have no mother or father, no true friends; and certainly the whole idea of his relationship with women is to avoid commitment.[15]

The individualistic nature of personality theory may have led to as many ills as cures for social problems. For example, one contemporary psychologist has suggested that the long-standing emphasis on individual self-fulfillment has led to an "epidemic of narcissism" (e.g., excessive self-love), which in turn leads to more social ills, not fewer.[16]

We note that focusing on internal and individual psychological qualities needs to be a central part of the discipline of psychology—especially personality theory. But the problem in the past has been that this emphasis has centered primarily on the individual, devoid of substantial consideration of the socially embedded nature of individuals. Fortunately, many newer studies coming from developmental psychology, social psychology, and even neuropsychology point to the value of reciprocal and deep relationships. This emphasis on relationality has also impacted a growing movement in psychology called positive psychology, which seeks to promote human strengths, including relationship formation.[17]

DETERMINISM

The psychoanalytic,[18] behavioristic, and trait approaches are all strongly deterministic. In psychoanalysis, we are determined by our unconscious impulses and past. In behaviorism, we are determined by our associations, contingencies, and social environment. In the trait approach, we are determined by genetics, biology, and very early experiences that generate relatively fixed or unchanging personality traits. The cognitive approach is less deterministic, and some within this approach suggest that we may indeed possess agency.[19] However, only the humanistic approach places great value on self-directed and freely chosen behavior.

Because humanistic personality theory recognizes our freedom of choice and responsibility, some Christians favor it. But we want to issue a caution not to ignore the flip side of the coin: our agency is *limited*. In fact, one of the significant failures of humanistic psychology is that it overemphasizes our potential to choose, seeing it as nearly limitless. On the other hand, the shortcoming of

---

15. Vitz, "Christian Theory of Personality," 205.

16. See Twenge and Campbell, *Narcissism Epidemic*, 9.

17. Bolt, *Pursuing Human Strengths*, 179–98.

18. Some feel that Freud was actually quite conflicted on this point, but he still gave little room for human choice. See discussion in Morea, *In Search of Personality*, 9–34.

19. Seligman et al., "Navigating into the Future," 123.

the other approaches is their adherence to absolute determinism, which robs human beings of their responsibility and opportunity for change (theme 4).

On a positive note, other voices within the field of psychology are providing welcome ideas regarding agency. In their intriguing review article, "Navigating into the Future or Driven by the Past," Seligman and colleagues introduce the notion of **prospection**, *which is the mental representation of possible futures* (i.e., the opposite of retrospection, or reflecting on the past). They feel that prospection is the best way to think about free will, and they speculate that

> viewing behavior as driven by the past was a powerful framework that helped create scientific psychology, but accumulating evidence in a wide range of areas of research suggests a shift in framework, in which navigation into the future is seen as a core organizing principle of animal and human behavior.
> . . . The past is not a force that drives [humans and intelligent animals] but a resource from which they selectively extract information about the prospects they face. . . . Prospection casts new light on why subjectivity is part of consciousness, [and] what is "free" and "willing" in "free will."[20]

Seligman and colleagues indicate that psychoanalytic, behavioristic, and cognitive approaches have so emphasized humans as being driven by past events that this focus has led to a deterministic dogma within psychology. In other words, psychologists have come to believe that we are who we are entirely because of our unchangeable past. It's not that Seligman and colleagues feel the past is irrelevant, but they believe that our ability to self-consciously (i.e., subjectively) reflect about future possibilities frees us to consider alternatives and to make choices based on long-term values and goals. This way to understand human action is much more compatible with the limited agency view found in Scripture. Less deterministic perspectives, such as Seligman's, are very positive developments in the field of personality, and Christians can help shape psychological thinking away from a purely deterministic view of the person.

MISUNDERSTANDING OUR MORAL TENDENCIES

Most personality theorists are relatively silent on moral tendencies, or they view humans as neither inherently good nor inherently evil; humans are simply responding to the environment in a way that matches their genetic and mental capabilities. Freud's emphasis on the very self-serving nature of humans is a notable exception. In his view, our basic survival motives—primarily sexual and aggressive urges—are directed toward self-satisfaction without regard for the

---

20. Seligman et al., "Navigating into the Future," 119.

needs of others. Of course, he felt that the ego and the superego could overrule these drives but that our primary motives are still directed toward selfish needs. Secular authors and religious authors have both noted the parallels between Freud's notion and the idea of sin.[21] In summarizing Freud's position, Richard Webster quotes from Freud's description of the unconscious mind, "in which all that is evil in the human mind is contained as a predisposition." Freud goes on to suggest that these evil predispositions are of the "crudest and most forbidden kind."[22]

While Freud's view may be an important balance to the humanistic emphasis on human goodness, and there certainly are parallels to Christian theology, this comparison to the theology of sin is only superficial. In Freud's view, this "evil in the human mind" is biologically based, unconscious, confined primarily to the id, and managed by social restraint through the ego and the superego—but never ultimately cured. This contrasts significantly with both the biblical picture of our brokenness and the possibility for reconciliation with God. Theologians Richard Plantinga and colleagues summarize Scripture's depiction of sinfulness this way: "If *shalom* in the Hebrew Bible refers to the vital flourishing of all things in right relationship with one another, then sin can be described as that which corrupts, distorts, and taints that universal flourishing. Where obedience is called for, disobedience reigns. Where faithfulness to God and other human beings ought to be the norm, faithlessness shatters our lives. Where freedom ought to be used for the benefit of others, the shackles of selfish desires, slothful inaction, and broken relationships tie human beings down."[23] In this view, sin affects the whole person—reason, emotions, moral tendencies, and relationships—not just one aspect of personality, as Freud's approach suggests. Sin is not just a tendency requiring restraint but a pervasive disfigurement of the image of God. Ultimate healing from sin comes in a restoration of shalom and relationship to God by way of the sacrifice of Jesus Christ. Any biblically grounded personality theory must recognize the inherent goodness created in humans, the corruption that now exists, and, by God's grace, the possibility for restored goodness.

The opposite of Freud's dark view is the much more positive view of human potential found within humanistic psychology. While most Christians agree that this human goodness was present in God's original good creation, we cannot ignore the real presence of brokenness. Any approach to understanding the person that ignores the true brokenness of individuals (theme 2) and the

21. Morea, *In Search of Personality*, 9–34.
22. Webster, *Why Freud Was Wrong*, 326.
23. R. Plantinga, Thompson, and Lundberg, *Introduction to Christian Theology*, 195.

distorted nature of our social being will ultimately fail to fully capture human behavior. Not only our individual nature but also the larger family, social, and economic structures that influence the personality are distorted.

A Faith-Based Response to Theories of Personality

It's an easy task to point out the flaws in each of these theories, but it's another thing to propose an alternative. If many elements of these theories conflict with a biblical picture of human nature, should we scrap them all and come up with a completely new and uniquely Christian personality theory? Certainly this is a tempting approach, and some Christian psychologists have put forth very interesting theories worthy of our consideration.[24] However, as psychologist Mary Stewart Van Leeuwen has suggested, developing alternative approaches is difficult because personality theories operate at several levels of detail or focus (i.e., from specific individual traits to broad themes of human function).[25] In addition, as we have alluded to at several points in this chapter, Christians don't always get it right either. Sometimes Christians have downplayed our embodiment, been too individualistic, become overly focused on complete freedom of choice (or the opposite), or ignored our relationship to creation. Van Leeuwen argues that "we [Christians] deceive ourselves if we believe that our social, cultural, and theological backgrounds will make no difference in the way, and the degree to which, we use Scripture as a source of control beliefs for personality theorizing."[26]

At other times, Christian psychologists have been quick to affiliate with one of the major personality theories without properly weighing the underlying perspectives and carefully examining the scientific evidence. As Malcolm Jeeves states in highlighting Van Leeuwen's concerns, "She pointed out the danger of selecting one of several personality theories currently in the psychological marketplace and seeking to baptize it with Christian orthodoxy."[27] Equally dangerous is the temptation to engage in "religious imperialism," as Stanton Jones has cautioned against, where we impose religious dogma that simply overrules all scientific ideas.[28] Rather, Jones calls for a dialogue in which Christian psychologists propose tentative models about human personality and behavior that are based on Christian **control beliefs**: *foundational commitments or presuppositions*

24. See Burke, *Man and Mind*.
25. Van Leeuwen, "Personality Theorizing," 172.
26. Van Leeuwen, "Personality Theorizing," 172.
27. Jeeves, *Human Nature at the Millennium*, 153.
28. Jones, "Constructive Relationship," 195.

that are assumed on the basis of faith.[29] However, Jones feels these models must still be put to the test of scientific scrutiny. He also maintains that a pluralistic discussion (i.e., coming from diverse worldviews) needs to take place regarding the utility and value for psychological practice of Christian models about personality.

Therefore, developing a cohesive theory that is biblically grounded, is consistent with scientific findings, and has practical value is a difficult task for Christians engaged in psychology. In its place, we hope to present a set of control beliefs that one can use to guide thinking about contemporary personality theory. While we feel that these control beliefs are biblically sound, our goal is to present ideas that can be considered useful within mainstream psychology and not just for Christians alone.

Each Person Is Unique—but We Are Also Related

While we believe that each person is unique, we also note that Scripture passages stress the importance of sameness. These passages emphasize the value of losing one's identity and becoming more like Christ. For example, passages such as Romans 8:29, 1 Corinthians 4:16, and 1 John 3:1–3 suggest that Christians should be like Christ, be conformed to Christ, and even be imitators of the apostle Paul, so one might assume that Christians should be more like one another and more like Christ.

While Christ's followers are to conform to Christ's character according to the "fruit of the Spirit" (e.g., love, joy, kindness; see Gal. 5:22–23), Scripture also points to a diversity of qualities and characteristics and celebrates differences. Passages such as Romans 12 and 1 Corinthians 12 speak about the variety of gifts given to Christians and the diversity of abilities each person has and the various roles each person plays within the body of believers. This diversity is seen even in the unique personalities of the apostles (e.g., Peter, with strong emotional reactions; Paul, the thoughtful theologian), which all served the kingdom of God. So, much the way psychologists have noted that each person is in some ways like everyone else and in other ways like no one else, Scripture reflects this same perspective. This balanced view of similarities and differences also points to the care and respect that Christians should show to others who seem very different from themselves, since differences among people are valued in Scripture.

Despite our individual nature, we can never fully understand our individuality apart from the context of relationality. The individual gifts described in the

---

29. See Wolterstorff, *Reason within the Bounds of Religion.*

New Testament are always talked about in the context of the unified body of Christ. As Christian psychologists Barrett McRay, Mark Yarhouse, and Richard Butman state, "Costly discipleship and sustained altruism can be nurtured and developed only within healthy communities that know how to balance affirmation with accountability and the priestly and prophetic witness of the truly committed."[30]

Applying these grand thoughts to the case of Lucy, we can say that she does not need to act like everyone else and that others should respect her individual qualities. She should develop and nurture the characteristics that are unique to her and then seek to utilize them for something (or someone) other than herself. For example, channeling her natural tendency to be angry into constructive action could turn Lucy into an assertive leader. At the same time, she should work to conform herself to the basic qualities and the fruit of the Spirit that Christ exemplified in his life. She can accomplish this only when she immerses herself in a positive community and works to build strong relationships with people who accept her but are also willing to hold her accountable.

Personalities Are Stable—but Change Is Possible

Personalities do become relatively stable—meaning they remain consistent over time—because of the influence of biology, environment, and our own patterns of acting. There is no escaping the fact that some of Lucy's personality traits may be inborn, since research suggests that approximately 50 percent of personality "variation" can be "explained" by our biological inheritance.[31] There is also no escaping the fact that environment strongly molds our personalities for better or worse. As McRay, Yarhouse, and Butman state when discussing personality disorders, "Careful developmental histories of persons struggling with personality disorders suggest that significant others, whether peers or adults, were largely absent or disinterested."[32] They also point out that problem personality traits become harder to change as people get older. But these same authors recognize that Christians simply cannot fall into a deterministic mindset when thinking about personality. They contend that both research and Scripture hold out hope for change for very difficult personalities, even though that work "can be hard and demanding."[33] The person must desire this change (i.e., express agency), but they also need positive relationships found in families, supportive communities, or church families.

30. McRay, Yarhouse, and Butman, *Modern Psychopathologies*, 300.
31. Tellegen et al., "Personality Similarity."
32. McRay, Yarhouse, and Butman, *Modern Psychopathologies*, 297.
33. McRay, Yarhouse, and Butman, *Modern Psychopathologies*, 299.

We Are Broken—but We Are Also Redeemable

We cannot assume that if Lucy reaches deep into her own mind, releases some of her inner conflicts, or places herself in a better environment that she will automatically become the type of good person that others would like her to be. Even though these activities may be useful in understanding her tendencies, recognizing the reality of sin means recognizing that her rational mind, her moral thinking, the seemingly good people around her, and her good intentions can all be subtly twisted by sin. As noted earlier, in addition to our own inner sinful tendencies, we must contend with our broken bodies and brains, and we regularly encounter a broken world. How should Lucy counteract these distortions of God's good world from within and from others? Not by self-exploration alone but by immersing herself in positive communities (for Christians, this likely involves a healthy church community), by conforming her will to the examples set by Christ and other positive role models, and by developing regular practices and habits that cultivate character (for Christians, a unique Christian character[34]).

Personality Direction Depends on Meaning

A Christian approach to personality theory should emphasize that human beings are designed to be more than "satisfaction maximizers" or "pain minimizers," as some behaviorists have emphasized. Lucy may be influenced by the physical, mental, internal, and social factors from the past, but she also can "prospect," or think about, future possibilities. When we imagine future actions, we set priorities based on what we have come to value. As both psychology and Scripture suggest, we are driven to understand the meaning of perceptions and memories, why we do what we do, and our overall purpose. We then direct our behaviors based on these purposes and priorities.

Having positive purposes and priorities leads to a healthy personality. As Seligman and colleagues state in relation to personality disorders, "There is growing evidence that a strong sense of meaning and purpose . . . is highly protective against psychopathology."[35] So Lucy needs to reflect on the basic values and life goals she has, what is most valuable and meaningful in her life, and what her ultimate purpose is. This will not make her anger vanish instantly, but it can help her choose patterns of living that can shape her personality over time.

34. See N. Wright, *After You Believe*.
35. Seligman et al., "Navigating into the Future," 135.

Summing Up: A Christian Personality Theory?

We have not tried to present a single, unified personality theory that can call itself uniquely Christian, and the ideas we presented cannot be called uniquely Christian because psychologists from many perspectives could easily find agreement with elements of these control beliefs. We have also tried to avoid a simple eclectic approach common among many contemporary personality theorists—in which they pick and choose parts of different theories that fit nicely with their own view without regard for whether they form a cohesive whole. What we have tried to do is put forth basic human nature tendencies that hopefully hang together to develop the beginnings of a cohesive personality theory that might be useful in everyday explanations of behavior.

Hopefully we have provided a set of principles that can help you think more about your own personality and the personality of others. So this is certainly not the end of any discussion on what shapes our personalities but only the beginning of your ongoing quest to understand the real you!

——————————— DISCUSSION QUESTIONS ———————————

1. Are there times you feel the same as everyone else? Are there times you feel very unique? Which of these experiences do you prefer?
2. Are there personality traits you possess that you greatly value? What do you think are the origins of these traits—your parents, your upbringing, your unconscious, your relationships, your own choices?
3. Is it better to simply accept and like yourself just the way you are, or is it important to change who you are?
4. Are there personality traits in yourself or others that you have seen remain the same over a long period of time? Are there personality traits that you have seen change over time?
5. If you took Paul Vitz's covenant theory of personality seriously, how would this influence the way you might change your own personality?
6. Have you ever contemplated your long-term life goals—not only career or family goals but also goals for the type of person you would like to be? How might you determine if these goals are right for you?

14

In Search of Normality

Psychological Disorders

SUMMARY: You might think that normality would be a simple concept, but it turns out to be hard to define. Perhaps, as one author has suggested, normal is just a setting on your dryer. This chapter focuses on the difficulty in defining both normality and psychological disorder and on how God views individuals with psychological disorders. We also explore whether mental disorders should be considered spiritual, biological, social, or willful problems of living. We emphasize the themes of embodiment, relational persons, and responsible limited agents to explore the causes of disorder as well as how we care for one another when we struggle with disorders.

In depression you cannot imagine that anyone would really love you, want to be there for you, find you still worthy of friendship and love. Truly darkness seemed my only companion. Of this I was quite convinced.

Kathryn Greene-McCreight, *Darkness Is My Only Companion*

Ah, Lord, my prayers are dead, my affections dead, and my heart is dead. But thou art a living God and I bear myself upon thee.

English preacher William Bridge (1600–1670), quoted in Kathryn Greene-McCreight, *Darkness Is My Only Companion*

The following is from a personal story placed anonymously on a public website called Mental Health America: Real Lives.

My first marriage was doomed from the start. I knew three months into the marriage that it would not last. But being a God-fearing Christian, I stayed in the marriage until my wife betrayed me for another man. I was faithful in my marriage. But during the 12 years I was married I tried to kill myself at least four times.

On the job, my depression cost me promotions as I could not get a handle on my emotions. I would be up and down in my feelings. I could not control them. So I would get passed over for promotions or turn them down because I knew I would fail. The last suicide attempt I had was three years ago in April. I was working and wanted to hurt myself really badly. I told a fellow supervisor what I was thinking and was called into the office where I had a confrontation with my managers. They wanted me to get help. I am thankful for that confrontation. It saved my life.

I did not have insurance and the local area had few resources for the uninsured or under insured. I was able to get into a local mental health facility that really changed my thinking. I will never forget my counselor, Kristin.

And then there are those in the Christian community who feel mental illness is a spiritual problem, not a real problem. My wife went to the leaders in my faith and told them how I was and that I was in really bad shape. Not one of them approached or cared to see how I was. They avoided me at all costs. Why? I am not [a] mind reader, but all I can think of is they believed I was spiritually damaged goods in God's view. I was not worthy of being spoken to, prayed with or any other type of help. I was shunned instead of helped.

I still have many ups and downs. I am married to an incredible woman who loves me despite my shortcomings. Mental illness is that—an illness. Help yourself. Help others.[1]

Every person's story of psychological disorder is unique, but most stories share two common features: very personal suffering and disrupted relationships. The story you just read describes significant pain and the social and personal issues that often accompany psychological disorders.

Kathryn Greene-McCreight describes how her depression created isolation from others and from God: "I am not necessarily sad when I am depressed. I am not necessarily 'down.' Sometimes I just have a gnawing, overwhelming sense of grief, with no identifiable cause. I grieve my loved ones as though they were dead and contemplate what their funerals would be like. I feel completely alone; darkness is my only companion."[2] She goes on to say, "In the midst of an impenetrable depression, one is often unable to sense the presence of God

1. Anonymous. Website no longer available.
2. Greene-McCreight, *Darkness Is My Only Companion*, 29.

at all. Sometimes all one can feel is the complete absence of God, one's utter abandonment by God, the ridiculousness of the very notion of a loving and merciful God. This cuts to the heart of the Christian and challenges everything she believes about the world and about herself. But if one is depressed, one should not expect to feel otherwise."[3]

Greene-McCreight feels that her struggles echo those of Job in the Old Testament, who struggled to understand his own suffering:

> I loathe my very life;
>   therefore I will give free rein to my complaint
>   and speak out in the bitterness of my soul.
> I say to God: Do not declare me guilty,
>   but tell me what charges you have against me.
> Does it please you to oppress me,
>   to spurn the work of your hands,
>   while you smile on the plans of the wicked? (Job 10:1–3)

Christians have struggled to understand psychological difficulties. Historically, people of faith have emphasized personal responsibility and free choice as well as the power of God's Spirit to transform lives. People who have never experienced such difficulties may find it hard to understand why someone with these struggles doesn't just "get over it." So Christians have often leaned toward explanations that involve a person's spiritual journey—which may account for the reaction of the church in the story told at the beginning of the chapter. At the same time, there is greater understanding that brain function plays a critical role in psychological disorders. If you were to ask many people of faith why some individuals become clinically depressed,[4] they would typically offer two distinct possibilities: (1) the person likely has some form of chemical imbalance, or (2) the person has willfully chosen a path that is not entirely virtuous, moral, or faithful. While these explanations contain an element of truth, we believe the situation is more complicated.

What Defines *Disorder*?

The American Psychiatric Association's *Diagnostic and Statistical Manual of Mental Disorders* (DSM-5) defines **psychological disorders** *as consisting of three key*

3. Greene-McCreight, *Darkness Is My Only Companion*, 93.
4. A condition in which someone experiences at least some of these symptoms for at least two or more weeks: depressed mood, loss of interest or pleasure, weight loss, insomnia, psychomotor agitation, fatigue, feelings of worthlessness, diminished ability to concentrate, recurrent thoughts of death. American Psychiatric Association, *Diagnostic and Statistical Manual*, 160–61.

elements: (1) disturbances in behavior, thoughts (cognition), or emotional regulation and (2) significant personal distress or impairment that (3) stems from an internal dysfunction (biological, psychological, or both)—not the typical response to a difficult event (e.g., loss of a job).[5] Although this manual is certainly useful because it can guide both treatment and research, it implies a greater understanding of disorders than might actually be the case. The reality is that while we know a lot more about causes and treatments than we did fifty years ago, psychiatrists and psychologists still don't understand all the causes in individual cases. In addition, many controversies and debates remain about this "medical model," in which psychological disorders are described in the same way we might describe physical injuries or diseases. Some critics have raised concerns that a diagnosis can become a crutch or a self-fulfilling prophesy—because people begin to act in ways that are consistent with their diagnosis.

People of faith often have additional questions and concerns. If psychological disorders are simply medical conditions, does this imply that all behavior is determined by brain function (or dysfunction)? What about issues such as free will and responsibility (theme 4), relationships with God and others (theme 1), and meaning (theme 5)? Many people understandably worry that if one adopts this medical model, it eliminates any discussion of these important dimensions of human nature. So while the typical professional description of psychological disorders is useful, it also seems slightly oversimplified. The problem comes in trying to understand the true complexity of these conditions and how all these factors interact.

Understanding Psychopathology

To help illustrate the complexity of psychological disorders, consider the issue of obesity. When we ask our students why many North Americans are obese, we get answers similar to those proposed for psychological disorders: causes such as genetics, physiological characteristics, or some form of willful (or "weak-willed") behavior. However, as the discussion continues, students often begin to offer additional explanations. Suggestions include (1) emotional issues (e.g., excited, bored, depressed), (2) increasing affluence and availability of food (e.g., snacks at social events), (3) increased portion sizes at restaurants, (4) decreased activity because of technology (e.g., riding lawn mowers, video games), (5) the structure of cities and towns (e.g., fewer sidewalks but more car access), creating longer commutes and less walking, (6) poverty (which is associated with poor nutrition), and (7) learned tendencies or habits (e.g.,

5. American Psychiatric Association, *Diagnostic and Statistical Manual*, 20.

taste preferences learned early in life or a habit of eating snack foods before bed). This list illustrates an important point about human behavior: the causes of our behavior are often much more complex than physiology and willful decisions alone.

These same issues apply to psychological disorders. Christian psychologists Barrett McRay, Mark Yarhouse, and Richard Butman suggest that we need to consider the whole person in understanding disorders, including the personal and collective impacts of sin. They state, "In addition to increased awareness of personal responsibility, an explanatory framework that takes sin seriously will increase our awareness of corporate responsibility. Sin not only affects the individual in terms of personal choices . . . [but] pervades the very structures of society."[6] In other words, brokenness is not just a personal failing but a "failure" of the natural world or of culture. So obesity and psychological disorders have a lot in common. We believe that, as with obesity, physiology and willful choices *do* play a role in psychological disorders, but there are also mental, social, and cultural forces that mold us, teach us, train us, and in many cases harm us psychologically and physically. Extreme stress brought on by war, broken relationships, an overly materialistic society, abusive parents, rejection or abandonment, and dire poverty or deprivation all illustrate ways that a broken world warps the fabric of our experience and can distort our thinking and emotions.

Comparing psychological disorders to something like obesity also helps us appreciate individual differences because the mix of influences may be different for each person. Some may be strongly influenced by genetics or physiology, others may be more influenced by their situation (e.g., they work at a fast-food restaurant), others may have learned bad habits at a very early age, and some may simply practice gluttony. Specific sins could be the key issue in certain situations, but it's rarely the case that individual sins are the only or the primary cause of either obesity or psychological disorders. After all, many immoral or irreligious persons have few if any emotional problems, and many righteous people have lots of problems, as Psalm 73:3–5 indicates:

> For I envied the arrogant
>   when I saw the prosperity of the wicked.
> They have no struggles;
>   their bodies are healthy and strong.
> They are free from common human burdens;
>   they are not plagued by human ills.

6. McRay, Yarhouse, and Butman, *Modern Psychopathologies*, 101.

Later in that same passage, we read:

> Surely in vain I have kept my heart pure
>   and have washed my hands in innocence.
> All day long I have been afflicted,
>   and every morning brings new punishments. (vv. 13–14)

Sinful tendencies are always a part of our lives, but the issue of personal sin alone will never help us completely understand disorders because living in a broken world involves experiencing many complex and interacting causes.

We have made progress in understanding some aspects of these complex interactions. For example, the genes we inherit are not the only way we become what we are; these genes can be "expressed" (i.e., uncovered) or blocked and thus influence brain function or behavior. A good deal of contemporary research suggests that our environment (e.g., maternal nurturing, childhood neglect, stress) influences whether genes associated with depression or other significant disorders are expressed or blocked.[7] If those genes were expressed by the wrong environmental conditions, individuals were much more likely to develop symptoms of depression or other disorders. This is just one example of the many complex interactions that can lead to disorder.

Interacting Influences and "Disordered Minds"

The place where interacting factors come together is within our mental life. In other words, the mind is the sum of all these factors but is also greater than the sum of all the interacting parts. This leads to a profound and still controversial notion: our mental life—while dependent on experience, biology, genetics, and other factors—has properties that cannot be explained completely by any of those factors. Christian psychologist Donald Lindskoog has suggested that the radical notion of psychology is that "in the evolving empirical discipline of psychology, a truly original and unique explanatory language has developed to name and understand an aspect of human experience that has never been named or understood before."[8]

He goes on to suggest that psychology, as a discipline, has captured an aspect of reality (i.e., "the mind") that is partially independent from other human fields of knowledge (e.g., biology, chemistry, philosophy, religion)—even though he acknowledges that there is interdependence among all fields of knowledge

7. Moffitt, Caspi, and Rutter, "Measured Gene-Environment Interactions."
8. Lindskoog, *Idea of Psychology*, 5.

(e.g., biology is dependent on chemistry, even though it is also unique). If our mental life has properties that are not explained by other aspects of reality, this implies that our mental processes can be disordered despite healthy brains and relationships. This notion, attributable to Freud and many others, is still a controversial one. To the dismay of many people of faith, it implies that aspects of our behavior are not entirely explained using theological concepts alone. To the dismay of people in biology or medicine, it implies that human behavior cannot be reduced to purely mechanical forms using scientific analysis.

Even some trained in the disciplines of psychology and psychiatry have questioned the notion of a disordered mind. In 1961, psychiatrist Thomas Szasz suggested that mental *illness* is a myth.[9] He argued that an immaterial thing (i.e., the mind) cannot be afflicted with illness; only the body experiences illness. He also argued that the development of diagnoses related to mental illness was not a triumph of modern medicine but a way to marginalize and discriminate against people who deviated from social norms. We believe that Szasz and a number of his followers (including some Christian psychologists) contributed important cautions about the way we diagnose mental disorders. However, we also maintain that understanding our mental life directly—in addition to understanding biological issues, spiritual concerns, or social explanations—is central to understanding psychological disorders and that it is very appropriate to speak of "disordered thinking." We also believe that our mental life is embodied (theme 3) rather than immaterial, as Szasz states. Thus it is highly dependent on its biological underpinnings as well as the environment. At the same time, our mental life cannot be reduced completely to our biological or spiritual dimensions because it has properties that cannot be explained by these basic qualities alone.

For example, there are no biological properties or actions that can fully explain self-awareness, emotional self-regulation, or theorizing about other minds. Similarly, there are no spiritual principles to fully explain perception, mental habits, or learning complex concepts. While we are embodied individuals and embedded in relationships, we still have a mental life that is greater than the sum of these many parts. All our experiences, brain functions, choices, and mental processes can interact together in a way that can ultimately be dysfunctional or disordered.

Therefore, someone with serious clinical depression may have a biological predisposition that lies at the heart of their condition. But they also have had a lifetime of learned habits, ways of thinking and perceiving, memories, positive and negative social relationships, and positive and negative spiritual experiences

9. See Szasz, *Myth of Mental Illness*.

that can influence their mood, which in turn can influence other aspects of their life. In addition, they have had a lifetime of struggling to understand who they are and the purpose or meaning of this condition, why life seems so difficult, and why others around them seem to have it so easy.

There are significant implications for this interacting and unifying approach. If we want to understand psychological disorders, we need to do more than study brain scans, engage in talk therapy, explore spiritual growth, or understand broken relationships. We also need to understand and deal directly with the mental life of persons in the context of their relationships, personal history, faith perspective, and view of the fundamental meaning of their existence. Christians who wish to focus exclusively on the spiritual dimension, neuroscientists or behaviorists who want to focus entirely on brain function or environment, and therapists who focus on only the social or family environment all fail to appreciate the complex and integrated nature of our psychological functioning.

Defining Disorder in the Context of Faith

Understanding something about the causes and the nature of psychological disorders still does not tell us how to distinguish disorders from normal behavior. Is an extremely religious person just being devout, or is this an example of some form of delusion? Is a person diagnosed with a mild form of autism really disordered? Perhaps they are just different—and maybe even superior in many ways.

Certainly, one way that faith impacts this area of psychology is in helping us sort out what society should value and how we should view individuals who struggle with psychological disorders. Faith perspectives have a lot to say about our greater purpose in life. At a very practical level, we agree with most textbook definitions or descriptions of psychological disorders (a simplified version of the DSM definition) as being "a significant disturbance in an individual's cognition, emotion regulation, or behavior," and these thoughts or behaviors are dysfunctional or maladaptive.[10] However, each of these terms is loaded with all sorts of value judgments. After all, who decides what is significant, dysfunctional, or maladaptive?

The answer—like the answer to every question asked in Sunday school—is God. God's intention was to create a harmonious universe where people were not only physically healthy but also emotionally, intellectually, and behaviorally healthy. In other words, they are not just doing okay; they are flourishing and

10. Myers and DeWall, *Psychology*, 552.

living their best life. So there is a normative feature about creation, meaning that God had an ideal plan for creation.[11] We can also suppose that God did not intend for people to experience suffering caused by uncontrollable anxiety, uncontrollable voices inside their heads, overwhelming and unexplained depression, or significant intellectual impairments. Someone who is experiencing mental illness may object to the notion that they are not normative. However, it is important to note that the brokenness of the current world affects all human beings. Since we all experience the brokenness of sin, disease, disorder, and death, none of us should be arrogant and suggest that others are more broken than we are.

It is also important to realize that God desired diversity within his creation. As described in chapter 13 on personality, Scripture repeatedly stresses the desirable diversity among people. But is a characteristic such as left-handedness a sign of some deviation from the path of normalcy (i.e., God created right-handedness as the norm and any deviation from that is a result of our broken world), or is this part of the variety God intended? Some Christians have raised similar questions about variations in intellect, personality, and even sexual orientation. For example, do we consider an individual who has been diagnosed as having autism as "nonnormative" despite their being quite capable of learning, speaking, and relating to other people? Is someone with dyslexia (i.e., a reading disorder) atypical or dysfunctional? Some individuals with autism are brilliant engineers (e.g., Temple Grandin); some individuals with dyslexia have been amazing artists. Years ago, people with dyslexia wouldn't have been considered disordered because proficient reading wasn't an essential part of everyday life. Maybe we should talk about the "reading obsession" prevalent in society as opposed to a reading disorder in the person. In other words, perhaps the brokenness in these situations lies more with the social stigma or the lack of social tolerance than with individual deficiencies.

These questions are very difficult to answer in our present existence because we don't have direct experience as to what a previously perfect world was like. While more extreme or disturbing examples of suffering brought about by atypical mental functioning are easily identified as outside God's intention, other cases are clearly more difficult. So a faith perspective doesn't by itself answer all the questions about what defines normal or abnormal. What we can say is that any condition that brings about suffering or inhibits us from fulfilling our most basic God-given roles (e.g., being a responsible parent, sibling, or friend; holding down a job; being a responsible and productive citizen and/or church member) is a *potential* example of a nonnormative outcome.

11. See Wolters, *Creation Regained*.

A faith perspective can also help to determine what a healthy mental life and healthy personality look like. Several thinkers in psychology have begun to suggest that clinical psychologists and psychiatrists have placed too much emphasis on unhealthy or disordered personalities and not enough on what a fully functioning human or "flourishing" person would look like. This movement is sometimes referred to as positive psychology, and these psychologists have outlined many personality strengths they believe a person should possess to thrive. Qualities such as wisdom, courage, temperance, transcendence,[12] and many others have been described and studied. We favor this general movement because it helps to guide treatment (i.e., if we want to make you less depressed, what qualities should replace the negative emotions?) and provides a framework for determining what is normative. (See chap. 15 for additional discussion of normative goals in therapy.)

God's View of Disorder

Going a bit deeper into the issue, it's also important to appreciate how God sees human beings in the context of brokenness. God's Son came to this earth to restore the relationship between God and humans by offering himself as payment. But Christ also experienced the range of genuine embodied pain that humans can experience. He felt physical pain (Matt. 27:30), anger (23:26–28), anxiety and deep sorrow (26:37; Luke 22:44), betrayal and abandonment (Matt. 26:56), as well as positive emotional experiences (Luke 10:21); he knows our pain. God never promises an easy life, even when we are his children (Rev. 2:10). However, because he has experienced the effects of a broken world that we all know, he does not judge us according to our frailty. Rather, "from everyone who has been given much, much will be demanded; and from the one who has been entrusted with much, much more will be asked" (Luke 12:48). This verse implies that those who have little (e.g., few resources, little emotional regulation, little intellectual capacity, little ability to perceive reality, etc.) will have less expected of them. This puts a new light on how we respond to individuals struggling with psychological or mental disorders. Christians sometimes wrongly see individuals who struggle with psychological conditions as damaged goods and not as worthy of God's grace. But we believe that Jesus taught that much more will be expected of those who are emotionally and psychologically well balanced and that special grace is given to those who struggle.

To make this concrete, we know of a woman who struggles with chronic schizophrenia. She has occasional delusions and sometimes hears voices (when

---

12. See Bolt, *Pursuing Human Strengths.*

not controlled by medication); in many ways, she has lived a very debilitated (and nonnormative) life. But this woman is also one of the most caring people we know. She is faithful in her church and spiritual life; her prayer life would put most others to shame. She has little to offer the world in terms of productive output, but she outshines most of us in childlike faith. She has been entrusted with very little in life, but we believe that she has far exceeded what many people have accomplished in God's eyes. We also believe that individuals with special needs or psychological disorders are an essential part of our current reality in that they define what others—who have been given much—should do. God will judge those given much by how they have treated those given less (see Matt. 25:40). Christian psychologists McRay, Yarhouse, and Butman provide an eloquent description of how we should respond to those who struggle.

> One of the integrative challenges facing Christian mental health professionals lies in recognizing the common humanity among those with even the most severe expressions of psychopathology. We must stand against a view of those who suffer from problems of psychosis as "other," as it leads to a diminished view of the image of God in them and of our responsibility for the care of the weak and vulnerable.
>
> Christians must cultivate a profound appreciation for the value of being human and of individual human beings (cf. Jones and Butman, 1991, chap. 2). Even in the midst of severe psychosis, the worth and dignity of the afflicted person is in no way diminished; the *imago Dei* may be tainted but is never removed. Given our own humanity, surely we can find some empathy for those who appear to us to be deluded or who have lost touch with reality. Christian philosopher and psychiatrist A. A. Howsepian (1997) argues persuasively that we all have disordered thinking and appetites (desires) to at least some degree. Thus there is room for some humility in this conversation.[13]

The Meaning of Suffering

One way for individuals struggling with mental illness to better understand their own condition is to place the symptoms and issues within the context of their lives. Because we are meaning seeking persons (theme 5), we can best understand our struggles—and the struggles of others—if we understand more about the purpose or meaning of our existence. As described in chapter 1, human beings not only react to their environment but also work to understand it and to appreciate an ultimate purpose. When people are struggling with disorders, these disorders can influence and be influenced by a broader understanding of

13. McRay, Yarhouse, and Butman, *Modern Psychopathologies*, 356–57.

life. So psychological disorders are disorders of meaning in addition to being disorders of brain function, personal failures, personal sins, social/structural sins, or mental dysfunction.

While we would never wish psychological disorders on any individual, there are times when suffering—whether by way of physical, mental, or social pain—can lead individuals to a better place. We know of people who have experienced very difficult and painful emotional struggles and have come through them as more thoughtful, more empathic, more helpful, and even more spiritual people. This growth happens only when people have social, spiritual, and—in some cases—professional support.

McRay, Yarhouse, and Butman also indicate that individuals struggling with psychological disorders need to reflect on the meaning and significance of their symptoms at two levels. On one level, this reflection on meaning relates to understanding the immediate causes, such as possible biological, social, and personal factors that may contribute to their thinking patterns or symptoms. Such reflection is helpful because it changes a person's perspective from an obsessive focus on the symptoms themselves—an understandable and common tendency—to a focus on root causes. This reframing of the meaning of their symptoms helps to make the symptoms seem more manageable and allows for better distancing from the problems and improved problem solving. On a deeper level, reflection related to sin, suffering, and struggle can help individuals cope with their situation and promote healing. McRay, Yarhouse, and Butman believe "that a clearly articulated Christian worldview and a congruent and credible Christian lifestyle constitute a form of primary prevention. Reflection on our struggles can help us see what truly matters from the perspective of kingdom values."[14]

They are not suggesting that a Christian worldview (or any other worldview) is a magic cure or treatment. They fully appreciate that there are biological, mental, interpersonal, and social factors that influence the development of a disorder. However, they believe that psychological disorders can be understood better in the context of broader life issues and that this can contribute to healing or even the prevention of symptoms. As described earlier, psychological disorders—similar to obesity—have complex and interacting factors, and our broader questions about life are an important part of that mix.

Yale graduate and ordained Episcopal priest Kathryn Greene-McCreight (cited earlier) worked to understand the meaning of her severe bipolar depression (i.e., cycling between periods of depression and mania) by writing a book about her experiences. She writes, "This book began, then, as my own agonizing

14. McRay, Yarhouse, and Butman, *Modern Psychopathologies*, 182.

search for the meaning of my mental illness."[15] She struggled with questions such as "Does God send this suffering? If so, why? And why this particular kind of suffering? Why, if I am a Christian, can I not rejoice? What is happening to my soul?"[16] Even though she was helped tremendously by psychotherapy and medication, she states that "while therapists and counselors, psychiatrists and medications abound, I found no one to help me make sense of my pain with regard to my life before the triune God." She knew that she could not completely divorce her experience from her faith: "How could I, as a Christian, indeed as a theologian of the church, understand anything in my life as though it were separate from God? This is clearly impossible. And yet how could I confess my faith in the God who is 'a very present help in trouble' (Ps. 46:1) when I felt entirely abandoned by that God?"[17]

Finding meaning in suffering does not eliminate other issues or treatments. As Lewis B. Smedes, former professor at Fuller Theological Seminary, once wrote about his own struggle with depression, "Then God came back. He broke through my terror and said: 'I will never let you fall. I will always hold you up.'. . . I felt as if I had been lifted from a black pit straight up into joy." But he also adds, "I have not been neurotically depressed since that day, though I must, to be honest, tell you that God also comes to me each morning and offers me a 20-milligram capsule of Prozac. . . . I swallow every capsule with gratitude to God."[18]

Caring in the Christian Community

We will discuss treatment of psychological disorders more in chapter 15, but we can say at this point that the support of a faith community (e.g., local church, small group, religious college, like-minded friends) can greatly ease symptoms of psychological disorders or even promote a significant amount of healing. This support requires that persons in those faith communities react in a way that is much more positive than the kind of response described in the opening story of this chapter. Christian psychologist Warren Brown has written that our humanity, or "soulishness" as he calls it, is defined by our ability to have a relationship with God and others.[19] He says that individuals who lose the ability to have reciprocal relationships (i.e., Alzheimer's patients, individuals with brain injury

15. Greene-McCreight, *Darkness Is My Only Companion*, 12.
16. Greene-McCreight, *Darkness Is My Only Companion*, 12.
17. Greene-McCreight, *Darkness Is My Only Companion*, 13.
18. Smedes, *My God and I*, 133.
19. Brown, "Cognitive Contributions to Soul," 99.

or disorder) still need to have relationships. In those cases, God can maintain a relationship with them even when they have difficulty responding. Likewise, the community of faith needs to provide a supportive relationship even if a person is unable to respond in kind. Greene-McCreight talks eloquently about how God never left her, even though she could not feel that presence or respond; her husband and many Christian friends did not abandon her but supported her, even when she could not immediately feel their love and support. "In God's eyes we are not how we feel, we are not what we think, we are not even what we do. We are what God does with us, and what God does with us is to save us from our best yet perverse efforts to separate ourselves from this presence, from his fellowship, communion, sharing."[20]

Implications and Applications

As imperfect human beings, we will not always respond to psychological disorders as we should. However, a faith perspective can provide some fresh insights into how we might respond better. A faith perspective can help us to

1. See the broader influences on psychological functioning and psychological disorder. A biblical perspective that sees humans as embodied, relational, spiritual (i.e., in relationship with God), and responsible persons helps us avoid the reductionism that places too much emphasis on one aspect of our being (e.g., brain function, social or cultural factors, spiritual issues alone).

2. Appreciate that factors beyond a person's control (e.g., biology, genetics, environment, culture) are typically more central to the development of disorder than personal failings or individual sins. The effect of living in a fallen world is broad and influences our relationships with God, one another, and creation.

3. Better understand the defining features of normative (i.e., as God intended) behavior and the types of personal traits that allow people to thrive. We need to evaluate what we collectively value and make sure those values are in line with biblical norms for living (e.g., showing justice, loving mercy, walking humbly, versus the pursuit of wealth or success).

4. Appreciate the value and humanity of each person. We should be able to see the image of God even in the most broken person and be able to respond with the support that only a community of faith can provide. We

20. Greene-McCreight, *Darkness Is My Only Companion*, 89.

also need to recognize the unique qualities and gifts that individuals may have even in the face of very debilitating and difficult situations, and first see the person well before we see the disorder within them.

5. Help each person understand the context and meaning of their psychological disorder. A supportive, understanding, and even admonishing community can do much to reduce symptoms and to help people work through difficult issues. When people come to understand the meaning of suffering—in themselves or others—they experience some healing and are better able to cope with the issues they face.

DISCUSSION QUESTIONS

1. If you or someone you know has experienced some form of psychological disorder or mental illness, how did others respond? Was there acceptance, blame, curiosity, or simply ignoring of the issue? How have you responded to others?

2. If you are part of a Christian community, how would most people in your community explain or account for psychological disorders? Do you mostly agree or disagree with these views? Why? Have your views changed over the course of reading this chapter or book?

3. List some of the ways that the brokenness of the natural world and the social world influences mental illness/health. Have you or someone you know experienced some or many of these influences?

4. How do you explain the type of suffering that some people experience with mental illness? Why might God allow people to have these difficulties?

5. If you have had experience with mental illness, are there things that others did that made the situation better or worse? What are ways that you can be supportive of others struggling with mental illness? Are there things you should or shouldn't say or do that make it better or worse?

15

"Meaningful" Healing

Therapy

▶ **SUMMARY:** There are many attitudes about psychotherapy. This chapter outlines the ways Christians and others have characterized therapy practice, and it examines various types of helping relationships to consider when needing help. We also attempt to critique common therapy techniques from a biblical worldview.

My therapist told me the way to achieve true inner peace is to finish what I start. So far today, I have finished 2 bags of M&M's and a chocolate cake. I feel better already.

Dave Barry, quoted in *The Essential Addiction Recovery Companion*

Finally, brothers and sisters, rejoice! Strive for full restoration, encourage one another, be of one mind, live in peace. And the God of love and peace will be with you.

2 Corinthians 13:11

Mrs. C. was a 39-year-old woman who complained of fear reactions to traffic situations."[1] As described by therapist Joseph Wolpe, Mrs. C. had experienced a traumatic accident and was now extremely anxious while driving or even walking across busy intersections. She would stay at

1. Wolpe, *Practice of Behavior Therapy*, 309.

home for weeks to avoid driving. She was also experiencing regular headaches, and her increasing anxiety was beginning to affect her marriage relationship and even her sex life. Wolpe used cognitive-behavioral therapy that included assessment of her emotional and marital history and training in guided imagery, relaxation, and cognitive techniques designed to change her thinking patterns. She also received homework assignments designed to help her practice these techniques outside of the therapy sessions. Seven months of intermittent therapy sessions led to a major reduction of fear, greatly increased driving frequency, and improved sexual and marital relationships with her husband. A nine-year follow-up showed that she remained symptom-free.

Results such as these seem impressive—even magical—but you may have some questions about the process. Perhaps Mrs. C. would have gotten better on her own after seven months of doing something else or even nothing at all. Perhaps there are cheaper or even more effective techniques than these (e.g., medication, spiritual healing, sharing with friends). These and many other questions have made people somewhat ambivalent about psychotherapy of any kind.

Attitudes toward Therapy

Have you sought or would you seek psychotherapy if needed? Attitudes in the United States toward mental health treatment have become more favorable over the years. In a 2003 survey, an estimated 41.4 percent of respondents reported that they would "definitely go" for professional help if needed.[2] A 2018 survey involving the US and Ontario, Canada, found that a combined 79 percent of respondents would "probably" (45%) or "definitely" (34%) go for professional help if needed.[3] Of course, this means that a fairly large proportion would still not seek professional help. In fact, the National Institute of Health reveals that even for individuals with a serious mental health condition, slightly less than half receive treatment of any kind.[4] Survey research has identified the most significant factors that cause resistance to mental health services: cost, personal stigma associated with a mental disorder, cultural beliefs that are suspicious of therapy, and being very religious.[5] Others have more privately questioned the value or effectiveness of therapy. Humorist Dave Barry captured this sentiment when he said that most people have "the impression that psychiatrists are just a bunch of bearded voodoo doctors who espouse confusing and wildly contradictory

2. Mojtabai, "Americans' Attitudes," 644.
3. Jagdeo et al., "Negative Attitudes," 760.
4. Kessler et al., "Prevalence and Correlates of Untreated Serious Mental Illness."
5. Eisenberg et al., "Stigma and Help Seeking."

theories that have nothing to do with common sense." To which he replied, "This is totally unfair. Many psychiatrists are clean shaven."[6] A slightly more serious poke at psychotherapy came in the 1950s from a clinical psychologist who said that therapy is "an unidentified technique applied to unspecified problems with unpredictable outcomes. For this technique we recommend rigorous training."[7] His not-so-subtle suggestion is that psychotherapists really don't know what they are doing, but they insist on making the practice look professional.

As the research mentioned above suggests, people who are very religious have been particularly ambivalent about seeking mental health treatment. Despite this tendency, there are certainly differences among Christians about the value of therapy. Many Christians are favorable toward psychotherapy because they view it as a helping profession that brings healing to hurting individuals. Many Christians also feel that Christian faith is valuable but not essential in therapy—so long as the therapy is effective. However, others have questioned psychotherapy on several grounds. Some feel that psychotherapists operate according to models that are in opposition to Christian faith[8] and that change happens only through prayer, Scripture reading, spiritual healing, or the support of a church community. Others see value in the insights of psychological theories but feel that therapy is best done by a Christian pastor, spiritual leader, or Christian counselor (i.e., under the direction of a church-related ministry)—not necessarily a person trained and licensed as a professional therapist. Finally, as discussed in chapter 3, some feel that actions are ultimately guided by a separate component called the soul, meaning that people should be able to transcend their bodily existence and, in some way, rise above any physically caused emotions.

One last doubt about professional therapy—and perhaps other forms of helping relationships—comes from Christians who believe that we should deal with problems on our own or perhaps with God alone. After all, they argue, God will not give us more than we can handle. Therefore, we should be able to deal with all difficulty, including psychological disorders, through self-reflection, prayer, and strong faith. One problem with this belief is that it is a misreading of the apostle Paul's statement in 1 Corinthians 10:13: "God is faithful; he will not let you be tempted beyond what you can bear." This verse is focused on the temptation to commit a specific sin, not necessarily our ability to handle tragedy or difficulty in our lives. Certainly, the story of Job in the Old Testament leaves a very different impression of the way tragedy affects persons of faith. In response to the tragedy in his own life, Job says, "I have no peace, no quietness; I have no

6. Barry, *Dave Barry's Bad Habits*, 141.
7. Eysenck, *Effects of Psychotherapy*, 698.
8. Farber, *Unholy Madness*.

rest, but only turmoil" (Job 3:26), and, "Why did I not perish at birth, and die as I came from the womb?" (3:11). It appears that even people of great faith can get "dumped on" with a force that is far more than they can bear—individually.

This brings us to the other key fallacy about bearing up in tragedy: it's not something we do alone. As a very old story recounted by Kathryn Greene-McCreight (and paraphrased here) goes, a drowning man refused help from several sources, saying, "God will save me." After he drowned, he inquired at the gates of heaven why God had not rescued him. The reply came, "I sent several people to save you. What more did you want?"[9] So we not only bear God's image collectively but bear up under tragedy—including the tragedy of mental illness—through helping relationships that can include professional psychotherapy. Greene-McCreight concludes her thoughts about the role of mental health treatment this way:

> Indeed, Christians sometimes reject therapy in toto, claiming that all they need for health, and mental health specifically, is Jesus, and then things will be fine. I had a student once who interpreted her own depression as a preconversion illness that disappeared upon her conversion. Maybe so, but what about those of us who have a vibrant faith and a strong relationship with Jesus and yet are still thrown in the pit? Surely the voice of the psalmist throughout reflects the plight of these mentally ill, as it does the plight of the physically ill, the poor, the outcast. . . . I don't see why God's grace cannot come in the form of a daily dose of antidepressant or in the form of a therapist, even an atheist. That cannot be impossible, surely.[10]

In addition to this wide diversity of views among people of faith (as well as with the broader public), there are diverse views among therapists about how therapy should be conducted and what the goals of therapy should be—perhaps the source of Dave Barry's complaint about "wildly contradictory theories." All of this makes evaluating different therapies from the perspective of faith very difficult. While you may not plan on becoming a therapist, you may already have faced or will face questions about when, where, and how to use therapy for psychological problems, so the descriptions and critiques that follow are designed as a "consumer guide" to helping and therapy.

Helping Comes in Many Forms

As mentioned earlier, one very simple reason why people are resistant to therapy is that many have experienced great benefit from just sharing their problems with a friend, a family member, a youth pastor, or someone they trust to have good wisdom. They may have also done some "self-therapy" by going to a movie or eating cake. A person might ask, "Why pay for a service when I can get the same thing for free?" While this is certainly an understandable sentiment, professional therapy does have some unique benefits.

Psychotherapy is a specialized helping relationship and is defined by John C. Norcross (and officially adopted by the American Psychological Association[11]) this way: "*the informed and intentional application of clinical methods and interpersonal stances derived from established psychological principles for the purpose of assisting people to modify their behaviors, cognitions, emotions, and/or other personal characteristics in directions that the participants deem desirable.*"[12] Note the use of "established psychological principles" that require extensive knowledge and training that makes psychotherapy distinct from casual conversations, supportive friendships, prayer, or spiritual counseling. Research over many years has confirmed that licensed professional therapists provide scientifically verifiable benefits to people that are not found in other types of helping relationships.[13]

Does this mean that other forms of helping are unimportant? Not at all; other helping relationships can be extremely therapeutic, but for different reasons. Research regularly confirms that strong relationships and social support promote well-being, reduce or prevent psychological dysfunction, and even reduce the incidence of physical illness.[14] Sharing with a friend can be extremely helpful. According to Christian psychologists Barrett McRay, Mark Yarhouse, and Richard Butman, this is one area where the church can be at the forefront of prevention and care. Offering social support can be a significant force in reducing other forms of distress, such as extreme financial need, poor coping skills, chronic health issues, and other physical needs.[15] These everyday concerns are strong predictors of future mental health. Pastoral or spiritual counseling, small groups, and formal church organizations that promote supportive and caring relationships can bring about tremendous healing or prevent future problems.

One example of this type of organization is Stephen Ministries. According to their promotional material, "Stephen Ministers are congregation members trained by Stephen Leaders to offer high-quality, one-to-one Christian care to people going through tough times. A Stephen Minister usually provides care to one person at a time, meeting with that person once a week for about an hour."[16]

---

11. American Psychological Association, "Recognition of Psychotherapy Effectiveness."
12. Norcross, "Eclectic Definition of Psychotherapy," 218 (emphasis added).
13. M. Smith and Glass, "Meta-Analysis of Psychotherapy," 752.
14. Cohen and Wills, "Stress, Social Support," 310.
15. McRay, Yarhouse, and Butman, *Modern Psychopathologies*, 89–113.
16. Stephen Ministries, "What Is Stephen Ministry?"

This ministry is not designed to replace psychotherapy, pastoral counseling, or other church ministries. Stephen Ministers are discouraged from giving advice, probing psychological function, or engaging in any other form of therapeutic intervention; the ministry is simply designed to build caring, safe, and confidential relationships.

The benefit provided by these types of informal helping relationships is consistent with the theme of being relational persons (theme 1). Being responsible limited agents (theme 4) and broken but redeemable persons (theme 2) also means that we need relationships to help hold us accountable. Church families often act as accountability groups to help us check our own behaviors and remind us of our responsibilities to one another and to God. Church ministries can also remind us of scriptural mandates concerning what God desires of us—always in the context of God's amazing grace for fallen people. Certainly, there are analogous groups outside the church that can serve similar functions.

Slightly more formal helping relationships may come through pastoral counseling or church-based counseling services. These counselors may or may not be professionally licensed for counseling and may not have all the specialized training described above, but they can provide great benefit. In addition to offering the type of safe relationship building provided by more informal support groups, spiritual or pastoral counseling can also help satisfy our meaning seeking desire (theme 5). McRay, Yarhouse, and Butman have indicated that having a strong sense of meaning and purpose is another significant predictor of mental health.[17] They argue that symptoms associated with physical or mental illness need to be understood not only from their biological and psychological basis but also in terms of their ultimate significance and purpose in a person's life. As described in chapter 14, people of faith who have struggled with mental illness or significant personal problems have found great comfort in grappling with the meaning of their suffering or difficulty. Church-based counseling can go a long way in helping people understand a deeper purpose for the difficulties they face.

Professional Psychotherapy

Where does this leave us with "professional" psychotherapy? While informal relationships have great value, there are some things that the church or friends cannot supply, such as specialized knowledge about cognition and learning, conscious and unconscious processes, developmental processes, social factors that alter our behaviors and attitudes, brain and bodily functions, and many

17. McRay, Yarhouse, and Butman, *Modern Psychopathologies*, 180–94.

other concepts. In addition, psychotherapists possess specialized knowledge about how to help a person change their thoughts and behaviors.

Consider the opening story about Mrs. C. We can assume that most pastors, spiritual healers, or even Stephen Ministers would not have expertise with techniques designed to reduce fear that occurs after a car accident. While social support, an improved relationship with God, understanding the overall meaning of her fear, and being held accountable would all help, they could not automatically eliminate the fear itself. As McRay, Yarhouse, and Butman confirm, "It becomes readily apparent to most pastors or Christian workers that meditation on key Scriptures rarely 'fixes' serious anxiety struggles, any more than the regular singing of 'Amazing Grace' helps a struggling person feel like she or he is God's beloved. . . . God's grace, and the truths of Scripture, must be incarnated (fleshed out) in the context of everyday living."[18]

Likewise, Greene-McCreight says that "those Christians who have not faced the ravages of mental illness should not be quick with advice to those who do suffer. Platitudes such as 'Pray harder,' 'Let Jesus in,' even 'Cast your anxiety on him, because he cares for you' (1 Peter 5:7), which of course are all valid pieces of advice in and of themselves, may only make the depressive person hurt more."[19] Scripture was not written as a science textbook or a psychotherapy manual, and it cannot provide specific answers to every life issue. But we are given minds to learn more about how our minds work, and we are given the task of using that knowledge to bring healing. Therefore, whatever psychotherapy is and whatever theories are behind a given technique, the first order of business is that it be based on sound principles and well-tested practices. For example, to ensure that treatment success is not due to the passage of time or client expectations alone, research needs to compare a nontherapy group to a therapy group under carefully controlled conditions.

Unfortunately, the history of psychotherapy is riddled with examples of bad practices and untested ideas. Robyn Dawes, in his book *House of Cards*, raises concerns about how professional therapy is practiced: "The impression is created that psychotherapy treatment is all a matter of opinion or conjecture. It isn't, but many practitioners treat it that way, while the professional associations support them in doing virtually anything at all that appeals to their 'clinical intuition,' as if there were no knowledge."[20] He goes on to say that a good amount of research does show that "psychotherapy works. . . . Those who believe they have problems are encouraged to try it—especially if they

18. McRay, Yarhouse, and Butman, *Modern Psychopathologies*, 186.
19. Greene-McCreight, *Darkness Is My Only Companion*, 21.
20. Dawes, *House of Cards*, 9.

have been unable to change their behavior by simply 'willing' a change."[21] Of course, one should be careful in selecting a therapist; Dawes provides useful—though slightly unrealistic—advice on this selection by saying, "For myself, in choosing a professional psychologist I would want one of the 30 percent of APA members who reads one or more of its scientific journals."[22] In other words, the practice of psychotherapy should be based on well-tested principles and thoroughly studied outcomes.

The same should be true for professional psychotherapy that is conducted by Christians. As mentioned in chapter 13, Christian psychotherapist Alan Tjeltveit indicates that Christian therapists have rarely tested the therapy techniques that they believe are consistent with the principles of Christian faith.[23] This is not to say that these techniques are wrong or ineffective, but they do need to be verified and perhaps refined. We would anticipate that practices that prove effective would also be consistent with biblical views of human nature—but they still should be tested to determine whether therapists are applying the concepts correctly. Therefore, if professional psychotherapy—whether by a Christian or not—claims that it offers specialized knowledge that goes beyond more informal forms of helping, it needs to demonstrate that this expertise is indeed worth the trouble (and the cost).

Christian Psychotherapy

Are there features that are unique to Christian psychotherapy? First, it's hard to precisely define "Christian psychotherapy" because no one description or technique can be characterized as uniquely Christian. While having a therapist who is a Christian certainly provides a strong possibility that therapy will adhere to biblical themes, we feel this is not the essential or even a necessary component for therapy to be practiced in this way. What is most important (at a minimum) is that the approach of the therapist (regardless of their religious beliefs) follows techniques and establishes goals that are not contradictory to a biblical understanding of persons and that are well tested and shown to be effective.

What qualities should individuals consider when selecting a therapist or therapy approach? What follows is a list of qualities that we believe are compatible with well-tested practices and are consistent with the scriptural themes concerning human nature. This is neither an exhaustive or detailed list nor a

---

21. Dawes, *House of Cards*, 73.
22. Dawes, *House of Cards*, 74.
23. Tjeltveit, "Faith, Psychotherapy, and Christian Counseling."

"therapy for dummies" manual but a set of basic qualities that should guide Christians when selecting therapies that are most helpful. The reader should consult chapter 13 on personality for some additional background on the various theories behind the main psychotherapy approaches. That said, the techniques that appear most consistent with these themes and that have the most research support do the following:

1. *Provide empathy, caring concern, and unconditional acceptance.* Substantial evidence shows that empathy, a sense of trust, and feeling cared for are key elements in the therapeutic process.[24] Dawes—a secular psychologist with a preference for a more scientific approach to therapy—summarizes a large body of research by saying, "Much of the success of verbal therapy is influenced by the personal qualities of therapists and how they relate to clients."[25] People who feel trust and some level of basic acceptance are more willing to explore issues and are less resistant to change. "Client-centered" therapy approaches that grew out of humanistic psychology, along with many other approaches—both secular and Christian—have emphasized these aspects of therapy. Behavioral approaches (e.g., behavior modification or behavior analysis) have genuine strengths in other ways, but they are not as strong in this regard. Of course, this acceptance and care also need to be balanced with accountability (more on this in a moment).

These qualities reflect the theme of being relational persons. We also receive this form of unconditional acceptance from God—through the blood of Christ—so this mirrors what God does for those who seek him.[26] This does not imply that the therapist and client need to be long-term friends, but it does imply that relationship building within the therapy setting should be part of the therapeutic process.

2. *Are present and future oriented rather than focused on the past.* An emphasis on being "driven by the past" (i.e., being shaped entirely by past experiences) may foster a sense of fatalism or determinism. (See chap. 13 for a full discussion of this issue.) While some exploration of past experiences and tendencies is an important part of the initial interview, the primary focus should be on the goals for therapy and how these goals are going to be accomplished. This approach has significant research support. As Martin Seligman and colleagues describe in their summary of this research, one specific example of a therapy type using this forward-looking or "intentional" approach was very effective in promoting better self-regulation of emotions and behaviors and achieved

24. Norcross and Lambert, "Psychotherapy Relationships," 4.
25. Dawes, *House of Cards*, 75.
26. Romans 5:8: "But God demonstrates his own love for us in this: While we were still sinners, Christ died for us."

greater success in accomplishing goals.[27] Many cognitive-behaviorally oriented therapy approaches use this approach to a large degree.

Emphasizing future action also seems consistent with being *responsible* limited agents (theme 4) because it involves consciously considering future alternatives to the present situation and setting priorities based on what is valuable and meaningful to the client.

3. *Stress responsibility and accountability.* Stressing responsibility and accountability should go together with "unconditional positive regard." One emphasis does not negate the other; parents discipline their children as they also show them unconditional love and acceptance. Accepting a person does not imply that one must approve of their behavior. Stressing accountability is consistent with the idea that we are broken and in need of redemption (theme 2) and that we are responsible limited agents (theme 4). As McRay, Yarhouse, and Butman state, "We see throughout Scripture and Christian theology that people are considered responsible for what they do with what they have been given. These are concepts that have been all but lost in contemporary discussions of psychopathology."[28]

Clearly, therapists should recognize and explore the structural and physical evil that may have influenced the present behavior. We cannot ignore, however, the reality that individuals—if left to their own devices—will not always select the best action. Many therapists who favor a cognitive-behavioral, client-centered therapy (humanistic), along with some other approaches, do stress this accountability to some degree. However, there is an essential flaw in any approach that assumes that if we look deep within ourselves and shed the constraints of the past, we will automatically choose adaptive, wise, or moral action. The influence of our sinful tendencies means that even what appears to us to be moral, reasonable, or correct can be very self-centered, damaging, or evil.

This emphasis does not imply that therapists need to dictate actions or solutions to clients, any more than clients should dictate entirely what they should do. Recall that the definition of psychotherapy provided earlier emphasizes that therapy should move in directions that the "participants deem desirable." Therefore, therapy should be a partnership or joint effort between therapist and client of setting goals consistent with fundamental moral values and of exploring useful alternatives. Human self-centered tendencies are reduced when we see things from the perspective of others.

4. *Appreciate biological constraints and social context.* Every person is not the same (see chaps. 9 and 13). Some people struggle with inborn temperaments

27. Seligman et al., "Navigating into the Future," 135.
28. McRay, Yarhouse, and Butman, *Modern Psychopathologies*, 101.

or tendencies that are difficult to manage individually. A person may have also experienced extremely troubled social or economic environments that make healthy adjustments very difficult. Being embodied individuals (theme 3) and being responsible *limited* agents (theme 4) mean that many of the issues a person faces are outside of their direct control. Therapists should be willing to work with psychiatrists, other medical professionals, and social workers in prescribing medication, changing diet or physical habits, or providing other social and environmental changes. As McRay, Yarhouse, and Butman note, "We do not believe God will be found in Prozac, or Prozac in God. But when medication is used judiciously and responsibly, it can make all the difference in the world for those who suffer needlessly and those who try to help them. Medication is often a necessary (but not always sufficient) prerequisite for healing and change with the problems of anxiety."[29]

The same principles apply to dealing with the limitations of the physical and social environment that are very evident in other conditions. For example, drug addiction is a good illustration of both the embodied nature of some problems (e.g., continued drug use may cause significant changes in neurological function) and the importance of the environment. Successfully treating the physical elements of drug addiction but not considering the social environment surrounding the person may result in a return to drug use once the person returns to their normal situation. Ongoing efforts should be in place to either improve the environment or reduce its negative impact. These constraints do not eliminate responsibility and accountability, but clients should be held accountable only for how they *respond* to their biological or social constraints.

5. *Are action oriented and (slightly) less insight oriented.* While self-insight is effectively used in cognitive-behavioral, humanistic (client-centered), psychodynamic, and many other types of therapies, an overemphasis on self-insight places too much attention on the self. As we discussed in chapter 13 on personality, Paul Vitz argues convincingly that we should reduce focus on the self, not increase it. He states, "This fundamental tendency based on pride creates the pervasive human expression of narcissism, the choice of self-love over love of God and others."[30]

Action-oriented therapies also take advantage of our embodied nature because (as described in chap. 3) engaging in physical action can lead to greater change. Developing positive thoughts and behaviors requires practice, training, and external support. (Anyone taking extensive music training or lessons understands this principle from experience.) Action-oriented therapies are also more present and future oriented (see quality number 2).

29. McRay, Yarhouse, and Butman, *Modern Psychopathologies*, 190.
30. Vitz, "Christian Theory of Personality," 206.

6. *Work on establishing purpose and meaningful goals.* As psychologist Seligman and colleagues state, "There is growing evidence that a strong sense of meaning and purpose . . . is highly protective against psychopathology." They go on to describe one study showing that soldiers who strongly disagreed with the statement "my life has meaning" were much more likely to commit suicide. They also describe therapeutic techniques that focus on "sustainable personal projects" that involve setting goals and contemplating what the client would like to "become or be."[31]

Establishing purpose and meaning is consistent with our meaning seeking tendency (theme 5). But what really distinguishes an approach that is consistent with biblical themes is not only the *process* of setting goals but also *which* goals are set. This issue is perhaps far more important than any specific technique in distinguishing a uniquely Christian approach to therapy. There is often little debate among therapists (Christian or secular) that a goal of therapy is to reduce symptoms of severe depression, persistent anger, or marital conflict. But what is being put in its place? Here is where a person's worldview and priorities become most evident. Some therapists strive for self-understanding or greater self-esteem. Some encourage greater independence, taking greater control of one's life, or perhaps pleasing oneself. But are these goals truly consistent with a biblical view? Christian psychologists Mark Cosgrove and James Mallory outline what they feel are the qualities that define mental health.[32] These include the following:

purpose and meaning in life

a realistic self-worth

a capacity for self-sacrificing love, empathy, and sensitivity

an accurate view of reality

strong internal standards

the ability to accept what is unchangeable

a sense of freedom to enjoy oneself

physical, emotional, and intellectual needs in balance

Christian counselor Edward W. C. McAllister has a similar list describing our basic needs, but he also includes forgiveness, community, and hope.[33] What is striking about these lists is how much the focus is away from the self and

31. Seligman et al., "Navigating into the Future," 135.
32. Cosgrove and Mallory, *Mental Health.*
33. McAllister, "Christian Counseling and Human Needs," 55.

toward others. Forgiveness, love, community, and empathy all supersede self-improvement and self-focus.

There are certainly many more issues related to psychotherapy that are beyond the scope of this chapter and this book, but we hope that presenting the range and value of various helping relationships and the contours for professional therapy provides a useful guide to helping. We all need help in various ways from time to time, so may we all be open to providing support to others and to accepting the help that God may send our way.

DISCUSSION QUESTIONS

1. If you or someone you know well has experienced psychotherapy, what was the experience like—positive, helpful, challenging, or negative?

2. In regard to question 1, do you think the way therapy was conducted matched up with the list of qualities that may define Christian psychotherapy? If yes, in what ways? If no, how was it different?

3. Think about the various attitudes that Christians have expressed about therapy (described early in this chapter). Where would you, your family, or your community (e.g., church, home, school) fit in that list of attitudes?

4. Some Christians have said that people "only need the Bible" when it comes to tackling personal problems. According to the authors, what are some possible counterarguments to that statement?

5. Are you someone others would describe as "a good listener" with whom others share their problems, or can you think of others described in that way? In what ways is that type of support helpful? In what ways is it better than, worse than, or just different from professional psychotherapy?

6. In being supportive of others, where would difficulties arise in trying to balance accountability and responsibility with relationality, support and care, and empathy?

Christian Approaches to Psychology

The Case of Evolutionary Psychology

▶ **SUMMARY:** We, the authors, have used a particular approach when relating faith to psychology. However, Christians have used other perspectives when thinking about psychology. These different perspectives can come into play in any area of psychology, but they become more obvious when dealing with controversial issues such as evolutionary psychology and sex differences. These issues raise deep questions about the use of natural science, scriptural interpretation, and moral principles—to name just a few. This chapter describes how Christian groups from various faith perspectives have approached such issues and shows how the themes of this book may be used to evaluate these ideas.

How do you arrange food on your plate at mealtime? Do you make sure no items touch any other items (e.g., the peas can't touch the potatoes), or are you happy to mix everything together into a makeshift stew? Perhaps you don't like peas at all, so you hide them under the edge of the plate. Just as with food, when exploring psychology and Christian faith, there are a variety of approaches for mixing—or not mixing—the two together. Throughout this book, we have described just one approach, but we feel it is important to see how committed Christians from different traditions have related faith to psychology.

Evolutionary Psychology

To illustrate different Christian approaches, let's first examine two topics that can provide an example of the dilemmas Christians face when relating faith to psychology: evolutionary psychology and sex differences. According to psychologist Glenn Geher, "**Evolutionary psychology** *is, essentially, the application of evolutionary principles to questions of human behavior.*"[1] Evolutionary theory dates to Charles Darwin's 1859 publication, which claimed that any inherited trait that helps an organism survive will be passed on to its offspring, but traits that do not help an organism adapt to the environment will die out.[2] Just as dog breeders can increase the likelihood or prevalence of certain traits by selecting animals with those traits—and then continuing to pair dogs from subsequent generations—so the natural world selects and increases the occurrence of certain traits. Dog breeders can create docile house pets or aggressive hunting dogs through selective breeding. But in the absence of an intelligent being, who does the selecting according to evolutionary theory? The natural world "selects" dogs who are good hunters if the environment they are in calls for that ability. In that context, good hunters will survive and pass on their genes, but more docile animals will be less likely to survive and produce offspring. Therefore, over thousands of years, the traits of the animal gradually change so that the animal is well adapted to its environment. Traits that help it survive "win out" over other traits. If the environment changes, then perhaps new traits will be selected and become dominant.

While biological evolution focuses on structures (e.g., the shape of the teeth or running speed), evolutionary psychology focuses on behavioral or psychological traits (e.g., a more aggressive tendency). Although still controversial, evolutionary psychology has become an important framework for how many psychologists understand the basis for a large set of human behaviors.[3] While evolutionary psychologists don't deny that social influences can alter behavior, they contend that human behavior was primarily shaped (1) over eons of time as "brain modules" were sculpted—with each module designed to govern a specific behavior for a specific need; (2) in prehistoric times with only small changes since then, giving us "stone age minds" that were suitable for prehistoric times; and (3) by random forces that have no greater purpose other than survival.[4] Thus while we have qualities that aid in our current context, unconscious behaviors still cause us to behave in ways that can be explained only by ancient

---

1. Geher, *Evolutionary Psychology 101*, 1 (emphasis added).
2. Darwin, *On the Origin of Species*, 1–6.
3. Geher, *Evolutionary Psychology 101*, 1.
4. Looy, "Sex Differences," 302–4.

survival instincts. Why do humans prefer sweet tastes? Because in ancient times fruit contained not only calories but also vitamins. Why do humans often cooperate? Because a hunter-gatherer society needed individuals who could work together on the plains of Africa to hunt efficiently.

Sex Differences

Evolutionary psychology has been applied to many areas of psychology— including helping, competition, warfare, intelligence, morality, and even humor, to name just a few. But its most talked about and most controversial application is to sex differences. According to evolutionary psychology, because each sex makes different biological contributions to reproduction, each has developed different behaviors to survive in their environment. While both parents pass genes to the next generation, women carry a child for nine months of pregnancy and nurse a baby for several months after that. Since men are not biologically equipped to serve these functions, they instead developed traits that help them provide food, protection, and support.[5]

Therefore, evolutionary psychologists contend that men and women developed different traits associated with these differing needs. Women developed greater sensitivity to emotional cues and more nurturing tendencies, while men developed greater spatial ability to track prey when hunting. In addition, the large amount of time that women invest in rearing children leads them to desire a long-term commitment from a mate for protection and support, improving the chance that offspring will survive—which means that these "commitment traits" survive as well. Men, however, have typically had less investment in child-rearing, so they developed a trait that favors passing on their genes through multiple partners. By having multiple sexual partners, they increase the chance that their genes—their "unfaithful genes"—will be passed on. As described in one psychology textbook, "The data are in, say evolutionists: Men pair widely; women pair wisely."[6] Men also develop greater jealousy over potential infidelity than females because, unlike women, they can't know with certainty if the genes carried by the offspring are theirs.

Because of these different biological roles, each sex also developed differences in what they find sexually attractive. Men favor younger women with full lips and breasts and with a certain waist-to-hip ratio—"all indicators of sufficient estrogen levels, fertility, and ability to successfully birth a child."[7] Women favor

5. Buss, "Sex Differences in Human Mate Preferences."
6. Myers and DeWall, *Psychology*, 139.
7. Looy, "Sex Differences," 304.

slightly older men with stronger body types and narrow hips—all of which indicate someone with healthy testosterone levels who is also able to provide protection.

Critiques of Evolutionary Psychology and Sex Differences

There have been critiques and criticisms of evolutionary psychology from several sources. Surprisingly, the greatest criticisms of evolutionary psychology, especially in relation to sex differences, have come not from religious circles but from various groups who emphasize the impact of environment on development. For example, psychologists arguing from a feminist perspective are concerned that evolutionary theory reinforces outdated gender stereotypes.[8] They contend that sex differences come from traditions handed down over the centuries. Psychologists who stress the social environment (e.g., some social psychologists, some developmental theorists) feel that we socially construct these realities and that gender-related behaviors are very flexible and are not biologically predetermined.[9] A concern raised by many people outside of psychology is that evolutionary psychology's emphasis on nondirected, random forces creating various tendencies in men and women reduces moral responsibility.[10] If men are more promiscuous due to evolutionary pressures, why should anyone—including a spouse—hold them accountable for their actions?

Another source of criticism is related to the methods of research and attempts to provide evidence for the theory. One concern is that researchers simply work backward from evidence rather than making testable hypotheses and then finding evidence that can directly confirm or disconfirm the hypothesis. For example, if researchers find that men are more promiscuous than women, does that confirm the hypothesis that the *mechanism* for how this came to be was adaptive pressures? Couldn't other theories related to culture or tradition (or mixed moral messages) just as easily explain the results?

Despite these concerns and criticisms, evolutionary psychology concepts have become an important theoretical tool for many psychologists who use these concepts to provide **functional explanations** for behaviors: *explanations that help elucidate the reason or the function for behaviors that seem to have few other explanations.* For example, why do women have greater desire for sexual activity

8. Eagly and Wood, "Feminism and Evolutionary Psychology," 550–51; Grossi et al., "Challenging Dangerous Ideas," 282–84.

9. Wood and Eagly, "Cross-Cultural Analysis," 699–721.

10. Braddock, "Evolutionary Psychology's Moral Implications," 531–33; Gunnoe, *Person in Psychology and Christianity*, 188–91.

when estrogen levels are high? Because estrogen levels are high just before they ovulate (release an egg from the ovary), meaning they have the greatest chance of becoming pregnant.[11] Centuries ago, people didn't have knowledge of the biology governing reproduction, so it was important that humans have built-in instincts that might motivate sexual behavior. Why do humans find some smells disgusting? Because certain smells are associated with substances that can cause illness or death (e.g., feces, toxic bacteria). Taking all this information together, how should we explore psychology and Christian faith when it comes to these controversial yet sometimes useful and widely used theories?

Christian Approaches to Psychology

As described at the start of the chapter, Christians with various perspectives on the application of religion to science, culture, or daily life have approached the field of psychology in quite different ways. We believe we can summarize these views by identifying three main approaches for relating faith and psychology: science and religion should be (1) in opposition, (2) separate but equal, or (3) related. These categories are not distinct but represent a continuum of views based on a person's understanding of science, especially social science, and their view of Scripture.

Approach 1: In Opposition

For religious people who stand in opposition to psychology, this approach typically takes a religion-over-science position. The flip side of this position—science-over-religion—also places science and religion in opposition, but this is not the position taken by religiously minded people. (See chap. 2 for a discussion of naturalism, which favors this science-over-religion approach.)

The religion-over-science view is illustrated by an approach called Biblical counseling. The way this term is typically used implies that "'established' psychology must be abandoned in favor of a completely new approach based strictly on the Bible."[12] This view emphasizes a more literal interpretation of the Bible (e.g., creation happened over six twenty-four-hour days rather than an extended time). Scientific investigation is acceptable unless it appears to contradict biblical descriptions of the world or proper behavior. Applied to psychology, this view strongly rejects many psychological theories, studies, and practices as being in opposition to God's Word. A strong proponent of this approach was a pastoral

11. Kalat, *Biological Psychology*, 336–37.
12. Jeeves and Ludwig, *Psychological Science and Christian Faith*, 74.

counselor named Jay Adams. In describing psychotherapy, he stated, "So, I say that the psychiatrist has usurped the work of the physician, but mostly the work of the preacher. And he engages in this work without warrant from God, without the aid of the Scriptures (in almost every case), and without regard to the power of the Holy Spirit. Thus he seeks to change the behavior and the values of people in an ungodly manner. Insofar as he succeeds, the results may be feared."[13]

When considering issues such as evolutionary psychology and sexuality, this approach suggests that a literal interpretation of Scripture rules out any consideration of evolutionary theories. Further, the only way to understand gender development, gender roles, or gender dysphoria (i.e., a mismatch between biological sex and gender identity) is by searching Scripture and understanding the moral principles outlined in relation to gender. Deviation from these biblical norms is not only a sin but also at the root of many mental health problems. Adams believed that these sins and tendencies need to be identified, challenged, confessed, and ultimately changed before emotional health can develop.

To be sure, there are variations of this oppositional view. Proponents of Christian counseling (which sounds like Biblical counseling but uses a slightly different approach) accept portions of psychological theory but feel that Scripture provides the majority of principles needed for therapy.[14] In critiquing this perspective, several Christian psychologists have provided some support, but others have raised concerns. Supporters have noted the strong emphasis on the work of the Holy Spirit and the importance of the Christian community and accountability in helping people address personal problems. Other supporters have indicated that this approach rightly identifies many biblically incompatible worldviews that have been prevalent in past theories (see chap. 15 for a similar critique). However, Christian psychologist David Entwistle summarizes the concerns of several individuals. He expresses concern about the undervaluing of science and says that even in a broken world, truth can be discovered by non-Christians. Second, Entwistle points out that it is an error to assume that Scripture and faithful living are completely sufficient and necessary for aspects of psychological well-being.[15] Many people sin or lack belief in God but do not suffer from significant mental disorder or distress. Many individuals with strong faith, who have confessed their sin, still struggle (see chaps. 14 and 15 for examples). Finally, critics note that Scripture, while "useful for teaching, rebuking, correcting and training in righteousness" (2 Tim. 3:16), is not a complete

13. Adams, *Big Umbrella*, 8.
14. Entwistle, *Integrative Approaches*, 210–14.
15. Entwistle, *Integrative Approaches*, 210–14.

how-to manual for natural science or psychology. For example, parents are told to love and discipline a child, but few details are given about exactly how to discipline or how best to demonstrate love in a particular situation. As author C. S. Lewis states about Scripture, "When it tells you to feed the hungry, it does not give lessons in cookery."[16] (See chap. 2 for a more complete quotation and additional discussion of the issue.)

Approach 2: Separate but Equal

The separate-but-equal view, sometimes referred to as a territorial model, implies that religion and science occupy completely distinct territories or domains.[17] This approach is distinct from the science-over-religion model in that both religion and science are highly valued and seen as legitimate avenues to truth. However, those who promote this view worry that religious views will bias the search for scientific truth. Therefore, science should be objective and free from personal, cultural, or religious perspectives. Science deals with the observable world that we can measure, while religion deals with belief, the spiritual—and unobservable—world, and moral principles. Science can help solve the problems of today, while religion promises hope for the life to come. When addressing issues such as evolutionary psychology and sex differences, people holding this position favor letting science lead where it leads. Religion provides the moral direction or purpose for sexual behavior even if natural forces were responsible for the development of these behaviors.

Reponses to this view have been mixed. Many Christian psychologists value the emphasis placed on science as well as on religion, and they agree that there are *potential* dangers of personal bias guiding us away from arriving at scientific truths. However, three concerns have been raised with this approach. The first is a general philosophical concern about objective truth. Many contemporary philosophers of science note that it may be impossible to have total objectivity in any science—but particularly in the science of human behavior.[18] We all filter reality through the lens of our past experiences, desires, and worldviews. Examination of many psychological theories often reveals hidden or not-so-hidden belief systems and unscientific assumptions about human nature (see chap. 13 for illustrations). A second concern, raised by biblical scholar Donald Carson,[19] is that keeping psychology and religion in separate worlds is intellectually unsatisfying. After all, reality is all part of a whole—shouldn't

---

16. Lewis, *Mere Christianity*, 64.
17. C. Evans, *Preserving the Person*, 102.
18. Ponterotto, "Qualitative Research," 126–28.
19. Carson, *Christ and Culture Revisited*, 210–11.

all knowledge about reality (observable and unobservable) match up and fit together? Finally, critics contend that religion not only is designed for our moral or spiritual dimensions but also should permeate our very being and transform the way we think as well as how we relate to God, others, and the world (see also Rom. 12:2).[20]

Approach 3: Related

The third approach suggests that science and religion are related and can be addressed together. However, there are some subtle differences among Christian psychologists about how these areas are related. The first view is that science and religion are **compatible**: *both science and religion provide avenues to truth, which is about a single reality, but they do so from different perspectives or levels.* Christian psychologists David G. Myers and Malcolm A. Jeeves capture this sentiment when they describe how we examine a masterpiece painting: "If you stand right up against it you will understand better how the paint was applied, but you will miss completely the subject and impact of the painting as a whole. To say the painting is 'nothing but' or 'reducible to' blobs of paint may at one level be true, but it misses the beauty and meaning that can be seen if one steps back and views the painting as a whole."[21]

They strive for a more complete understanding of life by seeing a "close up" (i.e., scientific) view of our world but simultaneously seeing a religious or holistic view. However, they also caution about the difficulties of attempting this approach:

> Nature is, to be sure, all of a piece. For convenience, we necessarily view it as multilayered, but it is actually a seamless unity. Thus the different ways of looking at a phenomenon like romantic love (or belief or consciousness) can sometimes be correlated, enabling us to build bridges between different perspectives. Attempts at building bridges between religion and the human sciences have sometimes proceeded smoothly. A religious explanation of the incest taboo (in terms of divine will or a moral absolute) is nicely complemented by biological explanation (in terms of the genetic penalty that offspring pay for inbreeding) and sociological explanations (in terms of preserving the marital and family units). Other times the bridge-building efforts extending from both sides seem not to connect in the middle, as when a conviction that God performs miracles in answer to prayer is met with scientific skepticism and psychological explanations of how people form illusory beliefs. To say that religious and scientific levels of explanation can be complementary does not mean there is never conflict or that any unsupported

20. Hall, "God as Cause or Error?"
21. Myers and Jeeves, *Psychology through the Eyes of Faith*, 8.

idea is to be welcomed as truth. It just means that different types of explanation may actually fit coherently together.[22]

As is illustrated by this quotation, sexuality, when viewed through an evolutionary psychology lens, can be understood using scientific or psychological analysis but also by understanding the religious context. In the view of Myers and Jeeves, since God created the natural world and created rules for living, the two worlds should naturally coincide. What distinguishes this approach from the separate but equal approach is that there is an attempt to place scientific understanding within the context of faith and to create a more unified understanding of reality using both perspectives. There is also a greater appreciation for the fact that objective truth in science is harder to obtain than many secular scientists suppose: "Worldviews even influence our psychological terminology: whether we label those who only say nice things about themselves on personality inventories as having 'high self-esteem' or as 'defensive'; whether we describe those who favor their own racial and national groups as 'ethnocentric' or as exhibiting strong 'group pride'; whether we view a persuasive message as 'propaganda' or 'education.'"[23] At the same time, these authors caution that there are potential dangers with this approach because "our values and assumptions cloud the spectacles through which we view reality. . . . Our calling is to clean the spectacles through careful scientific and biblical scholarship."[24]

A slightly different version of this related approach is one that seeks to integrate religious and theological ideas more intentionally with psychological principles. Christian psychologists who use the **integrated approach** *seek not only to show compatibility between the different levels of understanding (i.e., religion and science) but also to construct theories that are based on explicitly biblical or theological principles.* These theories still need to be tested with observable science, but they start with specific religious assumptions about the nature of human beings.

A clear example of this approach comes from Christian psychologist Heather Looy. Looy does not immediately dismiss ideas from evolutionary psychology (abbreviated EP in her article) or a competing theory known as social constructionism (SC) but starts her analysis with a different set of a priori (i.e., prior to) assumptions about the world:

Will our examination of human sexuality be illuminated and more complete if we assume, *a priori*, that there is an intelligent, purposeful cause shaping our

22. Myers and Jeeves, *Psychology through the Eyes of Faith*, 10.
23. Myers and Jeeves, *Psychology through the Eyes of Faith*, 14.
24. Myers and Jeeves, *Psychology through the Eyes of Faith*, 17.

sexuality, instead of random, purposeless processes? Will this assumption lead to a more fruitful and perhaps a more complete understanding of sexuality than provided by either EP or SC?

We can postulate that humans were made for particular purposes, and that our emerging, evolving nature contributes to our ability to manifest those purposes.[25]

Looy is suggesting that God may have used natural forces to accomplish a purposeful outcome. Note that Looy sees value in examining a theory like evolutionary psychology because it presents some interesting explanations that are hard to explain in other ways. So her approach is very different from the religion-over-science approach. But she also feels that evolutionary psychology starts from incorrect assumptions. Also note that her approach clearly starts with a nonscientific (i.e., not observable or testable) hypothesis, which distinguishes it from a compatible approach. However, she points out that evolutionary psychologists also start with an untestable hypothesis: that all life came about through natural mechanisms without purpose or direction. Using this approach, she presents some interesting possibilities about sexuality:

> Instead, we can reconceptualize our sexuality in light of a belief that we were designed to be in a loving relationship in order to develop our potential as humans through intimacy, vulnerability, and unconditional love. This enables us to generate a number of testable predictions about mate selection and to interpret several observations puzzling to EP. These include the fact that we do not always select our mates merely on the basis of EP criteria, and we usually do not seek another mate if a particular pairing produces no offspring. Also, some couples choose not to have children at all, some people select mates from their own sex, and we often stay together long after the childrearing years. EP claims that such observations constitute exceptions, special cases, or indirectly adaptive patterns, but that our real, albeit unconscious, motive is gene propagation. EP states that this is revealed in universal trends in mate selection and the dynamics of sexual relationships, including jealousy, divorce, extra-marital affairs, and serial monogamy.[26]

Looy contends that using her starting assumptions about relationships provides a better explanation of these so-called random variations or exceptions. She goes on to state that her framework does a better job of explaining nonsexual relationships: "This theory also accounts for the fact that many people choose not to engage in sexual relationships with the other sex. If we view humans as fundamentally relational and communal, then there are other ways in which these aspects of our humanity may be experienced and expressed, including in

25. Looy, "Sex Differences," 308–9.
26. Looy, "Sex Differences," 309.

friendships, through committed celibacy and service in religious communities, and between parents and children."[27]

In the end, Looy readily admits that this expansive theory about the purpose of human sexuality cannot be fully tested using scientific methods. However, keep in mind that evolutionary psychology suffers from the same problem, as was described earlier in the chapter. This reveals an important point about all science—but especially about psychological science: many useful theories are **underdetermined by the data**, *meaning that a theory may be very useful in summarizing patterns and processes but that there is no possible way of proving all elements of it using data.*

The Approach Used in This Book

Based on our view of science, religion, and how biblical concepts might inform the science of psychology, we favor the related approach. However, to be honest, we vacillate between the two subtypes of compatibility and integration. We very much appreciate Looy's idea of beginning with a new set of assumptions, but we also recognize the potential danger of clouding our view of the world rather than enlightening it with these assumptions. That is because, as broken individuals, Christians can still distort their understanding of God's intent, the purposes that God has for sexuality or marriage, or how we should apply biblical concepts to a complex world. Therefore, we don't have a single, definitive answer as to *how* one should do psychology from a Christian worldview. What we do believe is that one should strive to see how knowledge is related, to understand the whole, and to constantly explore God's Word as well as God's world for new insights. Sometimes the goal of our inquiry is not about a perfect final answer but about the *struggle* to constantly see the world as God intended for us to see it.

So the process we have used in this book is to start with a set of assumptions about human nature that appear to be both biblically sound and also compatible with many psychological principles. We then try to see how these may inform and shape our evaluation of larger theories and principles.

How is this illustrated when evaluating evolutionary psychology? Rather than rejecting or accepting the theory wholesale, we use our five themes of human nature to put the theory into the context of biblical principles. Here is a summary of how this looks:

Relational persons. Evolutionary psychology gets a mixed grade on this one. The theory does stress our relational nature to one another because of

27. Looy, "Sex Differences," 310.

our need to cooperate and because of the strong bonds that are necessary for sexual reproduction. It also stresses that we are in relationship with the natural world, which we have also stressed throughout this book. However, it denies or ignores any suggestion that we are in relationship to God, nor does it provide any description of the purpose for being in relationship—other than its survival value.

Broken, in need of redemption. In stark contrast to this theme, evolutionary psychology presents a neutral view of human nature: we are neither moral nor immoral. Instead, our qualities are simply designed for the long-term survival of our genes. Likewise, human sexuality is only as good or as bad as its functional outcome—does it promote the species?

Embodied. High marks can be given to evolutionary psychology for its understanding that we are designed bodily to function in a natural world. Christians have historically minimized our bodily existence, but we would do well to rediscover our embodied nature, which Scripture so clearly describes.

Responsible limited agents. Evolutionary psychology stresses, almost exclusively, our limited nature. In other words, we are determined by natural forces and by our genetic history, which have shaped our brains to act in certain ways. While over the course of time we have developed more flexible ways of learning and acting, we are ultimately driven by forces outside of our conscious control. For example, our sexual functioning is determined by our genetic endowment and by a small amount of social learning that dictates how we should behave. For many evolutionary psychologists, this leaves humans without genuine responsibility or accountability.

Meaning seekers. Again, evolutionary psychology gets a mixed grade on this one, since the theory postulates that our brains have evolved to see relationships, learn patterns, and ultimately explain why things happen. This quality evolved so that we survive better in this world. However, the ultimate meaning that we achieve is not directed by any larger power or purpose.

As you can see from this brief critique, we have not addressed several difficult points related to evolutionary psychology or sex differences. However, we encourage interested readers to examine similar but more thorough critiques by other Christian psychologists.[28] What we have done with these issues, and

28. See, e.g., Gunnoe, *Person in Psychology and Christianity*, 164–209.

issues throughout this book, is to provide a beginning point of evaluation so that we can begin to see how large philosophical and religious perspectives help us evaluate the foundations of psychology. Our hope and prayer are that, as students of psychology, you also begin to explore foundational principles that apply not just to this field but to all areas of study and life.

DISCUSSION QUESTIONS

1. Do you feel that evolutionary psychology concepts have some value, or should they be kept out of mainstream psychology? Why or why not?

2. In what ways are evolutionary psychology concepts about sex differences similar to more traditional Christian views, and in what ways are they very different?

3. Which approach of relating psychology and faith is closest to the views about psychology from your own tradition (i.e., your family, church, school, or social life)? After reading this chapter, or this entire book, has your own approach changed? If so, in what way?

4. Can or should psychological science be an objective science, free from our personal biases, religious beliefs, or worldviews? Why or why not?

5. What are the dangers or potential benefits of developing theories in psychology that start with explicitly biblical principles? Think of examples of both outcomes.

References

Adams, Jay E. *The Big Umbrella, and Other Essays and Addresses on Christian Counseling.* Nutley, NJ: Presbyterian & Reformed, 1975.

Allport, Gordon G. *Patterns and Growth in Personality.* New York: Holt, Rinehart & Winston, 1961.

American Psychiatric Association. *Diagnostic and Statistical Manual of Mental Disorders: DSM-V.* 5th ed. Arlington, VA: American Psychiatric Association, 2013.

American Psychological Association. "Recognition of Psychotherapy Effectiveness." August 2012. http://www.apa.org/about/policy/resolution-psychotherapy.aspx.

Anonymous. Mental Health America: Real Lives. Accessed August 30, 2013. http://www.mentalhealthamerica.net/reallives/index.cfm/2009/9/4/Learning-to-trust-others-and-forgive-himself.

Asch, Solomon E. "Opinions and Social Pressure." *Scientific American* 193 (1955): 31–35.

Ashforth, Blake E., and Fred Mael. "Social Identity Theory and the Organization." *Academy of Management Review* 14, no. 1 (1989): 20–39.

Augustine. *Confessions.* Introduction and commentary by Gillian Clark. Cambridge: Cambridge University Press, 1993.

Baer, John, James C. Kaufman, and Roy F. Baumeister, eds. *Are We Free? Psychology and Free Will.* New York: Oxford University Press, 2008.

Bakke, O. M. *When Children Became People: The Birth of Childhood in Early Christianity.* Translated by Brian McNeil. Minneapolis: Fortress, 2005.

Bandura, Albert, Dorthea Ross, and Sheila A. Ross. "Transmission of Aggression through Imitation of Aggressive Models." *Journal of Abnormal and Social Psychology* 63 (1961): 575–82.

Bargh, John A. "Free Will Is Un-Natural." In Baer, Kaufman, and Baumeister, *Are We Free?*, 128–54.

Bargh, John A., and Tanya L. Chartrand. "The Unbearable Automaticity of Being." *American Psychologist* 54 (July 1999): 462–79.

Barrett, Justin L. *Born Believers: The Science of Children's Religious Belief*. New York: Free Press, 2012.

——. "Cognitive Science of Religion: What Is It and Why Is It?" *Religion Compass* 1, no. 6 (November 2007): 768–86.

Barry, Dave. *Dave Barry's Bad Habits: A 100% Fact-Free Book*. New York: Henry Holt, 1993.

Bartlett, Frederic C. *Remembering*. Cambridge: Cambridge University Press, 1932.

Bastardi, Anthony, Eric L. Uhlmann, and Lee Ross. "Wishful Thinking: Belief, Desire, and the Motivated Evaluation of Scientific Evidence." *Psychological Science* 22 (2011): 731–32. https://doi.org/10.1177/09567976711406447.

Batson, C. Daniel, and Elizabeth R. Thompson. "Why Don't Moral People Act Morally? Motivational Considerations." *Current Directions in Psychological Science* 10, no. 2 (2001): 54–57.

Baumeister, Roy F. "Free Will in Scientific Psychology." *Perspectives on Psychological Science* 3 (2008): 14–19.

Baumeister, Roy F., and Mark R. Leary. "The Need to Belong: Desire for Interpersonal Attachments as a Fundamental Human Motivation." *Psychological Bulletin* 117, no. 3 (1995): 497–529.

Benner, David G., ed. *Christian Counseling and Psychotherapy*. Grand Rapids: Baker, 1987.

Benson, Herbert, Jeffrey A. Dusek, Jane B. Sherwood, Peter Lam, Charles F. Bethea, William Carpenter, Sidney Levitsky, et al. "Study of the Therapeutic Effects of Intercessory Prayer (STEP) in Cardiac Bypass Patients: A Multicenter Randomized Trial of Uncertainty and Certainty of Receiving Intercessory Prayer." *American Heart Journal* 151, no. 4 (2006): 934–42.

Bering, Jesse. *The Belief Instinct*. New York: Norton, 2011.

Bloom, Harold. *The American Religion: The Emergence of the Post-Christian Nation*. New York: Simon & Schuster, 1992.

Bloom, Paul. *Descartes' Baby: How the Science of Child Development Explains What Makes Us Human*. New York: Basic Books, 2004.

——. "Is God an Accident?" *Atlantic* 296, no. 3 (2005): 105–12.

——. "Religion Is Natural." *Developmental Science* 10 (2004): 147–51.

Bolt, Martin. *Pursuing Human Strengths: A Positive Psychology Guide*. New York: Worth, 2004.

Bolt, Martin, and David G. Myers. *The Human Connection: How People Change People*. Downers Grove, IL: InterVarsity, 1984.

Bonhoeffer, Dietrich. *Life Together: The Classic Exploration of Christian Community*. San Francisco: HarperOne, 1978.

Bower, Gordon H., Michael C. Clark, Alan M. Lesgold, and David Winzenz. "Hierarchical Retrieval Schemes in Recall of Categorical Word Lists." *Journal of Verbal Learning and Verbal Behavior* 8 (1969): 323–43.

Bowlby, John. *Attachment and Loss*. Vol. 1, *Attachment*. New York: Basic Books, 1969.

Boyle, Gregory. *Tattoos on the Heart: The Power of Boundless Compassion*. New York: Free Press, 2010.

Braddock, Matthew C. "Evolutionary Psychology's Moral Implications." *Biology & Philosophy* 24, no. 4 (2009): 531–40.

Bradley, Raymond Trevor. "Values, Agency, and the Theory of Quantum Vacuum Interaction." In Pribram, *Brain and Values*, 471–504.

Brakke, David. *The Gnostics: Myth, Ritual, and Diversity in Early Christianity*. Cambridge, MA: Harvard University Press, 2010.

Brown, Warren S. "Cognitive Contributions to Soul." In *Whatever Happened to the Soul? Scientific and Theological Portraits of Human Nature*, edited by Warren S. Brown, Nancey Murphy, and H. Newton Malony, 99–125. Minneapolis: Fortress, 1998.

Brown, Warren S., and Brad D. Strawn. *The Physical Nature of Christian Life: Neuroscience, Psychology, and the Church*. New York: Cambridge University Press, 2012.

Buehlman, Kim T., John Gottman, and Lynn F. Katz. "How a Couple Views Their Past Predicts Their Future: Predicting Divorce from an Oral History Interview." *Journal of Family Psychology* 5 (1992): 295–318. https://doi.org/10.1037/0893-3200.5.3-4.295.

Bufford, Rodger K. *The Human Reflex: Behavioral Psychology in Biblical Perspective*. San Francisco: Harper & Row, 1981.

Burke, Thomas J., ed. *Man and Mind: A Christian Theory of Personality*. Hillsdale, MI: Hillsdale College Press, 1987.

Burr, David. "Vision: In the Blink of an Eye." *Current Biology* 15 (2005): 554–56.

Buss, David M. "Sex Differences in Human Mate Preferences: Evolutionary Hypotheses Tested in 37 Cultures." *Behavioral and Brain Sciences* 12, no. 1 (1989): 1–14.

Bussema, Ken. "Perspectives on Developmental Psychology." *Pro Rege* 22 (September 1993): 1–8.

Calvin, John. *Commentaries on the First Book of Moses, Called Genesis*. Translated from the original Latin and compared with the French edition by John King. Grand Rapids: Eerdmans, 1948.

Carson, Donald A. *Christ and Culture Revisited*. Grand Rapids: Eerdmans, 2012.

Carter, John D., and Bruce Narramore. *The Integration of Psychology and Theology: An Introduction*. Grand Rapids: Zondervan, 1979.

Catechism of the Catholic Church. 2nd ed. Vatican City: Libreria Editrice Vaticana, 2019.

Christensen, Larry B., Burke R. Johnson, and Lisa A. Turner. *Research Methods, Design, and Analysis*. 13th ed. New York: Pearson, 2020.

Ciccarelli, Saundra K., and J. Noland White. *Psychology*. 5th ed. New York: Pearson Education, 2017.

Cohen, Sheldon, and Thomas A. Wills. "Stress, Social Support, and the Buffering Hypothesis." *Psychological Bulletin* 98, no. 2 (1985): 310–57.

Conway, Martin A. "Memory and the Self." *Journal of Memory and Language* 53 (2005): 594–628.

Corsini Encyclopedia of Psychology and Behavioral Science. Vol. 4. New York: Wiley, 2002.

Cosgrove, Mark P. *The Essence of Human Nature*. Grand Rapids: Zondervan, 1977.

Cosgrove, Mark P., and James D. Mallory. *Mental Health: A Christian Approach*. Grand Rapids: Zondervan, 1977.

Crick, Francis. *The Astonishing Hypothesis: The Scientific Search for the Soul*. New York: Touchstone, 1994.

Crowley, Michael J., Jia Wu, Erika R. McCarty, Daryn H. David, Christopher A. Bailey, and Linda C. Mayes. "Exclusion and Micro-Rejection: Event-Related Potential Response Predicts Mitigated Distress." *Neuroreport* 20, no. 17 (2009): 1518–22.

Damasio, Antonio R. *Descartes' Error: Emotion, Reason, and the Human Brain*. New York: Putnam, 1994.

———. *The Feeling of What Happens: Body and Emotions in the Making of Consciousness*. New York: Harcourt, Brace, 1999.

Darwin, Charles. *On the Origin of Species by Means of Natural Selection*. London: John Murray, 1859.

Dawes, Robyn M. *House of Cards: Psychology and Psychotherapy Built on Myth*. New York: Free Press, 1994.

Dawson, Michael E., and Paul Reardon. "Effects of Facilitory and Inhibitory Sets on GSR Conditioning and Extinction." *Journal of Experimental Psychology* 82, no. 3 (1969): 462–66.

De Neys, Wim. "On Dual- and Single-Process Models of Thinking." *Perspectives on Psychological Science* 16, no. 6 (February 2021): 1412–27. https://doi.org/10.1177/1745691620964172.

Dijksterhuis, Ap, and Henk Aarts. "Goals, Attention and (Un)Consciousness." *Annual Review of Psychology* 61 (2010): 467–90.

Dovidio, John F., Kerry Kawakami, Craig Johnson, Brenda Johnson, and Adaiah Howard. "On the Nature of Prejudice: Automatic and Controlled Processes." *Journal of Experimental Social Psychology* 33 (1997): 510–40.

Eagly, Alice H., and Shelly Chaiken. "Attitude Structure and Function." In *The Handbook of Social Psychology*, edited by Daniel T. Gilbert, Susan T. Fiske, and Gardner Lindzey, 2 vols., 1:269–322. 4th ed. Boston: McGraw-Hill, 1988.

Eagly, Alice H., and Wendy Wood. "Feminism and Evolutionary Psychology: Moving Forward." *Sex Roles* 69, no. 9 (2013): 549–56.

Eisenberg, Daniel, Marilyn F. Downs, Ezra Golberstein, and Kara Zivin. "Stigma and Help Seeking for Mental Health among College Students." *Medical Care Research and Review* 66, no. 5 (2009): 522–41.

Entwistle, David N. *Integrative Approaches to Psychology and Christianity: An Introduction to Worldview Issues, Philosophical Foundations, and Models of Integration*. Eugene, OR: Wipf & Stock, 2021.

Erikson, Erik. *Identity: Youth and Crisis*. New York: Norton, 1968.

———. "Reflections on the Last Stage—and the First." *Psychoanalytic Study of the Child* 39 (1984): 155–65.

Evans, C. Stephen. "The Concept of the Self as the Key to Integration." *Journal of Psychology and Christianity* 3 (1984): 4–11.

———. *Preserving the Person: A Look at the Human Sciences*. Vancouver: Regent College Publishing, 2002.

———. *Why Christian Faith Still Makes Sense: A Response to Contemporary Challenges*. Acadia Studies in Bible and Theology. Grand Rapids: Baker Academic, 2015.

Evans, Jonathan St. B. T., and Keith E. Stanovich. "Dual-Process Theories of Higher Cognition: Advancing the Debate." *Perspectives on Psychological Science* 8, no. 3 (May 2013): 223–41.

Eysenck, Hans Jurgen. *The Effects of Psychotherapy*. New York: International Science Press, 1966.

Farber, Seth. *Unholy Madness: The Church's Surrender to Psychiatry*. Downers Grove, IL: InterVarsity, 1999.

Farnsworth, Kirk E. *Whole-Hearted Integration: Harmonizing Psychology and Christianity through Word and Deed*. Grand Rapids: Baker, 1985.

Faw, Harold. *Sharing Our Stories: Understanding Memory and Building Faith*. Belleville, ON: Essence, 2007.

Fazio, Russell H. "Attitudes as Object Evaluations of Varying Strength." *Social Cognition* 25, no. 5 (2007): 603–37.

———. "Multiple Processes by Which Attitudes Guide Behavior: The MODE Model as an Integrative Framework." In *Advances in Experimental Social Psychology*, edited by M. P. Zanna, 23:75–109. San Diego: Academic Press, 1990.

Festinger, Leon. *A Theory of Cognitive Dissonance*. Stanford, CA: Stanford University Press, 1957.

Forgas, Joseph P. "Don't Worry, Be Sad! On the Cognitive, Motivational, and Interpersonal Benefits of Negative Mood." *Current Directions in Psychological Science* 22 (2013): 225–32.

Fowler, James W. *Becoming Adult, Becoming Christian*. Rev. ed. San Francisco: Jossey-Bass, 2000.

Freud, Sigmund. *The Complete Introductory Lectures on Psychoanalysis*. Translated and edited by James Strachey. New York: Norton, 1966.

Garrett, Brandon. *Convicting the Innocent: Where Criminal Prosecutions Go Wrong*. Boston: Harvard University Press, 2011.

Gazzaniga, Michael S. *Who's in Charge? Free Will and the Science of the Brain*. New York: HarperCollins, 2011.

Geher, Glenn. *Evolutionary Psychology 101*. New York: Springer, 2013.

Gelman, Susan A. *The Essential Child: Origins of Essentialism in Everyday Thought*. Oxford: Oxford University Press, 2003.

Gilbert, Daniel. *Stumbling on Happiness*. New York: Knopf, 2006.

Gilovich, Thomas, Dacher Keltner, Serena Chen, and Richard E. Nisbett. *Social Psychology*. 5th ed. New York: Norton, 2019.

Gollwitzer, Peter M. "Implementation Intentions: Strong Effects of Simple Plans." *American Psychologist* 54 (1999): 493–503.

Gopnik, Alison. *The Philosophical Baby*. New York: Farrar, Strauss & Giroux, 2009.

Gopnik, Alison, Andrew N. Meltzoff, and Patricia K. Kuhl. *The Scientist in the Crib*. New York: William Morrow, 1999.

Gottman, John M., and Robert W. Levenson. "The Timing of Divorce: Predicting When a Couple Will Divorce over a 14-Year Period." *Journal of Marriage and Family* 62 (2000): 737–45. https://doi.org/10.1111/j.1741-3737.2000.00737.x.

Gottman, John M., and Nan Silver. *The Seven Principles for Making Marriage Work*. Rev. ed. New York: Harmony, 2015.

Graesser, Arthur C., Murray Singer, and Tom Trabasso. "Constructing Inferences during Narrative Text Comprehension." *Psychological Review* 101 (1994): 371–95.

Grandin, Temple, and Margaret Scariano. *Emergence: Labeled Autistic*. Novato, CA: Arena, 1986.

Greene-McCreight, Kathryn. *Darkness Is My Only Companion: A Christian Response to Mental Illness*. Grand Rapids: Brazos, 2006.

Grossi, Giordana, Suzanne Kelly, Alison Nash, and Gowri Parameswaran. "Challenging Dangerous Ideas: A Multi-Disciplinary Critique of Evolutionary Psychology." *Dialectical Anthropology* 38, no. 3 (2014): 281–85.

Gunnoe, Marjorie Linder. *The Person in Psychology and Christianity*. Downers Grove, IL: InterVarsity, 2022.

Hall, M. Elizabeth Lewis. "God as Cause or Error? Academic Psychology as Christian Vocation." *Journal of Psychology and Theology* 32, no. 3 (2004): 200–209.

———. "What Are Bodies For? An Integrative Examination of Embodiment." *Christian Scholar's Review* 39, no. 2 (2010): 159–75.

Hamlin, J. Kiley. "Moral Judgment and Action in Preverbal Infants and Toddlers: Evidence for an Innate Moral Core." *Current Directions in Psychological Science* 22, no. 3 (2013): 186–93.

Hamson, Sarah E. "Mechanisms by which Childhood Personality Traits Influence Adult Well-Being." *Current Directions in Psychological Science* 17, no. 4 (2008): 264–68.

Harlow, Harry F., and Robert R. Zimmerman. "Affectional Responses in the Infant Monkey." *Science* 130 (1959): 421–32.

Hefner, Philip. "Imago Dei: The Possibility and Necessity of the Human Person." In *The Human Person in Science and Theology*, edited by N. H. Gregersen, W. B. Drees, and U. Görman, 73–94. Grand Rapids: Eerdmans, 2000.

Hennessey, Beth A., and Theresa M. Amabile. "Creativity." *Annual Review of Psychology* 61 (2010): 569–98.

Hirst, William, and Gerald Echterhoff. "Remembering in Conversations: The Social Sharing and Reshaping of Memories." *Annual Review of Psychology* 63 (2012): 55–79. https://doi.org/10.1146/annurev-psych-120710-100340.

Hodges, Bert E. "Perception, Relativity, and Knowing and Doing the Truth." In Jones, *Psychology and the Christian Faith*, 51–77.

Hoekema, Anthony A. *Created in God's Image.* Grand Rapids: Eerdmans, 1986.

Hofman, Wilhelm, and Lotte Van Dillen. "Desire: The New Hot Spot in Self-Control Research." *Current Directions in Psychological Science* 21, no. 5 (2012): 317–22.

Hofman, Wilhelm, Kathleen D. Vohs, and Roy F. Baumeister. "What People Desire, Feel Conflicted about, and Try to Resist in Everyday Life." *Psychological Science* 23, no. 6 (June 2012): 582–88.

Holmes, Arthur. *All Truth Is God's Truth.* Grand Rapids: Eerdmans, 1977.

Hong, David S., Signe Bray, Brian W. Haas, Fumiko Hoeft, and Allan L. Reiss. "Aberrant Neurocognitive Processing of Fear in Young Girls with Turner Syndrome." *Social Cognitive and Affective Neuroscience* 9, no. 3 (March 2014): 255–64.

Howell, Russell, and James Bradley. *Mathematics through the Eyes of Faith.* New York: HarperOne, 2012.

Hull, Jay G. "A Self-Awareness Model of the Causes and Effects of Alcohol Consumption." *Journal of Abnormal Psychology* 90, no. 6 (1981): 586–600.

Hulse, Stewart H., Harry Fowler, and Werner K. Honig. *Cognitive Processes in Animal Behavior.* Hillsdale, NJ: Erlbaum, 1978.

Jagdeo, Amit, Brian J. Cox, Murray B. Stein, and Jitender Sareen. "Negative Attitudes toward Help Seeking for Mental Illness in 2 Population-Based Surveys from the United States and Canada." *Canadian Journal of Psychiatry* 54, no. 11 (2009): 757–66.

Jeeves, Malcolm A., ed. *From Cells to Souls—and Beyond: Changing Portraits of Human Nature.* Grand Rapids: Eerdmans, 2004.

———. *Human Nature at the Millennium: Reflections on the Integration of Psychology and Christianity.* Grand Rapids: Baker, 1997.

Jeeves, Malcolm A., and Thomas Ludwig. *Psychological Science and Christian Faith: Insights and Enrichments from Constructive Dialogue.* West Conshohocken, PA: Templeton, 2018.

Jenny, Timothy P. "Sanctification." In *Eerdmans Dictionary of the Bible*, edited by David Noel Freedman, Allen C. Myers, and Astrid B. Beck, 1165–66. Grand Rapids: Eerdmans, 2000.

John Paul II (Pope). *Reconciliation and Penance.* Boston: Pauline Books & Media, 1984.

Jones, Stanton L. "A Constructive Relationship for Religion with the Science and Profession of Psychology: Perhaps the Boldest Model Yet." *American Psychologist* 49, no. 3 (1994): 184–99.

———, ed. *Psychology and the Christian Faith: An Introductory Reader.* Grand Rapids: Baker, 1986.

Kahneman, Daniel. *Thinking, Fast and Slow*. New York: Farrar, Strauss & Giroux, 2011.

Kalat, James W. *Biological Psychology*. 12th ed. Boston: Cengage, 2016.

Kandel, Eric R., Irving Kupfermann, and Susan Iverson. "Learning and Memory." In *Principles of Neural Science*, edited by Eric R. Kandel, James H. Schwartz, and Thomas M. Jessel, 1227–46. New York: McGraw-Hill, 2000.

Kanwisher, Nancy, and Paul Downing. "Separating the Wheat from the Chaff." *Science* 282 (1998): 57–58.

Kaufman, Joan, and Edward Zigler. "The Intergenerational Transmission of Abuse Is Overstated." In *Current Controversies on Family Violence*, edited by Richard J. Gelles and Donileen R. Loseke, 209–21. Thousand Oaks, CA: Sage, 1993.

Kawakami, Kerry, John F. Dovidio, Jasper Moll, Sander Hermsen, and Abby Russin. "Just Say No (to Stereotyping): Effects of Training in the Negation of Stereotypic Associations on Stereotype Activation." *Journal of Personality and Social Psychology* 78, no. 5 (2000): 871–88.

Kaye, Kenneth. *The Mental and Social Life of Babies*. Chicago: University of Chicago Press, 1982.

Keleman, Deborah. "Are Children 'Intuitive Theists'? Reasoning about Purpose and Design in Nature." *Psychological Science* 15 (2004): 295–301.

Keller, Timothy. *Making Sense of God: An Invitation to the Skeptical*. New York: Viking, 2016.

Kelman, Herbert C. "Attitudes Are Alive and Well and Gainfully Employed in the Sphere of Action." *American Psychologist* 29, no. 5 (1974): 310–24.

Kerkhoff, G. A. "Inter-Individual Differences in the Human Circadian System: A Review." *Biological Psychology* 20 (1985): 83–112.

Kessler, Ronald C., Patricia A. Berglund, Martha L. Bruce, J. Randy Koch, Eugene M. Laska, Philip J. Leaf, Ronald W. Manderscheid, Robert A. Rosenheck, Ellen E. Walters, and Philip S. Wang. "The Prevalence and Correlates of Untreated Serious Mental Illness." *Health Services Research* 36, no. 6, part 1 (2001): 987.

Kihlstrom, John F. "Consciousness and Me-ness." In *Scientific Approaches to Consciousness*, edited by Jonathan D. Cohen and Jonathan W. Schooler, 451–68. Mahwah, NJ: Erlbaum, 1997.

Kirkpatrick, Lee A. "God as a Substitute Attachment Figure: A Longitudinal Study of Adult Attachment Style and Religious Change in College Students." *Personality and Social Psychology Bulletin* 24 (1998): 961–73.

Kohlberg, Lawrence. "Stage and Sequence: The Cognitive-Developmental Approach to Socialization." In *Handbook of Socialization Theory and Research*, edited by David A. Goslin, 347–480. Chicago: Rand McNally, 1969.

Kroger, Jane. *Identity Development: Adolescence through Adulthood*. 2nd ed. Thousand Oaks, CA: Sage, 2007.

Kuhl, Patricia K. "Language, Mind, and Brain: Experience Alters Perception." In *The New Cognitive Neurosciences*, edited by Michael S. Gazzaniga, 99–115. 2nd ed. Cambridge, MA: MIT Press, 2000.

Kuhn, Thomas S. *The Structure of Scientific Revolutions*. Chicago: University of Chicago Press, 1962.

La Greca, Annette M., and Nadja Lopez. "Social Anxiety among Adolescents: Linkages with Peer Relations and Friendships." *Journal of Abnormal Child Psychology* 26, no. 2 (1998): 83–94.

Laureys, Steven. "Eyes Open, Brain Shut." *Scientific American* 4 (2007): 32–37.

Lavie, Nilli. "Distracted and Confused? Selective Attention under Load." *Trends in Cognitive Sciences* 9 (2005): 75–82.

L'Engle, Madeleine. *And It Was Good*. Wheaton: Harold Shaw, 1983.

Lepper, Mark R., David Greene, and Richard E. Nisbett. "Undermining Children's Intrinsic Interest with Extrinsic Reward: A Test of the 'Overjustification' Hypothesis." *Journal of Personality and Social Psychology* 28, no. 1 (1973): 129–37.

Leslie, Alan M., and Stephanie Keeble. "Do Six-Month-Old Infants Perceive Causality?" *Cognition* 25 (1987): 265–88.

Lett, Heather S., James A. Blumenthal, Michael A. Babyak, Timothy J. Strauman, Clive Robins, and Andrew Sherwood. "Social Support and Coronary Heart Disease: Epidemiologic Evidence and Implications for Treatment." *Psychosomatic Medicine* 67, no. 6 (2005): 869–78.

Lewis, C. S. *Mere Christianity*. New York: Macmillan, 1952.

Libet, Benjamin. "Unconscious Cerebral Initiative and the Role of Conscious Will in Voluntary Action." *Behavioral and Brain Sciences* 8 (1985): 529–66.

Libet, Benjamin, Curtis A. Gleason, Elwood W. Wright, and Dennis K. Pearl. "Time of Conscious Intention to Act in Relation to Onset of Cerebral Activation (Readiness-Potential)." *Brain* 106 (1983): 623–42.

Lindskoog, Donald. *The Idea of Psychology: Reclaiming the Discipline's Identity*. Washington, DC: Howard University Press, 1998.

Locke, John. *Some Thoughts concerning Education*. Edited by R. H. Quick. 1690. Reprint, Cambridge: Cambridge University Press, 1892.

Loftus, Elizabeth F., and G. R. Loftus. "On the Permanence of Stored Information in the Human Brain." *American Psychologist* 35 (1980): 409–20.

Looy, Heather. "Sex Differences: Evolved, Constructed, and Designed." *Journal of Psychology and Theology* 29, no. 4 (2001): 301–13.

Madole, Kelly L., and Lisa M. Oakes. "Making Sense of Infant Categorization: Stable Processes and Changing Representations." *Developmental Review* 19 (1999): 263–96.

Marsh, Charles. *Strange Glory: A Life of Dietrich Bonhoeffer*. New York: Knopf, 2014.

Martin, Rod A. *The Psychology of Humor: An Integrative Approach*. London: Elsevier Academic, 2006.

Maslow, Abraham H. *Motivation and Personality*. 2nd ed. New York: Harper & Row, 1970.

Mason, Malia F., Michael I. Norton, John D. Van Horn, Daniel M. Wegner, Scott T. Grafton, and C. Neil Macrae. "Wandering Minds: The Default Network and Stimulus-Independent Thought." *Science* 315 (2007): 393–95.

Matlin, Margaret W., and Thomas A. Farmer. *Cognition*. 9th ed. Hoboken, NJ: Wiley, 2016.

McAllister, Edward W. C. "Christian Counseling and Human Needs." In Benner, *Christian Counseling and Psychotherapy*, 53–56.

McDonagh, John. "Working through Resistance by Prayer and the Gift of Knowledge." In Benner, *Christian Counseling and Psychotherapy*, 200–203.

McLemore, Clinton W., and David W. Brokaw. "Psychotherapy as a Spiritual Enterprise." In Jones, *Psychology and the Christian Faith*, 178–95.

McNamara, Timothy P. *Semantic Priming: Perspectives from Memory and Word Recognition*. New York: Psychology Press, 2005.

McRay, Barrett W., Mark A. Yarhouse, and Richard E. Butman. *The Modern Psychopathologies: A Comprehensive Christian Appraisal*. 2nd ed. Downers Grove, IL: IVP Academic, 2016.

Melnikof, David E., and John A. Bargh. "The Mythical Number Two." *Trends in Cognitive Sciences* 22 (2018): 280–93.

Mental Health America, "Learning to Trust Others and Forgive Himself." Posted by Forgotten Dad, an anonymous user. Accessed December 15, 2022, https://web.archive.org/web/20130902000622/http://www.mentalhealthamerica.net/reallives/index.cfm/2009/9/4/Learning-to-trust-others-and-forgive-himself.

Middleton, J. Richard. *The Liberating Image: The Imago Dei in Genesis 1*. Grand Rapids: Brazos, 2005.

Milgram, Stanley. "Behavioral Study of Obedience." *Journal of Abnormal and Social Psychology* 67, no. 4 (1963): 371–78.

Miller, William R., and Harold D. Delaney, eds. *Judeo-Christian Perspectives on Psychology: Human Nature, Motivation, and Change*. Washington, DC: American Psychological Association, 2005.

Moffitt, Terrie E., Avshalom Caspi, and Michael Rutter. "Measured Gene-Environment Interactions in Psychopathology Concepts, Research Strategies, and Implications for Research, Intervention, and Public Understanding of Genetics." *Perspectives on Psychological Science* 1, no. 1 (2006): 5–27.

Mojtabai, Ramin. "Americans' Attitudes toward Mental Health Treatment Seeking: 1990–2003." *Psychiatric Services* 58, no. 5 (2007): 642–51.

Monahan, Jennifer L., Sheila T. Murphy, and Robert B. Zajonc. "Subliminal Mere Exposure: Specific, General, and Diffuse Effects." *Psychological Science* 11 (2000): 462–66.

Moon, Christine, Robin Panneton Cooper, and William P. Fifer. "Two-Day-Olds Prefer Their Native Language." *Infant Behavior and Development* 16 (1993): 495–500.

Morea, Peter. *In Search of Personality*. London: SCM, 1997.

Moxley, Roy A. "Skinner: From Determinism to Random Variation." *Behavior and Philosophy* 25, no. 1 (1997): 3–28.

Myers, David G. "A Levels-of-Explanation View." In *Psychology and Christianity: Five Views*, edited by Eric L. Johnson, 49–78. 2nd ed. Downers Grove, IL: InterVarsity, 2010.

——. *Psychology*. 10th ed. New York: Worth, 2013.

Myers, David G., and C. Nathan DeWall. *Psychology*. 13th ed. New York: Worth, 2021.

Myers, David G., and Malcolm A. Jeeves. *Psychology through the Eyes of Faith*. Rev. and updated ed. San Francisco: HarperSanFrancisco, 2003.

Myers, David G., and Helmut Lamm. "The Group Polarization Phenomenon." *Psychological Bulletin* 83, no. 4 (1976): 602–27.

Neisser, Ulric. *Cognitive Psychology*. New York: Appleton, 1967.

Norcross, John C. "An Eclectic Definition of Psychotherapy." In *What Is Psychotherapy? Contemporary Perspectives*, edited by J. K. Zeig and W. M. Munion, 218–20. San Francisco: Jossey-Bass, 1990.

Norcross, John C., and Michael J. Lambert. "Psychotherapy Relationships That Work II." *Psychotherapy* 48, no. 1 (2011): 4–8.

Norcross, John C., Marci S. Mrykalo, and Matthew D. Blagys. "Auld Lang Syne: Success Predictors, Change Processes, and Self-Reported Outcomes of New Year's Resolvers and Nonresolvers." *Journal of Clinical Psychology* 58 (2010): 397–405.

Oakes, Lisa M. "Using Habituation of Looking Time to Assess Mental Processes in Infancy." *Journal of Cognition and Development* 11, no. 3 (2011): 255–68.

Ochsner, Kevin N., Silvia A. Bunge, James J. Gross, and John D. Gabrieli. "Rethinking Feelings: An fMRI Study of the Cognitive Regulation of Emotion." *Journal of Cognitive Neuroscience* 14 (2002): 1215–29.

O'Hara, Ross E., Frederick X. Gibbons, Meg Gerrard, Zhigang Li, and James D. Sargent. "Greater Exposure to Sexual Content in Popular Movies Predicts Earlier Sexual Debut and Increased Sexual Risk Taking." *Psychological Science* 24 (2012): 984–93.

Ormrod, Jeanne Ellis. *Human Learning*. Upper Saddle River, NJ: Merrill, 1999.

Österlund, M. K., E. Keller, and Y. L. Hurd. "The Human Forebrain Has Discrete Estrogen Receptor α Messenger RNA Expression: High Levels in the Amygdaloid Complex." *Neuroscience* 95, no. 2 (1999): 333–42.

Otten, Sabine, and Gordon B. Moskowitz. "Evidence for Implicit Evaluative In-Group Bias: Affect-Biased Spontaneous Trait Inference in a Minimal Group Paradigm." *Journal of Experimental Social Psychology* 36, no. 1 (2000): 77–89.

Paul, Marla. "Your Memory Is Like the Telephone Game." Northwestern University News. September 19, 2012. https://uptowndallascounseling.com/your-memory-is-like-the-telephone-game-northwestern-university-news/.

Pearson, Birger A. *Ancient Gnosticism: Traditions and Literature*. Minneapolis: Fortress, 2007.

Penton-Voak, I. S., D. I. Perrett, D. L. Castles, T. Kobayashi, D. M. Burt, L. K. Murry, and R. Minamisawa. "Menstrual Cycle Alters Face Preference." *Nature* 399 (1999): 741–42.

Pinker, Steven. *The Blank Slate: The Modern Denial of Human Nature.* New York: Penguin, 2003.

Plantinga, Cornelius, Jr. *Engaging God's World.* Grand Rapids: Eerdmans, 2002.

———. *Not the Way It's Supposed to Be: A Breviary of Sin.* Grand Rapids: Eerdmans, 1995.

Plantinga, Richard J., Thomas R. Thompson, and Matthew D. Lundberg. *An Introduction to Christian Theology.* Cambridge: Cambridge University Press, 2010.

Ponterotto, Joseph G. "Qualitative Research in Counseling Psychology: A Primer on Research Paradigms and Philosophy of Science." *Journal of Counseling Psychology* 52, no. 2 (2005): 126–36.

Pribram, Karl H., ed. *Brain and Values: Is a Biological Science of Values Possible?* Mahwah, NJ: Erlbaum, 1998.

Pronin, Emily, Thomas Gilovich, and Lee Ross. "Objectivity in the Eye of the Beholder: Divergent Perceptions of Bias in Self versus Others." *Psychological Review* 111 (2004): 781–99.

Regan, Dennis T., and Russell Fazio. "On the Consistency between Attitudes and Behavior: Look to the Method of Attitude Formation." *Journal of Experimental Social Psychology* 13 (1977): 28–45.

Reisberg, Daniel. *Cognition: Exploring the Science of the Mind.* 7th ed. New York: Norton, 2019.

Riek, Blake M., Lindsey M. Root Luna, and Chelsea A. Schnabelrauch. "Transgressors' Guilt and Shame: A Longitudinal Examination of Forgiveness Seeking." *Journal of Social and Personal Relationships* 31, no. 6 (2014): 751–72.

Riek, Blake M., and Eric W. Mania. "The Antecedents and Consequences of Interpersonal Forgiveness: A Meta-Analytic Review." *Personal Relationships* 19 (2012): 304–25. https://doi.org/10.1111/j.1475-6811.2011.01363.x.

Rizzolatti, Giacomo, and Laila Craighero. "The Mirror-Neuron System." *Annual Review of Neuroscience* 27, no. 1 (2004): 169–92.

Roberts, Leanne, Irshad Ahmed, Steve Hall, and Andrew Davison. "Intercessory Prayer for the Alleviation of Ill Health." *Cochrane Database of Systematic Reviews* 2 (2009): CD000368. https://doi.org/10.1002/14651858.CD000368.pub3.

Roberts, Robert C. "Parameters of a Christian Psychology." In *Limning the Psyche: Explorations in Christian Psychology,* edited by Robert C. Roberts and Mark R. Talbot, 74–101. Grand Rapids: Eerdmans, 1997.

Roese, Neal J., and Kathleen D. Vohs. "Hindsight Bias." *Perspectives on Psychological Science* 7 (2012): 411–26. https://doi.org/10.1177/1745691612454303.

Rogers, Carl. "Notes on Rollo May." *Journal of Humanistic Psychology* 22 (Summer 1982): 8–9.

———. *On Becoming a Person: A Therapist's View of Psychotherapy*. Boston: Houghton Mifflin, 1961.

———. *A Way of Being*. Boston: Houghton Mifflin, 1980.

Rousseau, Jean-Jacques. *Emile*. Translated by William H. Payne. New York: D. Appleton and Company, 1892.

Sacks, Oliver. *An Anthropologist on Mars: Seven Paradoxical Tales*. New York: Vintage Books, 1995.

Sagi, Abraham, and Martin L. Hoffman. "Empathic Distress in the Newborn." *Developmental Psychology* 12 (1976): 175–76.

Santrock, John W. *Life-Span Development*. 18th ed. New York: McGraw-Hill, 2021.

Schacter, Daniel L. "Adaptive Constructive Processes and the Future of Memory." *American Psychologist* 67 (2012): 603–13. https://doi.org/10.1037/a0029869.

Schacter, Daniel L., Daniel T. Gilbert, Matthew K. Nock, and Daniel M. Wegner. *Psychology*. 5th ed. New York: Worth, 2020.

Schore, Allan N. "The Experience-Dependent Maturation of an Evaluative System in the Cortex." In Pribram, *Brain and Values*, 337–58.

Seligman, Martin E. P. *Authentic Happiness: Using the New Positive Psychology to Realize Your Potential for Lasting Fulfillment*. New York: Free Press, 2002.

Seligman, Martin E. P., Peter Railton, Roy F. Baumeister, and Chandra Sripada. "Navigating into the Future or Driven by the Past." *Perspectives on Psychological Science* 8, no. 2 (2013): 119–41.

Shotter, John. "Getting in Touch: The Metamethodology of a Postmodern Science of Mental Life." *Humanistic Psychologist* 18, no. 1 (1990): 7–22.

Simons, Daniel J., and Christopher F. Chabris. "Gorillas in Our Midst: Sustained Inattentional Blindness for Dynamic Events." *Perception* 28 (1999): 1059–74.

Simons, Daniel J., and Daniel T. Levin. "Change Blindness." *Trends in Cognitive Sciences* 1 (1997): 261–67.

Sire, James W. *The Universe Next Door: A Basic World View Catalog*. 5th ed. Downers Grove, IL: InterVarsity, 2009.

Skinner, B. F. *Beyond Freedom and Dignity*. New York: Knopf, 1971.

———. "Why I Am Not a Cognitive Psychologist." *Behaviorism* 5, no. 2 (1977): 1–10.

Smallwood, Jonathan, and Jonathan W. Schooler. "The Restless Mind." *Psychological Bulletin* 132 (2006): 946–58.

Smedes, Lewis B. *My God and I: A Spiritual Memoir*. Grand Rapids: Eerdmans, 2003.

Smith, James K. A. *Desiring the Kingdom*. Grand Rapids: Baker Academic, 2009.

———. *Imagining the Kingdom*. Grand Rapids: Baker Academic, 2013.

Smith, Mary L., and Gene V. Glass. "Meta-Analysis of Psychotherapy Outcome Studies." *American Psychologist* 32, no. 9 (1977): 752–60.

Smith, Noel W. *Current Systems in Psychology: History, Theory, Research, and Applications*. Belmont, CA: Wadsworth, 2001.

Stanovich, Keith E. *How to Think Straight about Psychology.* 11th ed. New York: Pearson, 2019.

Stanovich, Keith E., and Richard F. West. "Individual Differences in Reasoning: Implications for the Rationality Debate?" *Behavioral and Brain Sciences* 23, no. 5 (October 2000): 645–65.

Stephen Ministries. "What Is Stephen Ministry?" Accessed June 15, 2022. http://www.stephenministries.org/stephenministry/default.cfm/917.

Struthers, William M. *Wired for Intimacy: How Pornography Hijacks the Male Brain.* Downers Grove, IL: InterVarsity, 2009.

Szasz, Thomas S. *The Myth of Mental Illness: Foundations of a Theory of Personal Conduct.* New York: HarperCollins, 2011.

Tavris, Carol. *Anger, the Misunderstood Emotion.* New York: Simon & Schuster, 1982.

Tellegen, Auke, David T. Lykken, Thomas J. Bouchard, Kimerly J. Wilcox, Nancy L. Segal, and Stephen Rich. "Personality Similarity in Twins Reared Apart and Together." *Journal of Personality and Social Psychology* 54, no. 6 (1988): 1031–39.

Thomas, Manoj J., and Vicki Morwitz. "Penny Wise and Pound Foolish: The Left-Digit Effect in Price Cognition." *Journal of Consumer Research* 32 (2005): 54–64.

Tjeltveit, Alan C. "Faith, Psychotherapy, and Christian Counseling." In VanderStoep, *Science and the Soul,* 247–63.

Torrance, Alan J. "What Is a Person?" In Jeeves, *From Cells to Souls—and Beyond,* 199–222.

Tulving, Endel. "Episodic and Semantic Memory." In *Organization of Memory,* edited by Endel Tulving and Wayne Donaldson, 381–403. New York: Academic Press, 1972.

Twenge, Jean M., and W. Keith Campbell. *The Narcissism Epidemic: Living in the Age of Entitlement.* New York: Free Press, 2009.

Valenza, Eloisa, Francesca Simion, Viola Macchi Cassia, and Carlo Ulmità. "Face Preference at Birth." *Journal of Experimental Psychology: Human Perception and Performance* 22 (1996): 892–903.

VanderStoep, Scott W. "Psychological Research Methods and Christian Belief." In VanderStoep, *Science and the Soul,* 97–110.

———, ed. *Science and the Soul: Christian Faith and Psychological Research.* Lanham, MD: University Press of America, 2003.

Van Leeuwen, Mary Stewart. "Personality Theorizing within a Christian World View." In Burke, *Man and Mind,* 171–98.

Vitz, Paul C. "A Christian Theory of Personality: Covenant Theory." In Burke, *Man and Mind,* 199–222.

Volf, Miroslav. *After Our Likeness: The Church as the Image of the Trinity.* Grand Rapids: Eerdmans, 1998.

Warneken, Felix, and Michael Tomasello. "Varieties of Altruism in Children and Chimpanzees." *Trends in Cognitive Sciences* 13, no. 9 (2009): 397–402.

Weaver, Glenn D. "Embodied Spirituality: Experiences of Identity and Spiritual Suffering among Persons with Alzheimer's Dementia." In Jeeves, *From Cells to Souls—and Beyond*, 77–101.

Webster, Richard. *Why Freud Was Wrong: Sin, Science, and Psychoanalysis*. New York: Basic Books, 1995.

Wegner, Daniel M. "Who Is the Controller of Controlled Processes?" In *The New Unconscious*, edited by Ran R. Hassin, James S. Uleman, and John A. Bargh, 19–36. Oxford: Oxford University Press, 2005.

Whitaker, R. C., and W. H. Dietz. "Role of the Prenatal Environment in the Development of Obesity." *Journal of Pediatrics* 132, no. 5 (1998): 768–76.

Wilson, Timothy D. *Strangers to Ourselves: Discovering the Adaptive Unconscious*. Cambridge, MA: Harvard University Press, 2002.

Wolpe, Joseph. *The Practice of Behavior Therapy*. 3rd ed. New York: Pergamon, 1982.

Wolters, Albert M. *Creation Regained: Biblical Basics for a Reformational Worldview*. Grand Rapids: Eerdmans, 2005.

Wolterstorff, Nicholas. *Reason within the Bounds of Religion*. 2nd ed. Grand Rapids: Eerdmans, 1984.

Wood, Wendy, and Alice H. Eagly. "A Cross-Cultural Analysis of the Behavior of Women and Men: Implications for the Origins of Sex Differences." *Psychological Bulletin* 128, no. 5 (2002): 699–727.

Wood, Wendy, and David T. Neal. "A New Look at Habits and the Habit-Goal Interface." *Psychological Review* 114, no. 4 (2007): 843–63.

Wood, Wendy, and Dennis Rünger. "Psychology of Habit." *Annual Review of Psychology* 67 (2016): 289–314. https://doi.org/10.1146/annurev-psych-122414-03341.

Worthington, Everett L. *Coming to Peace with Psychology*. Downers Grove, IL: InterVarsity, 2010.

Wright, James L. "The Mortal Soul in Ancient Israel and Pauline Christianity: Ramifications for Modern Medicine." *Journal of Religion and Health* 50, no. 2 (2011): 447–71.

Wright, N. T. *After You Believe: Why Christian Character Matters*. New York: HarperOne, 2010.

———. *The Lord and His Prayer*. Grand Rapids: Eerdmans, 1996.

———. "Mind, Spirit, Soul and Body: All for One and One for All—Reflections on Paul's Anthropology in His Complex Contexts." Paper presented at the Society of Christian Philosophers Regional Meeting, Fordham University, Bronx, NY, March 18–19, 2011.

Yannaras, Christos. *The Freedom of Morality*. Translated by Elizabeth Briere. Crestwood, NY: St. Vladimir's Seminary Press, 1984.

Zajonc, Robert B. "Mere Exposure: A Gateway to the Subliminal." *Current Directions in Psychological Science* 10, no. 6 (2001): 224–28.

Zeskind, Philip S., Laura Klein, and Timothy R. Marshall. "Adults' Perceptions of Experimental Modifications of Durations of Pauses and Expiratory Sounds in Infant Crying." *Developmental Psychology* 28, no. 6 (1992): 1153–62.

Index

on support from Christian community, 193,
202, 204
on treatment with medication, 208

Calvin, John, 33
Carson, Donald, 217
catharsis, 140
"catholic," 11n7
causal stereotyping, 112–13, 114
chance, 34, 35
change
attitude and, 115, 161–62, 164–66
awareness and, 161, 165–66
brokenness and, 16
habits and, 16, 76, 96, 115, 159, 162
limited agency and, 19–20, 54, 64, 161, 165,
180
nondeclarative memory and, 96
overcoming confirmation bias, 115
in personality, 170, 171, 180
redirecting desires and impulses for, 65–66,
114–15
sensation and perception of, 72, 76
short-term versus long-term, 16
change blindness, 74n15
children
decision making by, 112
environmental shaping of, 118, 124
as meaning makers, 25, 121–24
mirroring and, 49
moral behavior of, 118, 122
religious belief of, 25, 123–24
teaching techniques for, 88
valued by Jesus, 129
Christian counseling, 216
Christians
bias of, 42
body downplayed by, 46–47, 222
calling of, 16, 77, 95
multiple perspectives among, 42
potential science-faith conflicts for, 38–39,
40–41, 43
scientific inquiry important for, 32–33, 43, 93
transformation of. See sanctification and
transformation
views of human nature, ix, 10. See also
agency, limited; brokenness; embodiment;
meaning seeking; relationality; responsibility; sin

church and Christian communities
attention influenced by, 77
discernment of impulses supported by, 115
as embodied, 53–54
faith-behavior alignment supported by,
165–66
interaction with other groups, 153–55
positive group influence of, 152–53
problems in, 153–55
relationality in, 11–12, 53–54, 151–52, 154
support for psychological disorders, 195–97,
202–3
unity in, 152, 153
as universal, 11
church-based counseling and support, 202–4,
205
classical conditioning, 80–81, 82, 83–84,
85–88
cognition, 105n2, 158
cognitive dissonance, 161–62
cognitive psychology
focus of, 105
learning theories shaped by, 83–84, 85, 86
meaning seeking and, 24–25
reasoning processes emphasized in, 170
cognitive unconscious, 59
"collective mind," 149–50, 152
coma, 57
Coming to Peace with Psychology (Worthington), 41
communion, 18
compassion, 113–14
compatibility approach to science and religion, 218–19, 221
conditioning
attitude toward, 84
classical, 80–81, 82, 83–84, 87–88
connectionist view of, 81, 83
operant, 80–81, 82, 85, 87–88
confession, 165
confirmation bias, 115
conformity pressure, 145–48, 152
connectionism, 81, 83
consciousness
brain function and, 47–48
defined, 57
dimensions of, 57–58
ego and, 169
limited agency and, 60–64

Christian minimization of, 46–47, 222
of church, 53–54
defined, 17
emotions and, 133, 143
faith practice and, 18, 95, 101
of God's interaction in the world, 70
of habits, 95, 163
human sexuality and, 222
importance for Christians, 55
of Jesus, 17n27, 18, 46, 70, 192
learning and, 85
limited agency and, 19, 52, 54, 71, 74
meaning seeking and, 24, 51
memory and, 95, 101
of mental life, 189
in nature-versus-nurture debate, 124
of psychological disorders, 189, 208
in psychology, 18–19, 120–21, 124, 172, 222
in psychotherapy approaches, 207–8
of relationship with creation, 55
of relationship with God, 14, 17–18, 52, 53, 55
of relationship with humanity, 49–51, 53–55, 120–21, 148
responsibility and, 54
salvation and, 53, 55
scriptural references to, 17, 46, 53
of sensory processes, 69, 72
of soul and consciousness, 17, 48, 51–52
of thinking processes, 110
emotions
brain function and, 47–51, 134, 136–39
Christian minimization of, 134
conscious and unconscious experience of, 133
embodied nature of, 133, 143
of God, 139
negative or difficult, 139–42, 148, 149
physical contact and, 122–23
reasoning and, 134, 136–37
regulation of, 140–41, 142–43
relationality of, 133, 135, 136, 138, 139, 142–43, 148
scriptural references to, 134, 139, 140, 142
sin and, 134, 140
views of, 133, 134–39
empathy, 49, 119, 193
empiricism, limits of, 7, 25–26, 173–74, 189
Entwistle, David, 216

environment
attention and, 73, 74–75, 76–77
considered in psychotherapy, 208
development and, 118, 121–22, 124, 125, 214
learning and, 81–82, 85
limited agency and, 6, 19, 21, 31, 34, 77
meaning seeking and, 22, 128
personality and, 169, 170, 176, 180, 181
psychological disorders and, 188, 189, 190
sensing and perceiving. See perception; sensation and sensory processes
stewardship of, 35
thinking as interaction with, 105
episodic memory, 93, 100
epistemic chance, 34n16
Erikson, Erik, 126–28, 130
estrogen, 50
Evans, C. Stephen, 16, 23, 31, 32
Evans, Jonathan St. B. T., 107n11
evolutionary psychology
assumptions in, 220
biblical view of human nature and, 221–22
critiques of, 214–15, 220
defined, 212
explanations for human behavior, 212, 214
explanations for religious belief, 123–24
explanations for sex differences and attraction, 50, 213–15, 219, 220, 221–22
evolutionary theory, 212

faith practice
attitude and behavior in, 159, 160, 161–62, 163, 164–66
development of trust and, 127
discernment of impulses supported by, 115
as embodied, 18, 32, 95, 101
Holy Spirit's role in, 164
hypocrisy in, 160–61
procedural memory and, 95, 101, 102
psychological disorders and, 187
as relational, 11–12, 53–54, 152–53, 154, 159
fall, the, 14
false justification, 110
Faw, Harold, 101
Fazio, Russell, 158
fear, 47–48
Forgas, Joseph, 141
forgetting, 100–102
forgiveness, 39, 166